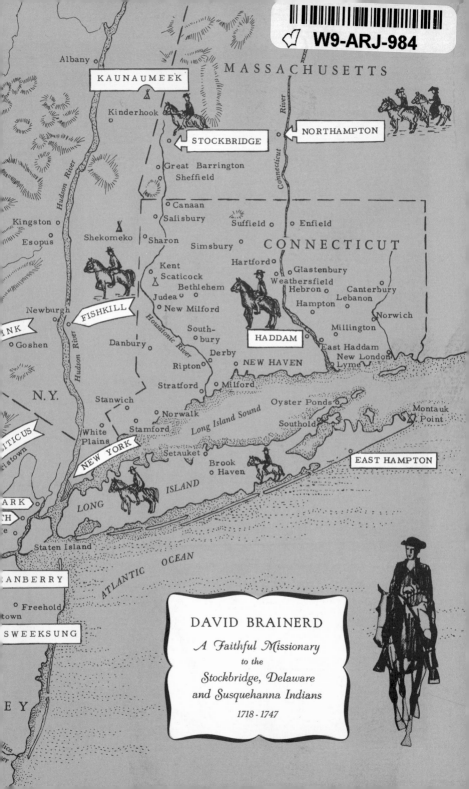

MASSACHUSETTS

W9-ARJ-984

Albany

KAUNAUMEEK

Kinderhook

STOCKBRIDGE

NORTHAMPTON

Great Barrington
Sheffield

Kingston

Canaan
Salisbury

Suffield
Enfield

Esopus

Shekomeko

Sharon

Simsbury

CONNECTICUT

Hartford

Glastenbury

Kent
Scaticock
Bethlehem

Weathersfield
Hebron

Canterbury
Lebanon

Newburgh

Judea
New Milford

Hampton

Norwich

FISHKILL

South-
bury

HADDAM

Millington

Goshen

Danbury

Derby

NEW HAVEN

East Haddam
New London

INK

Ripton

Lyme

N.Y.

Stanwich

Stratford

Milford

White
Plains

Stamford

Norwalk

Oyster Ponds

Long Island Sound

Southold

Montauk
Point

ITICUS

NEW YORK

Setauket

Brook
Haven

EAST HAMPTON

ristown

LONG

ISLAND

ARK

CH

Staten Island

ATLANTIC OCEAN

RANBERRY

Freehold
town

DAVID BRAINERD

A Faithful Missionary
to the

*Stockbridge, Delaware
and Susquehanna Indians*

1718 - 1747

SWEEKSUNG

EY

TENNESSEE POLYTECHNIC

INSTITUTE

David Brainerd
Beloved Yankee

— I sold my Tea-kettle & Mr Jo: Woodbridge, and am come hither to Mr Jno. Woodbridge, both which amounts to something more than it pounds, which I'll owe them to pay to you for the School if that succeed. I hope you will use the Money that way, if not, you are welcome to it your self.

As to my blankets I desir'd Mr Woodbridge to take the trouble of turning them into Beer-skins. If he has not done it, I wish he would and send the Skins to Mr Hopkins, and it might be to Mr Bellamy. —

I am, Sir, in greatest hast

your obedient humble Servt

David Brainerd

DAVID BRAINERD
Beloved Yankee

by

DAVID WYNBEEK

WM. B. EERDMANS PUBLISHING COMPANY
GRAND RAPIDS, MICHIGAN

Handwriting opposite title page represents the closing paragraphs of Brainerd's letter to John Sergeant at Stockbridge, Massachusetts, first published in The Library of American Biography, conducted by Jared Sparks, Volume 8: *Life of David Brainerd, Missionary to the Indians* by Wm. B. O. Peabody, 1837.

Endpaper Map by Macy Schwarz
and the author

Half Title Illustrations
by Marie Jonker

To
M. S. M.
AND
DAVID LEONARD

He was a Yankee ——

in New England, stated John Gottlieb Ernestus Heckewelder, the Moravian missionary-historian, the Indians *"first endeavoured to imitate the sound of the national name of the* English, *which they pronounced* Yengees . . . . *the name they now exclusively applied to the people of New England. . . . They say they know the* Yengees *and can distinguish them by their dress and personal appearance and that they considered them less cruel than the* Virginians *or* long knives," *or the Middle Colonists and the Iroquois whom they derisively called* Schwannach, *"salt or bitter beings"*

 —— *and he was beloved.*

Preface

THIS ACCOUNT OF THE BEST-LOVED MISSIONARY OF COLONIAL AMERICA has been written because so little is known about him. Few can recall the story of his brief years or identify him as accurately as the inscription on his gravestone: A FAITHFUL AND LABORIOUS MISSIONARY TO THE STOCKBRIDGE, DELAWARE AND SUSQUEHANNA TRIBES OF INDIANS. A generation ago George McLean Harper well said: "As for David Brainerd, it is astonishing that in America, where we have in general realized the need of discovering our national worthies and setting them up as examples to our level millions, his lovely and beautiful figure has been allowed to lie in the dust of oblivion."

As both a digest of and commentary on his diaries and journals, here is, we believe, a more complete story of Brainerd than has been previously attempted. We have endeavored to trace both his life and his thoughts, and to restore and illuminate pertinent features and events which have been obscured by time, or which Jonathan Edwards redacted in 1748 when he first compiled and edited Brainerd's diaries and remarked that the days of his years were still fresh in everyone's memory. It is our hope that we have attained toward that more "connected" narrative which Brainerd could not accomplish.

According to his employers in their Preface to his Journals, "the worthy author amidst his continued labours, had no time for such an undertaking." His Journals — there are two — cover only a single year. Part I is entitled *Mirabilia Dei inter Indicos,* or the Rise and Progress of a Remarkable Work of Grace amongst a Number of the INDIANS in the Provinces of New Jersey and Pennsylvania. It covers the period from June 19, 1745, to November 4, and was published early in 1746. Part II, from November 24, 1745, to June 19, 1746, is more modestly entitled *Divine Grace Displayed.* Both accounts were progress reports from the field as required by the Scottish Society that paid his salary, and they were published while he was still engaged in his work.

His personal diaries as edited by Edwards also leave much to be desired as an organized account of his life. Brainerd was precise and explicit, but Edwards was concerned to exhibit him as an

7

"example" of true religion and virtue in a day rampant with "false appearances and counterfeits of religion." He was primarily interested in Brainerd's thoughts and feelings, and therefore left only a skeleton of his physical movements and experiences, although he was fully aware that some parts of the diary which he omitted would "have been a great advantage to the history."

But though we have sought to recreate something of the times in which Brainerd lived, the momentous events that influenced him, the geography of his small world, and the identity of his friends, and have to that extent counterpoised Edwards' emphasis on Brainerd's "secret religion and the inward exercises of his mind," we have not wished to remove that emphasis or to alter Edwards' "example." Brainerd's life was pilgrimage and his way was service, self-denial and sacrifice, and we trust that our presentation of his thoughts and emotions sympathetically interpret Edwards' observations.

Our basic guide has been THE WORKS OF JONATHAN EDWARDS, A.M., with an Essay on His Genius and Writings by Henry Edward Hickman, in Two Volumes, Tenth Edition, London, 1865, first issued in eight volumes in 1817. The second volume of this work contains Edwards' Life and Diary of Brainerd, Brainerd's Journal in Two Parts with General Remarks and Three Appendices: Doctrines Preached, Method of Learning the Indian Language, and of Instructing the Indians (together with the Difficulties which Lie in the Way of Their Conversion), and Brainerd's Letter to Pemberton; Pemberton's Sermon at Brainerd's Ordination, Brainerd's Miscellaneous Letters and Papers, Edwards' Reflections and Observations, and Edwards' Sermon Preached at the Funeral of Brainerd. Published five years before Sereno E. Dwight's edition of most of these materials, it is free of Dwight's grammatical and stylistic "improvements."

Unless specifically noted, all quotations from Brainerd's diaries and Journals are presented in their original sequence. In paraphrases of his comments, the single words and phrases within quotation marks always indicate Brainerd's particular choice of words.

D. W.

Contents

BOOK FOUR: THE APOSTLE

BOOK FIVE: THE SAINT

Book One

The Initiate

His course of religion began before the late times of extraordinary religious commotion; yet he was not an idle spectator, but had a near concern in many things that passed at that time.

—Jonathan Edwards

1. IN A DARK THICK GROVE

HE WAS BORN IN A COUNTRY HOUSE which his grandfather, Daniel Brainerd, had built a half-century earlier. Presumably an English orphan who came to the Massachusetts Bay Colony in 1649 when he was eight years old, this progenitor of the large Brainerd clan in America had lived with a Wadsworth family until he was twenty-one, when he and twenty-seven other landseekers settled Haddam, Connecticut. Their tract of land at "Thirty-Mile Island" was twelve miles square and almost equally divided on the west and east shores of the Connecticut River, some twenty miles south of Hartford and fifteen miles north of the river's mouth. Daniel Brainerd prospered and eventually became Haddam's chief landholder, constable, surveyor, fence viewer, town assessor, collector, a Commissioner for the General Court, a justice of the peace, and a deacon in the Church of Christ which was gathered in Haddam in 1700.

Two years after he had staked his claim Daniel had married Hannah Spencer. The couple had a daughter and seven sons whom they named Daniel, James, Joshua, William, Caleb, Elijah, and Hezekiah. The last son, born in 1681, became the prominent member of the family. He also inherited the largest part of Daniel's estate, including the homestead. Jonathan Edwards referred to him as the Worshipful Hezekiah Brainerd, Esquire: one of his Majesty's Council. He was a Representative to the General Assembly, Speaker of the House in 1721 and 1722, and a member of the Governor's Council or Senate from 1723 to his death four years later. For special public services he and two other legislators were each awarded one hundred acres of land near Goshen. He was a country squire, a regiment commander, a justice of the peace at Haddam, and David Brainerd's father.

In all respects, David's mother was his father's equal. Dorothy Hobart Mason was the young widow of Daniel Mason, a grandson of Major John Mason who practically annihilated the Pequot Indians in 1637. Her son, Jeremiah Mason, was two and a half years old when she married Hezekiah Brainerd on October 1, 1707. Moreover, in a day when social station was inseparable from ministerial status, Dorothy brought luster to the Brainerd name, for she was the daughter of Haddam's first minister, Jeremiah Hobart, who had served Hempstead, Long Island, before coming to Haddam where

13

he spent the last fifteen of his eighty-five unremarkable years. He, in turn, was the son of preacher Peter Hobart of England and Hingham, Massachusetts, and three of his brothers were ministers. Another, Japheth, a young ship's doctor, was lost on a voyage to England and the East Indies. In addition, Dorothy's mother had been a child of the manse, the daughter of one of the ablest and most cultured Puritan ministers, Samuel Whiting, who had served congregations in Boston, England and Lynn, Massachusetts. Her three brothers were also ministers and an uncle, Oliver St. John, had been Chief Justice of England under the great Puritan leader, Oliver Cromwell.

Hezekiah and Dorothy Brainerd's sixth child was born on April 20, on the Sunday after Easter, 1718. Having bestowed their own names on their first-born son and daughter, and named their next three children Nehemiah, Jerusha, and Martha, they called their third son David, which in the Hebrew is *beloved*. He was born on Nehemiah's sixth birthday and a day before Jerusha's fourth, and he always remembered that he was born on Sunday. When he was two years old, John was born. Elizabeth arrived two years later and Israel, the ninth and last child, was born when David was seven.

Details of his youth are meager. He grew up with his nine brothers and sisters in the country house a hundred feet above the west bank of the Connecticut River, between Walkley Hill and Higganum, a mile below Higganum and two miles above Haddam village, the home of sixty families. To the south and across the river stood Mount Tom where the smaller Salmon River from the east silently joined the beautiful Connecticut as it flowed south to Long Island Sound through its valley of rugged hills and stately trees. It was a Rip Van Winkle land, the memory of which ever lingers in the sensitive soul of a native son. It was the heart of the Machemoodus country, the place of noises, and the ancestral domain of Connecticut's most superstitious, powwowing aborigines. An early historian explained that the numerous Indians of the valley had driven a prodigious trade at worshipping the devil and lived in awe of the strange noises and rumblings which emanated from the bowels of Mount Tom which, they said, was the residence of Hobbamock, the spirit of evil and the author of all human plagues and calamaties. Sometimes the houses actually did shake and great stones were removed from their ancient places. One aged father among them said that all this happened because Hobbamock was very angry that the Englishman's God had come to the valley.

The more practical aspects of a Haddam boy's life were his

parents' strict insistence on farm chores and lessons, on Bible reading and church attendance, on profound respect for elders, and on complete obedience to parental authority. David's self-educated father fits well into this picture. Brainerd family tradition states that he was "of great personal dignity and self-restraint, of rigid notions of parental prerogatives and authority, of the strictest puritanical views as to religious ordinances, of unbending integrity as a man and a public officer, and of extreme scrupulousness in his Christian life."

When David's half-brother Jeremiah Mason was twenty-two, he had courted and won the hand of Mary Clark. Their wedding day was set for May 24, 1727. David's eldest brother was then nineteen years old; baby Israel was barely two; David was nine. No doubt, the prospect of an elaborate wedding feast and busy merriment was pleasantly anticipated by the Brainerd family. But, on that day when Haddam's second pastor, Phineas Fiske, married the young couple, the Honorable Hezekiah Brainerd died in Hartford, "while attending in his place as Senator," stated Edwards, and was buried there in the grounds of the First Church. He had died on his forty-sixth birthday, at the home of David's uncle, Secretary Hezekiah Wyllys. Recalling those days, "after my seventh or eighth birthday," David wrote: "I became concerned for my soul, and terrified at the thoughts of death, and was driven to the performance of duties: but it appeared a melancholy business that destroyed my eagerness for play."

Perhaps the Brainerd children had a happier time in January 1731 when their eldest brother, Hezekiah Jr., married pastor Fiske's daughter Mary. However, when winter returned that year, much sickness came to Haddam, and the impressionable fourteen-year-old David again pensively contemplated the brevity of life and the inevitability of death. He prayed often, read much, especially Janeway's *Token for Children* and, like everyone else, *Pilgrim's Progress,* and perhaps Baxter's equally famous *Call to the Unconverted,* and he sometimes hoped that he was converted, yet "not knowing what conversion was." And then, just as the winter was beginning to loose its grip on the river and the valley, his mother died. She was fifty-two. Concerning that grief-laden spring, David stated simply: "I was also exceedingly distressed and melancholy at the death of my mother, in March, 1732."

Life went on. His early religious ardor cooled. Though secret prayer was his rule, it was perfunctory and in line with accepted, and expected, behavior. In July Hezekiah's and Mary's first baby was born in the homestead which they had inherited. In the fall Nehemiah graduated from Yale College, and on December 19, David's second eldest sister Jerusha, then eighteen, married Samuel Spencer of East Haddam, a village southeast and on better land across the river. Jerusha was David's favorite sister and his life-long confidant. Edwards observed that "a peculiarly dear affection, and much intimacy in spiritual matters" had "long subsisted" between them. Little wonder then that in the spring, just before his fifteenth birthday, David left the family home and also moved to East Haddam where, it is safe to assume, he lived for four years with Jerusha and Samuel and their first three children.

During those adolescent years in his remote, provincial valley, David began his earnest search for the ultimate meaning of life. He was, in his own estimation, "somewhat sober, and inclined rather to melancholy than the contrary extreme," but he did at least occasionally go to "frolics" with the young blades and girls of Haddam and East Haddam. Otherwise he would not have written his delicious bit of adult self-justification: "I was not much addicted to young company, or frolicking, as it is called, but this I know, that when I did go into such company, I never returned with so good a conscience as when I went."

On his nineteenth birthday David apparently inherited his share of his father's estate, a farm at Durham, about ten miles west of Haddam. About that time, too, the traditional description of his younger brother John as "tall in stature, large in frame, and active in his movements," may also have fitted him, even as John was "distinguished for exactness and propriety in everything." That same month, April 1737, he moved to his new farm. However, it seemed to have held little appeal for him and he worked it that summer only. His inclinations, he said, were more naturally toward a liberal education, and for that he frequently longed.

While his brother Hezekiah was about to become Clerk of Haddam and a justice of the peace, and had in 1734 already succeeded his father as Representative to the General Assembly, a position he would almost continuously occupy for forty years, Nehemiah had chosen to become a minister, the career to which their mother's father, two grandfathers and six uncles had dedicated their lives. During the winter David decided to follow Nehemiah's example. In that day when the average Yale student graduated before his twentieth birthday, he came late to his decision. Perhaps he finally decided that the ministry provided the easiest and most reasonable escape from his primitive and rude environment to a more congenial social and cultural life. He seemed to imply the dubiousness of his motives when he reflected a decade later: "I became very strict, and watchful over my thoughts, words, and actions; and thought I must be sober indeed, because I designed to devote myself to the ministry; and *imagined* I *did* dedicate myself to the Lord."

In April 1738, his birthday month, he returned to Haddam to live and to study with the pastor of his youth, Phineas Fiske. This able man and Joseph Noyes, minister of New Haven's First Church, had been the pillar tutors of infant (Yale) academy at Saybrook. Leader of the Haddam church for twenty-three years, ever since he had succeeded David's grandfather Hobart, Fiske knew the Brainerd family intimately. Three of his six daughters married Brainerds. Abigail had married David's cousin, the Reverend Chilliab Brainerd, Mary had married Hezekiah Jr., and the wedding of Elizabeth Fiske and Nehemiah Brainerd was imminent or had already taken place.

Having known David through his first twenty years, Fiske offered his advice to the youth who felt uncomfortable in frolicking young company: "He advised me wholly to abandon young company," said David, "and [to] associate myself with grave elderly people, which counsel I followed."

Having determined his course, he pursued his goal with intensity. He said: "I became wholly regular and full of religion, such as it was." He read his Bible more than twice through within the year and on Sunday evenings he met privately with a small group of friends for religious devotions. This was the more significant because the New England Sabbath began on Saturday night and ended at sundown on Sunday, an observance that had led to the prevalent Sunday evening dissipations and mirthmaking which Jonathan Edwards and other ministers greatly deplored. "In short," said Brainerd, "I had a very good *outside*."

He studied under Fiske's tutelage only a half year, for the old gentleman died in the autumn. David therefore joined with his brother Nehemiah and as he studied under his tutorship he became smugly satisfied with his inner life as well as his good outside. Increasingly he lamented the spiritual carelessness of others and imagined that his own dedication and sober behavior qualified him very favorably before both men and God.

It was on a Sunday morning in the beginning of winter when it happened. He was walking out for prayer. With a suddenness that amazed him, he knew himself as a self-righteous upstart, and he fully expected that the vengeance of God would soon descend upon him for the hideous hypocrisy of his life. In the days and weeks that followed he envied the birds and animals for their freedom from the guilt he now felt. He pleaded for relief from his guilt and meticuously observed his religious "duties." He stormed the gates of heaven in prayer and in grief; yet, at the same time, he calculated with Yankee shrewdness that the way could not be so very difficult: "I should by diligence and watchfulness soon gain the point."

By February 1739 he was setting aside days of secret fasting and almost incessant prayer as he strove for acceptance. He thought God must be pleased with his arduous strivings, but he could find no peace except in passing moods. When he thought of renouncing himself, of "standing naked before God, stripped of all goodness," he experienced veritable anguish. It was too dreadful for him to imagine. On another day when he realized how helpless he was to "gain the point" by himself, his fawning turned to anger that God should reveal Himself to others while excluding him. Whenever he grew indifferent to the matter his conviction of sin soon seized him with increased violence. One night he was so obsessed with the grim spectre of the earth opening under his feet, to drop his soul into hell, that he hurried to bed to escape notice. He schemed how he could dodge the Almighty, or, that being impossible, how he might thwart His judgments.

Distressed, bewildered, frightened, and resentful, he was particularly irritated with the Puritan doctrines of strict obedience to God's law, salvation only through faith, and the absolute sovereignty of God. He knew that he could not live a perfect life, and that all his fasting and prayer could not substitute for the faith he sought but which he could not comprehend — "I thought I would gladly come, if I knew *how!*" He flared in anger against Jonathan Edwards' grandfather, Solomon Stoddard, who suggested no way to bridge the gulf in his *Guide to Christ* — yet "which I trust was, in the hand of God, the happy means of my conversion." Least of all could he accept the idea of divine election: "I could not bear that it should be wholly at God's pleasure to save or damn me, just as he would." To admit that he was a sinner and a criminal and that God was his great Judge was revolting to him in the extreme. It was to jump off a cliff, or as he put it, to venture off some high precipice: "The truth was, I could see no safety in owning myself in the hands of a sovereign God, and that I could lay no claim to anything better than damnation."

In the end, that which he had tenaciously refused to acknowledge brought a melancholy peace to his soul. When he knew he could do nothing to bribe the Great Judge, and that he had nothing with which to argue his case, he could only ask for mercy: "I saw that I

had been heaping up my devotions before God, fasting, praying, pretending, and indeed really thinking sometimes, that I was aiming
at the glory of God; whereas I never once *truly* intended it, but only
my own happiness . . . the whole was nothing but *self-worship,* and
a horrid abuse of God."

He was completely disconsolate.

Winter again gave way to spring, and spring to summer. And,
then, on Sunday evening, July 12, 1739, as he retreated to his
secret place of prayer, God came to him. "As I was walking in a
dark thick grove, *unspeakable glory* seemed to open to the view
and apprehension of my soul. I do not mean any *external* bright-
ness, for I saw no such thing. . . . It was a new inward apprehension or view that I had of *God,* such as I never had before. . . . I
stood still, wondered, and admired! . . . It was widely different from
all the conceptions that ever I had of God. . . . My soul *rejoiced with
joy unspeakable,* to see such a God, such a glorious Divine Being;
and I was inwardly pleased and satisfied that he should be God
over all for ever and ever. My soul was so captivated and delighted
with the excellency, loveliness, greatness, and other perfections
of God, that I was even swallowed up in Him."

His distress regarding his personal salvation had vanished. At
that moment he was hardly aware of his own existence. He felt
himself in a new world. As for the way of salvation — entirely
by the righteousness of Jesus Christ, the effulgence of this divine
glory — he wondered that all the world did not see and comply with
"this lovely, blessed, and excellent way."

As the evening merged into night's darkness, there was light in
Brainerd's soul. He had encountered absolute love and divine glory,
and his life thereafter was passionate longing for and a fervent
dedication to that glorious Divine Being.

In the beginning of September he entered Yale College.

2. DISTINGUISHED IN ZEAL

YALE COLLEGE had been moved to New Haven and officially
named at the September Commencement of 1718, the year of
Brainerd's birth. Student life centered in the blue College Hall,
a three-storied frame building 165 feet long and 22 feet wide, con-

sisting of a hall, a library, and a kitchen. Here forty-five resident students lived and studied, attended sunrise prayers, and recited their lessons. The freshmen especially lived much in common and had little privacy. They were also continually hazed by upper-classmen and compelled to perform menial services upon slightest demands. And since two-thirds of the freshmen were but thirteen to seventeen years of age, and he already twenty-one, freshman Brainerd was older than most of the seniors, an awkward position at best.

Jonathan Edwards, who had graduated from Yale two decades earlier, had reported that the students engaged in such sophomoric pranks as night forays to steal "hens, geese, turkies [and] pigs," and "breaking windows, playing at cards, cursing, swearing, and damning." Only a year before Brainerd matriculated, sophomore Ezra Clapp had described a midnight revel in choicest language: "Last night some of the freshmen got six quarts of Rhum and about two payls fool of Sydar and about eight pounds of sugar and made it in to Samson . . . and we made such prodigius Rought . . . and yeled and screamed so that a bodey would have thought that they were killing dodgs there. . . ."

Amid such levity and high jinks, Brainerd's first winter at Yale must have been a rough one. He was distressed, he said, to see how carelessly most of his fellow students lived and, he added, "I longed exceedingly that they should enjoy what I enjoyed."

The winter, moreover, was an exceptionally cold one. The Quaker John Woolman reported in his journal that the Delaware River as far south as Philadelphia was frozen from December 15 to March and that market was conducted half-way between its shores. Long Island Sound was also frozen all winter, from the Connecticut shore to Long Island. In addition, an epidemic of measles broke out in New Haven, and Brainerd fell victim to it. He was laid low, both physically and spiritually, by the disease, by the intensity of his studies, and by the harassment of the upper-classmen.

He explained: "In January 1740, the measles spread much in college; and I having taken the distemper, went home to Haddam . . . and was very ill indeed, so that I almost despaired of life; but had no distressing fears of death at all. However, through divine goodness I recovered; yet, by reason of hard and close studies, and being much exposed on account of my *freshmanship*, I had but little time for spiritual duties . . . indeed, my ambition in my studies greatly wronged the activity and vigour of my spiritual life."

Obsessed with redeeming the time he had lost during his illness, he exhibited symptoms of an even worse malady before the summer ended. In August his tutor advised to go home again, for, said Brainerd, "I was grown so weak that I began to spit blood." Was he then already aware that he was infected with the same dread disease which likely had brought early death to his parents? Consumption or tuberculosis of the lungs was the plague of colonial New England.

After two months he returned to Yale, in the first week of November. He noted that he was still at Haddam on October 30 and on November 4, but in a curiously vague fashion for one who kept a precise diary, he marked the end of his long absence by stating: "I returned to college about November 6." Did he thereby circumvent his arrival at the campus on November 5, on Guy Fawkes Day? That was the one big holiday in Colonial America. It would be a great day for a college sophomore to rejoin his fellows. It was celebrated with great relish, with gunfire and bonfires and effigies of Guy Fawkes, the conspirator in the Gunpowder Plot of 1605 who was executed for attempting to blow up the British Parliament and King James I. It is still England's maddest night.

But whether he participated in the holiday, with zest or with the same reluctance he had expressed when he had first enrolled at Yale, he must have been amazed to discover the change that had come over his classmates. A new seriousness was unmistakably evident. The spiritual atmosphere of the place was different.

While he had convalesced among the quiet scenes of his boyhood, an event had occurred which would in large measure determine the course of his life. His career would probably not have been recorded had this event not taken place. It was the Great Awakening of New England, powerfully and unexpectedly ushered in by the arrival of George Whitefield of England, who had literally preached his way from Georgia and South Carolina and through Philadelphia and the Middle Colonies. His reputation had preceded him and during six unprecedented weeks, as this young Anglican priest visited Boston and more than thirty other New England towns, the people dropped their daily tasks and came from miles around to hear him. His effect on the lives and conduct of his listeners was amazing. "The very face of the town seems to be altered," exclaimed Benjamin Colman in concert with other ministers of Boston. Taverns were closed for lack of patrons and the ministers of Boston were soon beseiged by anxious inquirers of all ages and stations in life. When he was ready to leave Boston, 23,000 people jammed the Common to hear his farewell speech. From Boston he traveled to Northampton and there spent four days in Jonathan Edwards' home and occupied his pulpit five times.

Many among the crowds came only to be entertained by Whitefield's "amorous style of praying" and his "luscious style of preaching," as John Wesley once caricatured his fervent appeals and exhortations. But as Whitefield's silver voice proclaimed the old familiar gospel of salvation through the shed blood of Jesus Christ, from the pulpit or on the town green or in an open field, his message continued to strangely warm the hearts and minds of his listeners. And on October 27 when he traveled south along the Connecticut River to New Haven and preached to the students of Yale, a pentecostal flame had also descended upon them, and few were left without a strong and deep concern for the salvation of their souls.

Brainerd responded immediately to the warmth of this first manifestation of the Great Awakening. He wrote that through the goodness of God he felt the power of religion almost daily for the space of six weeks. Soon again, however, his ambition to excel in his studies seriously interfered with his religious ardor, at least for a time. His disclosure pin-points a momentous bit of Yale's history.

"Some time toward the latter end of January, 1741, I grew more *cold* and *dull* in religion, by means of my old temptation, namely, ambition in my studies. But through divine goodness, great and general *awakening* spread itself over the college, about the latter end of February, in which I was much quickened, and more abundantly engaged in religion."

The fact was that this second awakening at Yale College really took hold. The enthusiasm which possessed him and almost the entire student body became plainly evident in March when tall, thirty-eight-year-old Gilbert Tennent of New Jersey came to Boston, New Haven, and many other towns. A graduate of his father's Presbyterian Log College at Neshaminy, Pennsylvania, he had been strongly influenced by the evangelistic success of Theodore Frelinghuysen in the Dutch parishes near New Brunswick and had himself soon become the leading English revivalist in New Jersey. He had been even more stimulated by his personal contacts with Whitefield whom he declared he was willing to die for.

Tennent was a fiery Irishman with long flowing hair and the force of Elijah the Tishbite as he expounded primarily the stern warnings of the justice of God and the demands of His law. In one week as he preached seventeen powerful sermons from Joseph Noyes' pulpit in the First Church of New Haven and several more in the College Hall his success equalled that of Whitefield who had sent him. Senior student Samuel Hopkins who would become New England's greatest theologian after Jonathan Edwards wrote: "When I heard Mr. Tennent, I thought he was the greatest and best man, and the best preacher, that I had ever seen or heard. His words were to me 'like apples of gold in pictures of silver.' And I thought that, when I should leave the college, as I was then in my last year, I would go and live with him, wherever I should find him."

Some thirty students were seemingly of the same mind. When Tennent left New Haven they followed him on foot to hear him preach again in Milford, some ten miles away.

It is not known whether Brainerd accompanied these ready disciples. But he was by now one of the leading scholars of his class and he soon became its undisputed leader in contacting other students about their religious life and personal commitment to Christ. Samuel Hopkins wrote in his *Memoirs* that David distinguished himself in his zeal and that two seniors were intimately associated with him in visiting the students "for conversation and prayer." They were Samuel Buell and David Youngs. All three were older students — Buell was twenty-five; Youngs was twenty-two; Brainerd was twenty-three.

Hopkins also revealed that he owned his conversion to Brainerd. At first, he said, he resented Brainerd's visit, but afterwards he walked to his room in tears and "took up Watts' version of the Psalms, and opened it at the Fifty-first Psalm, and read the first, second, and third parts in long meter with strong affections, and made it all my own language, and thought it was the language of my heart to God." Isaac Watts' thirty-two verses for Psalm 51 contained those familiar and precious lines: Great God, create my heart anew, And form my spirit pure and true. Jesus, my God, thy blood alone — Thy blood can make me white as snow. A broken heart, my God, my King, Is all the sacrifice I bring.

On April 19 Ebenezer Pemberton visited Yale. A former Congregationalist, he was the pastor of the Presbyterian church in New York. His experiences to and from New Haven typified the Great Awakening's increasing momentum. One of his parishioners, an eyewitness, reported: "Whole colleges are under conviction, and many savingly converted. Our minister (Mr. Pemberton of New York), being sent for to Yale College on account of the many distressed persons there, in his going and coming preached twice a day on the road, and even children followed him to his lodgings, weeping and anxiously concerned about the salvation of their souls."

Pemberton's special visit to Yale is significant to Brainerd's story in that this Harvard graduate and distinguished gentleman and several other former New Englanders in the Middle Colonies had recently taken steps to send missionaries to the American Indians, and with this purpose in mind they had petitioned the Society in Scotland for Propagating Christian Knowledge for financial aid. It is entirely natural therefore that Pemberton would also challenge the most promising young men in New England outside Harvard to a life of missionary service. He may have suggested to them the example of John Sergeant, a brilliant former Yale student and tutor who was now teaching and baptizing Indians at Stockbridge, Massachusetts.

As the highlight of his visit Pemberton preached in the College Hall from I Corinthians 2:2 — *I am determined not to know any thing among you, save Jesus Christ and him crucified.* His theme was "Christ is all," and his exhortation was Colossians 3:2 — *Set your affections on things above, not on things on the earth.* His message made a profound impression upon the students. It was immediately published by T. Green in New London under the title *The Knowledge of Christ Recommended,* and an appended list of one hundred subscribers included all the students of Yale except three. Each of them subscribed for three to twelve copies. Buell, Young and Brainerd each ordered six. Hopkins ordered eight.

The crucial impact of Pemberton's visit in Brainerd's life can only be surmised. Pemberton was doubtless a popular speaker and highly regarded and in his address he reminded the scholars: "Your united requests have bro't me into this desk at this time, and for your service this discourse is peculiarly designed." He repeatedly and particularly challenged the ministerial aspirants to emulate the life of the apostle Paul, "the Great Doctor to the Gentiles," who *counted all things but loss and damage, for the excellency of the knowledge of Jesus Christ.* Indicative of his own temperament and poise was his pointed warning that Paul's commitment "was not a sudden flash of thought, occasioned by some present surprise" or "when his understanding was disordered with the fumes of enthusiasm." Brainerd would recall this warning, but it would seem that in a time of mounting "enthusiasm" he lost sight of it in his drive to imitate primarily the Great Doctor's zeal.

Another emphasis of Pemberton's address would particularly concern Brainerd's driving ambition. He had frequently longed for a liberal education and had pursued his studies with utmost intensity and though he had been laid low twice, he was now at the top of his class. But Pemberton's estimate of all such scholarly attainments would cause him no little discomfort. Pemberton said: "Men are apt highly to value themselves upon the account of their human knowledge and to look down with contempt upon others, whom they esteem ignorant and unlearn'd: But the wisest Philosopher, the greatest Scholar, if ignorant of Christ and the way of salvation appointed by him, will be finally rejected by God . . . neither the writings of Plato or Seneca, the celebrated Philosophers of Rome and Athens: nor the most accurate delineations of the religion of Nature by the admir'd teachers of morality in the present Age, will afford you a solid foundation of peace and comfort."

But, above all, Pemberton's fervent pleas to accept and to proclaim the glories of Jesus Christ — "a commission that would dignify an angel, and adorn the character of the highest seraph" — remained and grew in David's heart. Pemberton's impassioned prayer to "let thy kingdom be set up in my soul, reign absolute in my heart, and let every rebellious passion be subject to thy just and righteous government" would always be his, and the day would come when he would publicly record that he had always and only preached *Christ crucified*, as Pemberton had admonished — *"Let Christ and him crucified be the favourite subject, of your private meditations and public administrations, without which your sacred performances, how beautifully soever they are contrived, how artfully soever delivered, will be no better than the sounding brass and tinkling cymbal.* Remember the character you are to bear is that of a minister of Christ, and the commission you receive, is to preach *his unsearchable riches* — to proclaim the glories of the Amiable Jesus . . . Let his name therefore triumph in all your discourses, and let it be the height of your ambition to bring sinners to a saving acquaintance with him. . ."

But what sinners? Who were these lost souls whom he like the Apostle Paul must seek for the Amiable Christ? They were not Ephesians or Corinthians, Romans or the foolish Galatians. The Gentiles of his world were well defined. They were contemptuously referred to as the heathen Canaanites, Amorites and Philistines who plagued the land with their idolatrous worship of devils. They were the despised Indians.

Had he so long pursued after a liberal education, and had he left his farm at Durham and every reasonable assurance of secular success only to go to savages? Could this ever be the height of his ambition? What then of his scholastic achievement and the standing before men which he seemed to have so assiduously identified with his ministerial career?

He left no record of his initial decision to become a wilderness missionary. But there is a clue which could mean that Pemberton's stirring address and personal interest in the American Indian may have reached Brainerd as the call of the Spirit. The next day was April 20, his twenty-third birthday. On that day he vowed "to be *wholly* the Lord's, to be *for ever* devoted to his service."

3. NOT ONLY YOUNG IN YEARS

WHATEVER THE CRITICISMS against the Great Awakening, one overriding fact is assuredly true. The Spirit of God came as a wind and burned as a flame in the hearts of men, not only in New England but in the Middle Colonies, among Pietists, Arminians, and Calvinists alike; and it was manifest in Germany and England before it became evident in America. Its first stirrings had come to the colonies in the 1720's under the zealous preaching of pious Theodorus Jacobus Frelinghuysen in the Raritan Valley settlements of New Jersey and it spread, yet it was more a simultaneous moving than a progression. It could not be confined. In 1720 Increase Mather had lamented, "Oh, degenerate New England, what art thou come to . . .?", but a year later the minister at Windham, Connecticut, reported "a remarkable concern," and from the two hundred families in the village, eighty persons were added to the church. Other "refreshings" appeared unexpectedly in unrelated and out-of-the-way places. In 1734 the Spirit visited Northampton under the preaching of Jonathan Edwards and three hundred persons were converted in six months. It is difficult today to realize what a shaking and awakening took place at that time. When Edwards' *Narrative* of these events reached England, Isaac Watts wrote: "Never in the history of Christianity did we hear such a thing." It was the beginning of the most stupendous upheaval since the Reformation of the sixteenth century.

In 1740 Whitefield came to America and after a successful tour of the Southern and Middle Colonies he had come to New England. It was then that the Great Awakening burst into full flame and wonderfully and permanently transformed thousands to whom religion had been little more than empty formalism. New life had come. The hearts of men burned with a new devotion and a revitalized, personal faith in Jesus Christ, and in the early half of that revolutionary century the American church was impregnated with the evangelical witness.

But the Great Awakening was not an unmixed blessing, for the Prince of Darkness, the Great Deceiver, quickly saw his opportunity to despoil the Spirit's true work. He posed as an angel of light, and in his light men saw so clearly the faults of others and were blinded to their own. They began criticizing others who failed to display any great enthusiasm for revival and soon it was as Jonthan Edwards judged it to be. "Censuring others," he said, "is the worst disease with which this affair has been attended."

Whitefield was not spared from this temptation and serious fault. He fervently preached Christ's redeeming love, the new birth, and sanctification in Christian living. But when he made his first tour of New England he was only twenty-five years old and was probably more censorious than at any time in his long career. He singled out the New England clergy and condemned them as hypocritical and unconverted and, except for his specific endorsement, his reckless criticisms cast a pall of suspicion on the majority of the ministers. Later he admitted that his condemnations had been too sweeping and severe.

When he returned to New Jersey he persuaded Gilbert Tennet to tour New England, "to blow up the divine flame recently kindled there." Two years earlier at Nottingham, Pennsylvania, Tennent had preached his impassioned sermon, *The Danger of an Unconverted Ministry,* which had been published by Benjamin Franklin in Philadelphia. In that devastating attack he had called down the denunciation of heaven upon an ungodly ministry — "These Caterpillars labour to devour every green Thing." His New England tour lasted four months and as he reiterated this theme, and endorsed Whitefield's charges against the clergy, people began to turn against their ministers and began to hold "Separate" meetings. Many of these assemblies were conducted by self-appointed lay preachers and in some cases also by women exhorters.

At Yale the new and alarmed Rector Thomas Clap soon forbade his students to attend Separate meetings, and he levied fines against the scholars who had flaunted his orders by following Tennent to Milford. A strict disciplinarian, Clap was also a most rigid conservative who would increasingly oppose revivalism, Whitefield, Tennent, and those students who were already beginning to propagate the revivalists' uncomplimentary views about the clergy of which he was a member. The seeds of discord were planted especially during the spring of 1741, and they would blossom before the year's end.

The Great Awakening received even greater impetus on July 8 when Jonathan Edwards preached his famous Enfield sermon, *Sinners in the Hands of An Angry God*. His theme of the wrath of God who holds sinners over the pit of hell, "much in the same way as one holds a spider, or some loathsome insect," was quite different from his sermons on God's love which had brought refreshing rededications in his Northampton congregation five years earlier. He was now preaching in a different vein. He was now painting word pictures of hell to *scare* careless sinners into seeking the way to heaven.

Seeking the way, even as Brainerd had sought and had been found, was Edwards' constant theme, regardless of his code of presentation. But that night as he continued and concluded with his urging to repentance — "Now you have an extraordinary opportunity, a day wherein Christ has thrown the door of mercy wide open", and stands calling, and crying with a loud voice to poor sinners" — the people of Enfield broke into unprecedented shrieking and convulsive crying. In a sense there was no accounting for it. A few weeks earlier the same sermon had produced no perceptible effect when Edwards preached it to his own congregation.

Only ten days after the Enfield sermon, and scarcely twenty miles south of that town, David Brainerd's brother Nehemiah was also planning a series of revival meetings in his church. Pastor of the Second Congregational church in Eastbury, at that time a parish of Glastonbury, Nehemiah addressed a letter on July 17/18 to Eleazer Wheelock, the thirty-year-old crusading minister of nearby Lebanon, urging this subsequent founder of Dartmouth College to come to "Glassenbury," there to join forces with him in gathering Christ's chosen against the "daring, hardy soldiers of Satan." Significantly, Nehemiah also wrote: "If you can't come till ye week after next, probably our Friend Buel and my Brother will be here."

As noted earlier, Samuel Buell was one of Yale's oldest students and quite probably, in Rector Clap's estimation, also one of the most troublesome, for he had already earned the reputation of being a lively preacher. In Clap's view, Buell was at least an unordained enthusiast. But Nehemiah Brainerd implied in his letter to Wheelock that he was also expecting David to preach and that his younger brother was apparently readily available for such preaching services as were planned.

How avid an "enthusiast" was David? Little is specifically known about this aspect of his student days because he destroyed his college diaries before his death. He explained, however, that after he left Yale he was "more refined from some *imprudencies* and *indecent heats*," and he recalled his indiscretions with extreme distaste and remorse. The historian Richard Webster strove valiantly to defend both Buell and Brainerd by discrediting their scoffers. He wrote: "Of the extravagances charged . . . many are plainly untrue, coming from scoffers and worldly-wise men . . . denunciations fell like hail on Whitefield . . . Buell and Brainerd were held up as strollers and fanatics whom it was not allowable to improve." But Lucy Brainerd's monumental *Genealogy of the Brainerd-Brainard Family* strongly implies that David was one of the "most disorderly strolling preachers," and Jonathan Edwards, likewise, made no attempt to absolve him.

During the Great Awakening bands of young hecklers and orators harassed preachers who were not to their liking. Edwards seems plainly to identify Brainerd with such strollers or such disorderly conduct when he stated that "while complying in his conduct with persons of a fierce and imprudent zeal" whom he foolishly looked up to with great veneration, he "joined, and kept company with some who were tinged with no small degree" of enthusiasm and was not lacking in misguided zeal during his college days, although his extravagances were more imitative than genuine.

Edwards then tempered his judgment by explaining: "At the *beginning* of that extraordinary religious commotion . . . neither people nor ministers had learned thoroughly to *distinguish* between solid religion and its delusive counterfeits. . . . Even many ministers of the gospel, of long standing and the best reputation, were for a time overpowered with the glaring appearances of the latter; and therefore, surely it was not to be wondered at, that young Brainerd, but a *sophomore* at college, should be so; who was not only young in years, but very young in religion and experience."

Delusive counterfeits increased that summer, and ecclesiastical prejudices also entered the picture. A generation earlier the Congregational churches of Connecticut had adopted the Saybrook Platform of 1708 which increased the authority of ministerial associations or councils and thereby curtailed the complete autonomy of the local congregations, as based on the older Cambridge Platform. During the Great Awakening many persons justified the formation of Separate churches as the only means of protest against the Saybrook Platform and the authority of the associations, from which the Baptists and Quakers were already free.

Those who opposed the Separatists and looked with disfavor on revivalistic enthusiasms and innovations were called the Old Lights. They were the majority group which held political as well as religious control during Brainerd's years at Yale. Rector Clap was the champion of this class in New Haven. Between these two extreme parties were the New Lights or evangelicals who were stirred by the revival and desired a more vital Christianity in the churches, but deplored the extravagances and excesses that occurred almost daily. Jonathan Edwards was the outstanding New Light and moderating spirit.

Naturally, the lines of demarcation were often blurred. Joseph Noyes had welcomed Whitefield to his pulpit, but turned against even the New Lights in his opposition to the Separatist spirit. Gilbert Tennent, the New Side Presbyterian from New Jersey, abhorred the rapid rise of unqualified lay preachers, but himself encouraged Separatism in his attacks against the "unconverted" clergy. Eleazar Wheelock, the mutual friend of Nehemiah Brainerd, Samuel Buell and, doubtless, also David, was a New Light who veered dangerously toward extreme Separatism in his itinerant preaching, until he took himself in hand. But Wheelock's brother-in-law became a most voluble extremist.

James Davenport, a thirty-three-year-old bachelor who had graduated from Yale when he was fifteen or sixteen years old, was the minister of the Presbyterian congregation at Southold, Long Island, where Brainerd's great-uncle Joshua Hobart had once served. He was a great-grandson of John Davenport, the founder-minister of the New Haven colony a century earlier, and his father had been minister at nearby Stamford. James was therefore cordially received in New Haven when he took leave of his congregation and began his first deleterious preaching spree through Connecticut that summer. Preaching at the First Church in September he condemned Joseph Noyes from that good man's own pulpit and called him a wolf in sheep's clothing, an unconverted hypocrite, and a devil incarnate. The townspeople were put in uproar and a split in the congregation soon became imminent. And, according to the historian William Sprague, Davenport "produced a powerful effect upon the mind of David Brainerd . . . though an effect which was at best of a mixed character."

Amid the babel of bickering and dispute that followed in the wake of Davenport's tirades, Brainerd began his third year at Yale College. At the Commencement of September 10, Edwards preached the baccalaureate sermon from I John 4:1, *Beloved, believe not every spirit, but prove the spirits whether they are of God; because many false prophets are gone out into the world.* It was published before the end of the year under the title, *Distinguishing Marks of a Work of the True Spirit.* Graduate Samuel Hopkins was so impressed with the lecture that he changed his mind about going to live with Gilbert Tennent and arrived unannounced at Edwards' house that fall and stayed to study with him.

Since Samuel Buell and David Youngs also graduated that September, Brainerd lost their companionship and perhaps the protection of their seniority. Of this trio distinguished for their zeal, he now alone remained. And it was specifically against his kind and his type of enthusiasm that the Trustees of Yale passed this stern resolution when they met during Commencement Week: "Voted, that if any student of this College shall directly or indirectly say, that the Rector, either of the Trustees or Tutors are hypocrites, carnal or unconverted men, he shall for the first offense make a public confession in the Hall, and for the second offense be expelled."

Within a short time Brainerd ran headlong against the Trustees' new ruling and its provisions, and sometime during the winter he was expelled from Yale. Stressing that Brainerd was conversing only in private, with special and intimate friends "who associated together for mutual conversation and assistance in spiritual things," Edwards explained: "It once happened, that he and two or three more of these intimate friends were in the [College Hall] together, after Mr. Whittelsey, one of the tutors, had been to prayer there with the scholars; no other person now remaining in the hall but Brainerd and his companions. Mr. Whittelsey having been unusually pathetical in his prayer, one of Brainerd's friends on this occasion asked him what he thought of Mr. Whittelsey; he made answer, 'He has no more grace than this chair.' One of the freshmen happening at that time to be near the hall (though not in the room), over-heard those words."

"Unusually pathetical" meant that Whittelsey had prayed with emotion and a passionate, earnest spirit — not that his prayer elicited pity for a poor performance. Brainerd's censorious retort did not mean that Whittelsey merely lacked grace, charm or elegance in his prayer. As he leaned upon that innocuous colonial chair Brainerd had rashly pronounced Tutor Whittelsey to be without saving grace, in other words, a hypocrite and a carnal or unconverted man.

David's severe censure may never have come to light, had it not been for the green and no doubt harassed freshman who did not hold his tongue. He told a certain woman, perhaps his landlady, "that he believed Brainerd had said this of someone or other of the rulers of the college." She told Rector Clap and he sent for the freshman and "examined" him. The freshman told Clap what he had heard and the names of Brainerd's friends. Edwards showed little sympathy toward Clap when he concluded: "Upon which the rector sent for them: they were very backward to inform against their friend what they looked upon as private conversation, and especially as none but they had heard or knew of whom he had uttered those words: yet the rector compelled them to declare *what* he said, and of *whom* he said it."

That was it. Brainerd was quite defenseless. First, there was the new law made only weeks earlier by the Trustees. Second, "a little before I was expelled," he had attended a "Separate" meeting in New Haven, perhaps the new Second church then forming, in defiance of Clap's specific orders. Third, and understandably infuriating to Clap, another person reported that Brainerd had said that he wondered Clap "did not expect to drop down dead for fining the scholars who followed Mr. Tennent to Milford." David admitted having attended the Separate meeting but definitely denied recollection of the third charge. At any rate, the least punishment he could expect was the stipulated public confession in the College Hall.

Notwithstanding his later bitterness, Brainerd must have been truly humiliated when he finally realized that Tutor Chauncey Whittelsey was quite innocent of his rash judgment. Only six months his senior, Whittelsey began his tutorship when David had enrolled. He specialized in Latin, Greek and Hebrew. Although a moderate and cautious person, he did not openly oppose the New Lights. Perhaps as a deterrent to mounting intemperate zeal in the college, he had prayed that it might be controlled. He also kept a journal, and about the time when he was licensed to preach (September 30, 1740), he had written regarding his ministry of the Gospel: "Let me not enter upon it without thy direction and blessing. Lord Jesus! mighty Head of the Church! fit me for thy service. . . . May I be willing to spend and be spent in the work of the Lord, and for the good and salvation of souls. . . may I speak the truth boldly for Christ, and be blessed of him."

Whittelsey's lines could well have been Brainerd's own, as every reader of his diaries will instantly recognize. But they were written by the man whom he had condemned.

Rector Thomas Clap who is generally charged with David's expulsion was at that time thirty-eight years old. He was Connecticut-born, Harvard-trained, and, like David, had been converted through reading Solomon Stoddard's writings. Before his rectorship he had served Windham as a faithful but overbearing pastor for fourteen years. Although learned, pious and capable, Clap was unduly strict and set in his ways. He was especially opposed to every innovation in doctrine, itinerant preachers, lay exhorters, and the enthusiasm of which Brainerd was probably Yale's leading exponent.

In spite of Clap's antagonism, he did only require that Brainerd publicly confess his guilt. But, "as long as he lived," Brainerd considered himself ill-used in the affair. As Edwards apparently quoted him, he thought that it was "injuriously *required* of him — as if he had been guilty of some open notorious crime — to make a *public* confession, and to humble himself before the whole college in the hall, for what he said only in *private* conversation."

Since Brainerd was not then of a mind to make amends, Clap had little choice, as he saw it; and Brainerd's days at Yale came to a sudden end. He was not without fault. Edwards described his shortcoming in one neat sentence when he said, "Brainerd had the unhappiness to have a *tincture* of that intemperate, indiscreet zeal, which was at that time too prevalent; and was led, from his high opinion of others whom he looked upon as better than himself, into such errors as were really contrary to the habitual temper of his mind."

As Edwards also stated, Brainerd recalled only too well that during those days he was out of his element — "as a fish out of water."

4. THE PROSPECT OF THE HEATHEN

IN THE SPRING, after his expulsion from Yale, Brainerd lived and studied with Jedediah Mills. A graduate of Yale in 1722, Mills was pastor at Ripton, now Shelton, some ten miles west of New Haven. He was a strong evangelistic preacher, a friend of Edwards and other evangelical leaders. In Mills' parish of Stratford on the Housatonic River, Brainerd began the third little book of his diary. It reveals how he marked time during the next seven months, but it also discloses how greatly he had been chastened and that he had turned his back on extravagances and "party-spirit." He had also taken steps which would lead him from the circle of his friends to a solitary existence far from his native New England. The first preserved entry of his diary — "I seem to be declining, with respect to my life and warmth in divine things. . . ." — is dated April

1, 1742, but he may have started his new volume on March 25, the
first day of the year according to the Julian or Old Style calendar
which was still being used in the English colonies.

The highest pitch of the revival had passed and a more sober and
questioning mood was becoming apparent. In February, Jonathan
Dickinson, the leading minister of New Jersey, had visited New
Haven to seek advice about a split among the Presbyterians in the
Middle Colonies. He carried with him a letter from Gilbert Tennent
which expressed Tennent's weariness, not with the revival itself,
but with the controversies which the revival, and he, had caused.
He was greatly distressed about his own "mismanagement." Rector
Clap had the letter published in the *Boston Evening Post* in July.

Significantly, Dickinson was one of the ministers who had suc-
cessfully petitioned the Society in Scotland for Propagating Christian
Knowledge for funds. In August he and his colleagues had been
appointed as commissioners for the society in America. They had
in turn commissioned Azariah Horton as their missionary to the
remnant Indians on Long Island, and they were now looking for a
second man to extend the work. That Brainerd conferred with
Dickinson about their unique undertaking is more than suggested
by the fact that while he was in New Haven, Dickinson unsuccessfully
interceded for Brainerd. D. D. Fields in his *Genealogy of the
Brainerd Family* states that Dickinson "pleaded before the authorities of Yale College in behalf of the Society . . . which had [already]
appointed him as their missionary."

Jonathan Edwards observed that as Mills' protege, Brainerd frequently rode to visit Jedediah's neighboring ministers: Samuel Cooke of
Old Stratford, and John Graham and Joseph Bellamy of the ten-year-
old towns of Southbury and Bethlehem. But, even more so, David
was occupied in searching his soul, in reviewing the recent debacle
of his career and, apparently, in reaching toward the missionary cause
which Pemberton and Dickinson represented. In the first week of his
diary the reader re-discovers the mystic of the Haddam grove, and a
growing and groping ascetic. At times his language approaches the
romantic.

"What are the storms of this lower world, if Jesus by his Spirit
does but come walking on the seas. Some time past, I had much
pleasure on the prospect of the heathen being brought home to
Christ, and desired that the Lord would employ me in that work:
but now my soul more frequently desires to die, to be with Christ.

"I . . . began to find it sweet to pray and could think of under-
going the greatest sufferings in the cause of Christ with pleasure and

found myself willing, if God should so order it, to suffer banishment from my native land, among the heathen, that I might do something for their salvation, in distresses and deaths of any kind."

On April 20, his twenty-fourth birthday, he remembered how a year ago he had vowed to be wholly the Lord's, and he wrote: "This day I am twenty-four years of age. . . . And how poorly have I answered the vows I made this time twelvemonth. [But] this has been a sweet, a happy day to me. . . . I hardly ever so longed to *live to God* and to be altogether devoted to him; I wanted to wear out my life in his service and for his glory."

Always his thoughts were God-ward. The northern lights of an evening suggested to him the glorious morning of the resurrection, and he kept prayer trysts with God in sylvan retreats. On Easter Sunday he wrote "I retired early this morning into the woods for prayer," and on the following Sunday likewise: "It was early in the morning and the sun scarcely shined at all, yet my body was quite wet with sweat." At other times, morning, afternoon, or evening, he could say: "I withdrew to my usual place of retirement in great peace and tranquility." In a dedicated moment he quoted or composed some verse: "Farewell, vain world," and "Lord, I'm a stranger here alone."

He freely employed the popular religious and biblical expressions of his day. It was "the dialect of Canaan" — the dialect of faith, and prayer, and evangelical sympathy, as Lyman Beecher defined the sanctified speech of those possessed by the mind of Christ. On April 27 he passionately declared: "If I had a thousand lives, my soul would gladly have laid them all down at once to have been with Christ." Similar phrases, such as "O for a thousand tongues to sing my Great Redeemer's praise," are preserved today in Charles Wesley's stirring and familiar hymns and in many others. White-field, too, can be quoted almost at random — "Had I a thousand lives, had I a thousand tongues, they should be employed in inviting sinners to come to Jesus Christ." A century earlier when tempted to exchange Christ for the things of this life John Bunyan had stated it in the negative: "I will not; I will not . . . no, not for thousands, thousands, thousands of worlds" — trifling tributes to Him who views a thousand years as a day when it is past.

Brainerd's references to his expulsion, "my great trial at college," are slight, perhaps only because Edwards deleted most of them at this time. But that he waged a constant fight against the bitterness of his disappointment cannot be doubted. On April 25 he exclaimed: "O it is a sweet disposition, heartily to forgive all injuries done us; to wish our greatest enemies as well as we do our own souls!

Blessed Jesus, may I daily be more and more conformed to thee." On April 28 he again disowned his chagrin: "I had no more value for the favour of men, than for pebbles." But, as if recognizing the hollowness of his words, he added: "O that God would *purge away my dross, and take away my tin*, and make me seven times refined." The month ended. His studies went well. On Saturday, May 1, he noted, "This has been a profitable week to me," and as the green-leafed spring again spread up the Connecticut Valley he mounted his horse, left his peaceful retreat at Ripton, and traveled for three weeks. On Monday, May 10, he rode ten miles to New Haven, and spent most of the next day in covering the forty odd miles to Weathersfield. There, however, he revealed that he was "sometimes afraid of everything," and, desperate for a little of his former quiet, he exclaimed: "Alas! I cannot live in the midst of a tumult. I long to enjoy God alone."

On Thursday afternoon he arrived at Hartford. His father's grave was here. The capital city was also his principal objective on this trip, for his diary for Friday, May 14, reads: "I waited on a council of ministers convened at Hartford and spread before them the treatment I had met with from the rector and tutors of Yale college; who thought it advisable to intercede for me with the rector and trustees, and to entreat them to restore me to my former privileges in college."

New life, new friends, interested ministers, encouraging hopes — yet on Saturday, riding from Hartford to Hebron, he was all dejection. "Indeed," he lamented, continually fighting what he termed the spiritual pride of his soul, "I never saw such a week as this before." During the rest of the month he visited the towns of Lebanon, Norwich and Millington in eastern Connecticut and perhaps lingered along his own river shores at his old home in Haddam and with his dear sister Jerusha in East Haddam. By May 28, having returned to New Haven, he thought he scarce ever felt so calm in his life.

Even as he made this first circuit, the Legislature at Hartford passed stringent laws toward controlling the bands of "strolling exhorters" and other imitative zealots who had been the chief disturbers throughout the parishes of Connecticut during the past year. The legislators' action was a bit tardy for by now most of the offenders had grown weary of their avocations. The lawmakers made sure by forbidding even licensed clergymen to preach in any parish than their own unless they first obtained permission from the resident minister.

When he had visited Weathersfield a month ago and had com-

plained that he could not live in the midst of a tumult, Brainerd
may have left the barest hint that he had witnessed a riot or at least
a noisy demonstration. It was a happy circumstance then that he
had not yet returned to the home of Jedediah Mills when that
gentleman invited James Davenport and his "armour-bearer,"
Benjamin Pomeroy of Hebron, to conduct a series of evangelistic
meetings at Ripton. Soon after they had arrived complaints arose
that their preaching was inflammatory. As a consequence, both
Pomeroy and Davenport were hailed before the General Assembly
at Hartford. So great was the excitement over their arrest that the
sheriff at Hartford had difficulty in conducting them to their
lodgings, and a militia force of forty armed men was called out to
protect the Assembly from hostile demonstrators in sympathy with
the arrested brethren.*

After a three-day trial Pomeroy was acquitted on June 3, but the
Assembly declared Davenport "under the influence of enthusiastical
impressions and impulses, and thereby disturbed in the rational
faculties of his mind, and therefore to be pitied and compassionated,
and not to be treated as otherwise he might be." They ordered
him home, and a week later the sheriff and two files of the militia
armed with muskets conducted him to the bank of the Connecticut
River and put him aboard a boat to Long Island. Before long, however, he returned to the mainland and continued his fanatical preaching. During the summer he was again arrested in Boston where the
court also judged him *non compos mentis,* and therefore not guilty.

Davenport's friends, both the New Light Congregationalists of
Connecticut and the New Side Presbyterians of New Jersey, were
dismayed. He was well-known in the Middle Colonies where,
sometimes in company with Whitefield, he had preached effectively
but sanely, unaccompanied by the shriekings, faintings and rollings
he now encouraged in New England. As a result of his rabble-
rousing, true piety suffered, and the evangelicals were indiscriminately lumped together in the minds of the irreligious as being a nuisance
to society. Brainerd felt the sting of criticism, too. His diary gives
a small hint: "The disgrace I was laid under at college — it opens the
mouths of opposers."

He returned to Jedediah Mills' home on June 1 and began to

* Pomeroy and Davenport were both brothers-in-law of Brainerd's friend,
Eleazar Wheelock of Lebanon. Davenport's half-sister Sarah was Wheelock's
wife; Pomeroy's wife Abigail was Wheelock's sister. Because of some weakness in his legs, Davenport frequently leaned upon Pomeroy for support and
called him "my armour-bearer."

spend days in prayer and fasting, and he arrived at some assurance of progress in his desire to be "more engaged to *live for God* for ever, [and] for many that I thought were the children of God, *personally*, in many distant places." Yet he felt quite undecided, "very helpless, and at a great loss *what the Lord would have me to do.*" His entry for June 18 seems to epitomize his alternating "frames", his realization of personal inadequacy, and his hope for release from all the hobbles of mortal life.

"Considering my great unfitness for the work of the ministry, my present deadness, and total inability to do anything for the glory of God that way, feeling myself very helpless, and at a great loss what the Lord would have me to do; I set apart this day for prayer to God, and spent most of the day in that duty, but amazingly deserted most of the day. Yet I found God graciously near, once in particular; while I was pleading for more compassion for immortal souls, my heart seemed to be opened at once, and I was enabled to cry with great ardency, for a few minutes. O I was distressed to think that I should offer such dead cold services to the living God! My soul seemed to breathe after holiness, a life of constant devotedness to God. But I am ready to sink, because I continually fall short, and miss my desire. O that the Lord would help me to hold out, yet a little while, until the happy hour of deliverance comes!"

He was still in the same frame of mind as the month ended. At times he almost despaired of ever accomplishing anything in the world or for the heathen. "I thought that I had no power to stand for the cause of God," he said, "but was almost 'afraid of the shaking of a leaf.'"

Book Two

The Probationer

In the former part of his religious course, he imputed much of that kind of gloominess of mind, and those dark thoughts to spiritual desertion, which in the latter part of his life he was abundantly sensible were owing to the disease of melancholy.

—Jonathan Edwards

5. A KIND OF PLEASING PAIN

BRAINERD'S DIARY for July is rather sketchy. Yet it was the important month in which he was licensed, "for the trial and improvements of his gifts," as the usual form letter stated. It meant that he could preach in the churches as an accredited and regular preacher, although he was not permitted to administer baptism and the Lord's Supper.

On July 14 he heard Joseph Bellamy preach at Bethlehem and it would seem that he then spent most of the month with Bellamy in preparation for his examination. Journeying from Southbury to Ripton on July 22 he revealed a self-deprecation painful to today's reader. "I called at a house by the way," he wrote, "where being very kindly entertained and refreshed, I was filled with amazement and shame, that God should stir up the hearts of any to show so much kindness to such a dead dog as I." He wondered that God would suffer anyone to feed and sustain him.

He and Rueben Judd, a classmate of Hopkins and Buell, were both licensed on Thursday, July 29, by the Association of the Eastern District of Fairfield County at its meeting in Danbury. The New Light leaders of this association had also previously licensed Buell, and had presided at the organization of the new church in New Haven. They were all David's familiar friends: the lone New Light trustee of Yale, Samuel Cooke of Stratford who vigorously opposed the persuasive preaching of his townsman Samuel Johnson (one of Yale's most notable defectors who occupied the single Anglican pulpit in Connecticut, until he became the first president of King's College, Columbia University); John Graham the Glasgow-trained physician and minister of Southbury's second church who supported Cooke with his anti-Episcopal pamphlets; Elisha Kent who had graduated from Yale in 1729; and their eloquent junior colleague, Joseph Bellamy.

Of the four men, Bellamy was closest to Brainerd. Immediately after he was licensed, David joined with him in prayer, "in a convenient place." Although a year younger than Brainerd, Bellamy had already served Bethlehem for three years. He had graduated from Yale when he was sixteen years old and was licensed to preach at eighteen, after two years of study with Jonathan Edwards. When "Bethlem," the new parish of Woodbury, received permission to have

41

a winter preacher, they called Bellamy. He accepted, and stayed for fifty years. He was a giant in intellect, a valiant New Light, and one of Edwards' closest friends. Open-hearted, confident and outspoken, and still unmarried, he was also the "peculiarly dear friend" of Brainerd's diary, as Edwards disclosed in one of his numerous letters to John Erskine in Scotland.

Through the summer the two bachelors lived together, and worshipped and preached in the barn which served as a meetinghouse for Bellamy's small congregation. However, David's first sermon on the day after his licensure was not delivered in Bellamy's barn but in John Graham's church at Southbury. His text was I Peter 4:8, *And above all things have fervent charity!* His sermon was a success. He wrote, "I seemed to have power with God in prayer and power to get hold of the hearts of the people in preaching," and it left him "calm, composed, greatly refreshed and encouraged." A week later he occupied Bellamy's pulpit twice on Sunday and again felt "very comfortably."

Four days later, however, on Thursday, August 12, he seemed "shut out from God." He had also lost much of his hope that God would send him among the heathen afar off, "and of seeing them flock home to Christ." He also saw "so much of my vileness" that he wondered that people did not stone him and that they would so much as hear him preach.

The people he referred to that morning were Indians. Accompanied by Bellamy he had gone out to visit these people who were living along the Housatonic River near Kent, a small village which had been settled only four years near the Connecticut-New York border, about fifteen miles west of Bellamy's home. *If a man die, shall he live again?* His text, Job 14:14, was the same he had twice rehearsed before Bellamy's congregation on Sunday. Then, in a style somewhat reminiscent of Luke describing his journeys with the apostle Paul, he wrote: "Some Indians cried out in great distress, and all appeared greatly concerned. After we prayed and exhorted them to seek the Lord with constancy, and hired an Englishwoman to keep a kind of *school* among them, we came away about one o'clock and came to Judea, about fifteen or sixteen miles."

His first "missionary" contact with these Indians was apparently of no great import. Perhaps he and Bellamy had been delegated by their Association to hire the Englishwoman to teach the natives whose very proximity to the white villages indicated their status as remnant Mahicans, Wampanoags, and Narragansetts living as wards of the provincial government in the common village called Scaticock (or Scatocook). They were quite domesticated, performed chores for the neighboring white people of Cyrus March's church at Kent, and fished at their perpetually guaranteed "Good Fishing Place" which their last great sachem Waramaug had secured for them before his death in 1735.

Nor were Brainerd and Bellamy the first to preach to these Indians. Benaiah Case, another young licensee of Fairfield East, had worked among them during the spring and had expressed his desire to settle among them. These Indians of Scaticock had also been evangelized by prior Moravian missionaries, who called the village Pachgatoch. Chief among these Germans (whose unsolicited invasion of Yankee Connecticut greatly annoyed Old Light Cyrus March and others), was Christian Henry Rauch. In February his first Indian converts, christened Abraham, Isaac, and Jacob, had traveled to Olney, Pennsylvania, where their baptism was the high point of the ecumenical conference of German colonists which had been called by the Moravian leader, Count Nicholas-Louis of Zinzendorf.

Just before Brainerd's visit to Scaticock, this remarkable European together with his daughter Benigna and their party of thirteen followers, had traveled the tortuous trails through the forests of Pennsylvania and New York to Shekomeko, a larger Indian village in New York fifteen miles northwest of Scaticock. Zinzendorf spent eight days at Shekomeko, baptized six more Indians, and there established the first Moravian mission church. Eventually, the Moravians baptized more than 120 Indians, most of whom understood something of the area's Dutch dialect.*

It would be almost a year before Brainerd would again preach to any Indians. As a licensed itinerant of the Fairfield East Association he would preach where he could. A week after their Scaticock visit, he left Bellamy, visited Jedediah Mills at Ripton, and on Saturday rode outside the bounds of his Association to New Haven. There he stayed about ten days and, in defiance of the Assembly's new law, he preached secretly in private houses. It was the week before Yale's Commencement, the beginning of the new school year, a week of gay reunion and, for Brainerd and his intimates, a season of spiritual meetings, of rededications, and of fervent prayers. As he remembered how he had prayed privately with Christian friends at a particular

---

* Zinzendorf's journal, based on the Gregorian or New Style calendar, indicates that he left Bethlehem, Pennsylvania, on August 10. He concluded his stay at Shekomeko about August 23, which, according to the Old Style calendar, would be August 12, the day Brainerd visited Scaticock. (The Gregorian calendar was advanced eleven days over the Julian calendar.)

home, he wrote: "I scarce ever launched so far into the eternal world as then; I got so far out on the broad ocean that my soul with joy triumphed over all the evils on the shores of mortality. I think time, and all its gay amusements and cruel disappointments, never appeared so inconsiderate to me before."

Back in safe territory on Wednesday, September 1, he witnessed the installation of his fellow-licensee, Rueben Judd, who was installed by Bellamy as the first pastor of the thirteen-member church at Judea, now Washington, five miles west of Bethlehem. After the service, David rode with Bellamy to Bethlehem and preached there twice on Thursday — "I saw myself a poor worm." While in New Haven he had doubtless seen his young brother John who had just enrolled at Yale. He prayed that God would also make John "more of a pilgrim and stranger on the earth." He was willing, even rejoiced, that both he and John would perhaps suffer for Christ: "My heart sweetly exulted in the Lord, in the thoughts of any distress that might alight on him or me, in the advancement of Christ's kingdom."

After he preached "all day" at Bethlehem on Sunday he revealed the probable reason for his strong martyr complex when on Monday he wrote, "I was informed, that they only waited for an opportunity to apprehend me for preaching in New-Haven lately, that so they might imprison me. This made me more solemn and serious, and to quit all hopes of the world's friendship."

Despite his fear of arrest and imprisonment, he returned toward the city, but discreetly stayed at a farm house outside the town limits. He visited there from Tuesday to Friday, that he "might remain undiscovered, and yet have opportunity to do business privately with friends which come to Commencement." Although he spent what he described as a lonely but contented Commencement Day by himself in the woods on Wednesday, he probably enjoyed himself much more on Thursday evening when he sneaked "very privately" into New Haven to pray and to sing hymns with friends, and made "my escape to the farms again, without being discovered by any enemies." But during that week he also apparently learned that the Hartford council of ministers had failed in their attempt to have him re-instated at Yale, and he experienced a mingling of bitterness and perplexity.

On the last day of September, at an unidentified place, he dealt for nearly two hours with things "unsuitable and irregular in Christians' conduct." On October 19 he reflected: "My life is a constant mixture of consolation and conflicts, and will be so till I arrive in the world of spirits." Preaching from place to place — "I scarce ever preach without being first visited with inward conflicts, and sore trials" — he again substituted for Bellamy on Friday, October 22. He was "making the first prayer" when Bellamy returned from one of the many preaching tours which he and Edwards, Wheelock, Pomeroy, Mills and the many other New Light ministers were much engaged in those days.

The next day he also left on a preaching tour, during which he traveled a hundred and seventy-five miles. Starting up the Connecticut Valley, he rode thirty miles north to Simsbury and to "Turky-Hills." At West Suffield he again felt "infinitely vile" and unworthy to preach — "Oh, what dust and ashes I am, to think of preaching to others!" He feared he would certainly "daub with untempered mortar" — a common epithet usually directed against "unconverted" preachers.

His apprehension was groundless, for that evening though "it looked to me near as easy for one to rise out of the grave and preach, as for me," he acquitted himself with "life and power." Again, the next day, although he felt himself a helpless and "an unspeakably worthless wretch," he concluded that he had delivered his sermon with "clearness, power, and pungency." And his delivery won approval, but of a kind he did not appreciate — "There was some noise and tumult in the assembly, that I did not well like; I endeavoured to bear public testimony against it with moderation and mildness, through the current of my discourse."

In the meanwhile his own reflections and thoughts from day to day were hardly mild or moderate. In the homes he visited and on the way, he entertained "a pleasing, yet painful concern" in his striving to spend every moment with God. Upon several occasions he repeated that he was "filled with a kind of pleasing pain" and that his soul was hungry for God almost continually. At other times his insatiable desires in conflict with his carnal being, together with his sense of insufficiency and unworthiness, made him desire that his journey to heaven might not be too long, that he might soon be holy in the presence of his Maker. Increasingly it would become the growing passion of his life — "It makes my soul press after God; the language of it is, "Then shall I be satisfied, when I awake in God's likeness," but never, never before. . . . O that I may never loiter in my heavenly journey!"

As he continued on his earthly way he turned easterly to Suffield and to Eastbury where his now ailing brother Nehemiah lived, and to nearby Hebron, the home of Benjamin Pomeroy whom the Assembly had acquitted as "comparatively blameless" in the Ripton disturbance. His next stop was at Lebanon Crank (later Columbia) where Pomeroy's brother-in-law Eleazar Wheelock was the minister of the North or Second Parish. After that he turned from his easterly course and rode southwest to spend Sunday, November 7, and Monday, at Millington near Haddam.

Edwards omitted all of Brainerd's diary for the following ten days. Did Brainerd perhaps travel to New Fairfield, west of New Haven, to witness the ordination of Benaiah Case and of his friend Samuel Buell on November 9? Buell's ordination was considered "irregular" by many and was the subject of much criticism, for he was ordained by the Fairfield East Association not as a minister but as an evangelist and without having accepted a call from a congregation. Nor had he yet secured the customary theological training toward ordination. Late in January he had gone to study with Jonathan Edwards at Northampton, but once there and with Edwards away at Leicester for several weeks, he had begun to preach. His immediate success was so marked that it forced Mrs. Edwards to examine her heart and attitude toward this young man who so suddenly had usurped her husband's popularity in the town. In the end Mrs. Edwards was herself transported to such ecstasies under Buell's preaching that she was thrown into a state of immobility which caused her friends to fear for her life.

It is more likely, however, that Brainerd returned to his brother's home at Eastbury. On Monday he was much preoccupied with the "heavenly country" and with death, and on Tuesday, the same day Case and Buell were ordained, his brother Nehemiah, father of two small sons, died of consumption. He was thirty years old and, like his cousin Chilliab whom he had succeeded, he died after only two years residence at Eastbury.

6. TO GO, RATHER THAN STAY

TEN DAYS AFTER HIS BROTHER'S DEATH, Brainerd was again in New Haven. There, on Friday, November 19, he received the summons which he may have anticipated since his conversation with Jonathan Dickinson in April and his September visits in New Haven: "Received a letter from the Reverend Mr. Pemberton of New York, desiring me speedily to go down thither, and consult about the Indian affairs in those parts; and to meet certain gentlemen there who were intrusted with those affairs. My mind was instantly seized with concern; so I retired with two or three christian friends, and prayed; and indeed it was a sweet time with me. I was enabled to leave myself and all my concerns with God."

After lodging with Mills at Ripton through Sunday, he started out on Monday. Edwards deleted all details which Brainerd may have written about his first journey of eighty-five miles to New York City. Riding his horse (regular stage coach runs to New York were not inaugurated until forty years later), he would follow the Housatonic River to Stratford and continue through the old shore towns and cross the Saugatuck River, very much as Madam Sarah Kemble Knight described her trip in her colorful Journal of 1704. At Norwalk (Norrowalk, "from its half-Indian name North-walk," according to Sarah), he may have enjoyed the hospitality of its minister, Moses Dickinson, a brother of Jonathan. On her second night after leaving New Haven, Madame Knight had laid her "poor carcass (never more tired)" at Rye, New York, where she found her coverings "as scanty as my bed was hard." Brainerd seems usually to have traveled the more northerly route through the Bronx River town which, set amid white balsam groves, was called White Plains.

After breakfast in the French town of New Rochelle, spunky Sarah had arrived in New York about an hour before sunset on her third day of travel. David also arrived in New York after three days, on Wednesday, November 24. As he rode through rural Harlem and down the pebbled streets toward the southern tip of Manhattan Island, he was confused with the "noise and the tumult" of the busy Dutch-English city of some 11,000 souls where eighteen languages could be heard.

On Thursday he met with the commissioners of the Scotch Society, as it was popularly known, regarding the "important affair of evangelizing the heathen." As part of his examination he delivered a sermon, most probably in Pemberton's church on the north side of Wall Street between Nassau and Broadway. He was grieved for the congregation, "that they should sit there to hear such a dead dog as I preach." He thought he was totally unworthy to preach to others so much better than himself, and he felt infinitely indebted to them.

He left New York about nine o'clock on Saturday and rode back some thirty miles to White Plains, musing through the day: "Surely I may well love all my brethren; for none of them all is so vile as I: whatever they do outwardly, yet it seems to me none is so conscious of so much guilt before God. O my leanness, my barrenness, my carnality, and past bitterness, and want of a gospel temper. These things oppress my soul."

But as he slowly made his way to Haddam he must have also reviewed repeatedly his conversations with the "grave and learned" Presbyterians, both laymen and clergy, particularly Ebenezer Pemberton, the president of the commissioners, and his partners, young Aaron Burr of Newark and Jonathan Dickinson of Elizabethtown across the bay in New Jersey. He had accepted their invitation to bring the Gospel of Jesus Christ to the American Indians. In the spring, after the winter was past, he would go to seek lost souls along the shores of the Delaware and the Susquehanna rivers in distant Pennsylvania. His later regard for November 5, Guy Fawkes' Day, may indicate that it was the effective day of his appointment.

Having decided to spend his life among the Indians, he decided that he would have no use for the money he had inherited from his father's estate. At Southbury where he had preached his first sermon in Graham's church, he knew of a worthy young man, "a dear friend," who wanted to become a minister. Jonathan Edwards disclosed in a letter to John Erskine of Scotland that his name was Nehemiah Greenman, a native of Stratford. David went to Southbury a fortnight after he had left New York and offered to pay the cost of Greenman's education in the school from which he himself had been expelled.*

Leaving Southbury, he stayed overnight with Bellamy at Bethlehem and preached there on Sunday from Matthew 6:33, *Seek ye first the kingdom of God; and all these things shall be added unto you.* His offer to Greenman and the choice of his text could hardly have been merely co-incidental. A few years later, however, he confided to Edwards that he had regretted his precipitate generosity as he could have used his money to good advantage in his work. His second sermon for the day was from Romans 15:30, *That ye strive together with me in your prayers.*

Bellamy went on another of his preaching tours the next day and David rode the few miles back to Woodbury for the night. He had witnessed "much affection" in Sunday's audiences. On Tuesday, December 14, as he retraced his way farther to Southbury to conclude his arrangements with Nehemiah Greenman, he felt distressed, "especially on account of the false appearances of religion, that do but

---

* Brainerd was able to pay for three years of his friend's education. Greenman graduated from Yale in 1748, became a minister, and served the Presbyterian church at Pile's Grove (Pittsgrove), N. J., from 1753 to 1779.

rather breed confusion, especially in some places." Just prior to this time, Edwards had published *Some Thoughts Concerning the Present Revival in New England*. In that discerning treatise he admonished those who uncritically credited the Holy Spirit for the hysteria that plagued the Connecticut Valley. He believed that ecstasies and trances such as his wife had experienced under Buell's preaching were genuine spiritual manifestations, but he deplored the mass hysteria which he said was induced by the devil, who, when he could not stop the Great Awakening, joined it and carried it out to extremes to discredit and spoil it. The early manifestations, in 1740, were pure, he said, "but when the people were raised to this height, Satan took the advantage, and his interposition, in many instances, soon became very apparent: and a great deal of caution and pains were found necessary, to keep the people, many of them, from running wild." By 1742, he said, there was much imitation as the people were "dazzled" by "flaming exhorters" and by what they saw and heard.

Distinguishing between real and counterfeit must have been extremely difficult for young itinerant preachers, but Brainerd was no longer deceived. He had learned from bitter experience, and his approach that night at Southbury was to preach from I Thessalonians 4:8, stressing God, *who giveth his Holy Spirit to you*, that he might "undermine false religion."

As he took leave of his friends on Wednesday, they supposed it might be likely that they should not meet again till they reached the eternal world. Farther south at the shipping town of Derby he spent "much time," he said, with "dear Mr. Humphreys." A graduate of Yale in 1732, Daniel Humphreys was the New Light minister of Derby for fifty years. His obituary noted that he "exhibited that hilarity which made him the delight of his acquaintances."

After a return visit with Jedediah Mills, preaching at both Derby and Ripton, and spending the week-end of New England's uncelebrated Christmas at New Haven, Brainerd left from there on Sunday after evening prayers with friends in the woods. On Monday he again preached his "Seek ye first" sermon at Branford, and then returned to his home at Haddam. There he experienced a decided reaction. His spiritual life "sensibly declined" so that on January 14 he described his conflicts as "unspeakably dreadful [and] heavier than the mountains and overflowing floods," and he added: "I seemed enclosed, as it were, in hell itself; I was deprived of all sense of God, even of the being of a God; and that was my misery. . . . My soul was in such anguish I could not eat; but felt as I suppose a poor wretch would that is just going to the place of execution."

After another fortnight at home he started out with better feelings on a preaching tour to the north and east of Haddam. This part of the Connecticut colony was the scene of extreme excess and intolerance during the revival. On Wednesday, January 19, 1743, at Canterbury, he exhorted the people to love one another, and not to set up their own frames as a standard by which to try their brethren. But as he spoke along these lines he remembered his own past foolishness, and he was again "much oppressed." The next evening, he preached in his brother's house between Norwich and Lebanon, likely the home of his half-brother Jeremiah Mason, and on Friday, in Lebanon, he conversed not with parson Wheelock of the Second Society but with Solomon Williams of the First Parish. He was "greatly delighted with his serious, deliberate and impartial way of discourse about religion," stated Edwards. Friendly, accessible, a Harvard graduate and a highly respected New Light, Williams was a first cousin of Edwards. Two of his sons, Eliphalet, and Solomon who died that year, had been David's classmates at Yale.

When Sunday came David felt "unfit to exist." He thought himself unworthy of even a place among the Indians or the very savages of Africa, and he said: "None know, but those who feel it, what the soul endures that is sensibly shut out from the presence of God: alas! it is more bitter than death."

On the second Wednesday of his trip he preached to Joseph Fish's congregation at Stonington. One can readily imagine why Edwards retained Brainerd's account of this event. It was a sermon well applied to a story widely known at that time. Brainerd wrote: "Preached to a pretty large assembly at Mr. Fish's meeting-house: insisted on humility, and stedfastness in keeping God's commands; and that through humility we should prefer one another in love, and not make our own frames the rule by which we judge others. I felt sweetly calm, and full of brotherly love; and never more free from party spirit. I hope some good will follow; that Christians will be freed from false joy, and party zeal, and censuring one another."

On February 4 he also wrote in a letter to Bellamy: "And last week I preached for Mr. Fish at Stonington. . . . There was much false zeal among them, so that some began to separate from that dear man."

For ten years Joseph Fish, a Harvard graduate of 1728, had been the well-received minister of the parish of North Stonington, until she summer of 1741 when James Davenport visited Stonington. The people immediately received him as an inspired apostle, 104 souls were added to the church, and fanaticism was rampant. When Fish remonstrated, many left his congregation. But during the following year, on December 20, 1742, Fish himself became extremely distressed about his own salvation and conversion. He informed his congregation about his concern and did not preach to them for six weeks. It was in the latter part of this period, just before Fish found "relief," that David visited him and exhorted his people. Fish's biographer, a relative, stated: "He speaks of having been favoured with 'Christian conversation,' from which he derived benefit, just before his change of feelings." It was on February 7, twelve days after Brainerd's visit, that Fish resumed his place in his pulpit. He preached from Jeremiah 1:5, 6 — *Then said I, Ah, Lord Jehovah! behold I know not how to speak; for I am a child.*

Brainerd's visit to Stonington, so briefly noted in his diary as it is preserved today, may well have been the occasion for the conversation that restored Fish to his people. Seven years later the loyal among them "utterly refused to give him up" to another church, and he served Stonington for a total of fifty years. It is said of Fish that his experience made him "an excellent guide thereafter," and it was so also with Brainerd, as Edwards said: "For by his thus joining for a season with enthusiasts, he had a more full and intimate acquaintance with what belonged to that sort of religion; and so was under better advantages to judge of the difference between that and what he finally approved, and strove to his utmost to promote, in opposition to it."

Two days after he preached for Fish, Brainerd disclosed how radically his attitudes had changed since his days at Yale. His comments refer to his visit to New London, the seaport which had been greatly agitated by James Davenport on his several arrivals from Long Island. "Here I found some fallen into extravagances; too much carried away with a false zeal and bitterness. Oh, the want of a gospel temper is greatly to be lamented. Spent the evening in conversing about some points of conduct in both ministers and private Christians; but did not agree with them. God had not *taught them with briars and thorns* to be of a kind disposition towards mankind."

The commissioners had decided that Brainerd should not go to the Pennsylvania Indians in the dead of winter. With their permission he would first spend six weeks as a supply preacher at East Hampton, Long Island. He therefore returned from New London to East Haddam for a last Sunday at his old home, and on Tuesday evening, February 1, he preached his farewell sermon to his family and his friends at the house of an aged man who had been unable to attend public worship for some time. On Wednesday, accompanied by a messenger from East Hampton, he followed the Connecticut River to the shore town of Lyme, arriving there at night. His deep distress emphasizes how fully he anticipated going directly to Pennsylvania after his short stay on Long Island.

"On the road I felt an uncommon pressure of mind; I seemed to struggle hard for some pleasure in something here below, and seemed loath to give up all for gone; saw I was evidently throwing myself into all hardships and distresses in my present undertaking. I thought it would be less difficult to lie down in the grave; but yet I chose to go, rather than stay."

7. SPEEDILY DISMISSED

BRAINERD AND HIS GUIDE FROM EAST HAMPTON waited two days for passage from Lyme to Long Island. Perhaps bad weather prevented their earlier crossing, although the winter was a mild one that year and the waters of Long Island Sound were open. When they obtained ferriage for themselves and their horses on Saturday, February 5, they sailed some ten miles across the Sound to the point at Oyster Ponds, now Orient, on the northeast shore of Long Island, and then rode more than twice that distance to East Hampton on the south side of the island, twenty miles from its eastern tip. East Hampton was a prosperous whaling village settled by Connecticut and Massachusetts pioneers in 1648, and it was, said Edwards, "the fairest, pleasantest town on the whole island, and one of its largest and most wealthy parishes." It original name had been Maidstone.

David was expectantly welcomed by the Congregationalists at this place. As his diary subsequently reveals, they were looking for a young minister to settle among them. Their present pastor, Nathaniel Huntting, had served them for forty-three of his sixty-seven years, but he was now ailing and wished to retire. But that was not all. James Davenport and Jonathan Barber of Oyster Ponds had considerably disrupted East Hampton during the past three years. Barber had recently left to supervise George Whitefield's orphanage in Georgia, but Davenport's presence at Southold continued to be felt. Huntting's position was the typical uncomfortable one. Though he was not unsympathetic to the revival, he opposed its irregularities. As a result, some of his parishioners judged him to be hostile to it.

The East Hampton people were therefore quite divided among themselves. They were in need of a good counsellor, such as Jonathan Dickinson who in October had moderated the strife between James Davenport and his abused congregation across the bays at Southold. And there was still another interesting and important matter to be settled in East Hampton. It had been established originally as an English Congregational church in intimate fellowship with the Connecticut churches. Now, however, the trend was away from Congregational Connecticut to Presbyterian New York. This was inevitable since Long Island had become part of the latter colony. Davenport's church was already Presbyterian, and East Hampton was about ready to follow suit. As a "Presbyterianized-Congregationalist" Brainerd was a highly suitable man for East Hampton during this period of transition, and the pleasant possibilities of his settling here must have been very tempting to him.*

During his first week, however, he was in complete dejection until, as he phrased it then and several times again, his soul arose above those deep waters and he enjoyed some glimpses of divine glory. On Wednesday he may have observed the day of fasting and prayer which Jonathan Lee, the first New Light governor of Connecticut, had proclaimed for that February 9: to counteract the "unhappy Divisions and Contentions which still prevail, both among Ministers and People." Lee's recent election marked the shift of power in the colony from the Old to the New Light elements.

Throughout his stay at East Hampton, Brainerd kept busy and, for the most part, he seemed rather at ease with himself — "More refined and weaned from a dependence on my frames and spiritual feelings." In fact, on his third Sunday, February 20, he felt uneasy about his carelessness, not suitably concerned about the important work of the day. But he was also "exceeding infirm" that week-end and complained that he was "greatly troubled with pain in my head and dizziness, scarce able to sit up" — his first reference to his health since his breakdown at Yale.

A fortnight later the unhappy divisions and contentions which still

---

* Other Long Island churches at Southhampton, Hempstead, Jamaica, Newtown and Setauket, all established as English Presbyterian congregations, also gradually joined the Scotch-Irish Presbyterians of the Middle Atlantic Colonies.

prevailed worsened when restless James Davenport again crossed Long Island Sound to New London. There, after arousing the people to a high pitch of excitement on Sunday, March 6, Davenport exhorted them to destroy their idols. Upon his instructions they brought their wigs, cloaks, breeches, hoods, gowns, rings, jewels and necklaces, and heaped the articles in his room where he was confined with illness and his bad leg. After donating his own velvet breeches he ordered the pile to be burned on the town wharf. He also incited the people to burn religious books and tracts which were generally held in high esteem, but which he considered subversive. Among the volumes burned that day were those of Increase Mather, Matthew Henry, and lively Jonathan Parsons, the New Light minister of Lyme, whom Brainerd may have visited while awaiting passage from that town to Long Island. Parsons, like Joseph Fish of Stonington, had been "reconverted" less than two years before, which may explain Davenport's condemnation of Parsons' previously published writings, even as Parsons himself had destroyed every sermon he had preached before he adopted the Calvinism of Whitefield, Edwards and Tennent. Several weeks after Davenport's book burning, the Court fined six participants five shillings each and costs of six shillings, five pence, three farthings, for profaning the Sabbath Day. This time the Connecticut Assembly again deported Davenport and prohibited his return.

Brainerd could hardly have been immediately aware of these notorious events. On the day after the book burning his heart had ascribed "glory, glory, glory" to the blessed God and he wrote: "Time appeared but an inch long, and eternity at hand; and I thought I could with patience and cheerfulness bear anything for the cause of God." Two days later he rode sixteen miles to Montauk Point at the east end of the island where Azariah Horton, a native of Southold, ministered to two towns of 162 Indians. David wrote that on the way to Montauk he had "some inward sweetness on the road," but that he felt "somewhat of flatness and deadness" after he arrived and had seen Horton's Indians.

Perhaps he felt as he did because these natives were Horton's charges and not his own. His frequent later references to "my people" is indicative of a strong possessiveness in his nature. However, this change of mood, not at all uncommon to him, has been cited by some serious analysts as valid evidence that he was utterly "unromantic" about both the Indians and his calling to minister to them. It has also been charged that his self-denying mission to them was so self-centered as to be devoid of genuine compassion for their lives or for their souls.

It probably is true that he was not thrilled about the Indians *per se*. They were no novelty to him. He had seen their unkempt bodies and had witnessed their low level of existence since his boyhood days. But is that sufficient reason to strip him of all idealistic concerns about them? There surely was, as Edwards observed, "some mixture of the natural fire of youth with his zeal for God." And, closely akin to his mystical and ascetic bent, would there not echo in his soul the poetry of Isaiah the prophet: "The Lord hath anointed me to preach good tidings unto the meek — to give unto them beauty for ashes, the oil of joy, the garment of praise — that he might be glorified." With his Puritan background he would be essentially the prophetic preacher pointing the way to God through salvation in his Son, but as for his priestly concern and his natural sympathy, one need not read long in his diaries to discover that his pity for the poor Indian, "poor without Christ," indeed, but also in their physical plight, was as immediate as his passion to proclaim the Gospel to them.

The reason for his "deadness," particularly at this juncture, would rather be his "uncommon pressure of mind," his loathing "to give up all for gone." His scholarly ambitions and his hankering for recognition and leadership in an exciting era of an awakened society would fight long and hard against his taking upon himself the role of the obscure servant. He could hardly do it with equanimity, and East Hampton's cordial invitation to settle doubtless aggravated his struggle. Before he left Montauk Point he was so oppressed by the "blackness of my nature" that he thought he was not fit to speak so much as to the Indians.*

Despite his leanness, David stayed overnight, and preached from Isaiah. He would preach to the Indians from this prophet-poet again and again — "Ye have sold yourselves for nought, and ye shall be redeemed without money." "Ho, every one that thirsteth, come ye to the waters, and he that hath no money!" "Seek ye the Lord while he may be found." "Let the wicked forsake his way . . ." But today, perhaps reflecting his own strife of spirit, he told them of the Suffering Servant — "Yet it pleased the Lord to bruise him" — and,

---

* Horton's Indians included another 400 Narragansetts, Pequots, Nantics, and Mahegans scattered along the more than 100 miles of Long Island's south shore. Horton baptized 35 adults and 44 children, but only 20 gave any lasting evidence of their conversion. Most defections were caused by their weakness for liquor. In 1750 he became pastor at South Hanover, afterwards Bottle Hill (now Madison), New Jersey. After his retirement he volunteered to nurse Continental soldiers sick with the smallpox. He became infected by the disease and died March 27, 1777.

he said, he trusted that something of the divine presence came among them.

Just before he left East Hampton, he was again very ill. On his last Sunday morning, March 13, he could hardly stand up, but he gained strength and preached for an hour and a half from Genesis 5:24, *And Enoch walked with God.* The reader cannot but receive the impression here as elsewhere that the awful weight of making a final break, to go "rather than to stay," practically paralyzed him. Early on Monday as he packed his horse for his journey to Pennsylvania he was almost constantly in ejaculatory prayer. As he bade farewell to the people of East Hampton his heart "grieved and mourned, and rejoiced at the same time." They had by now "frequently invited" him to settle. But he left them, not as his grandfather Hobart had left Hempstead over trouble with Quakerism, but because like Paul he wanted to preach the Gospel where Christ was not named, *to whom he was not spoken of, and they that have not heard.* He noted later: "I never, since I began to preach, could feel any freedom to enter into other men's labours and settle down in the ministry where the gospel was preached before."

That same day he rode almost fifty miles, a good day's journey for an experienced post rider, and he may have reached a special destination that night when he lodged in a part of Brook Haven. This large township on the old island which has been so beautifully described as a fresh, green breast of the new world, included the small village of Setauket at Conscience Bay, the home of David Youngs since his ordination into the Presbyterian church in October. According to Samuel Hopkins it was Youngs, Brainerd and Buell who had distinguished themselves in zeal at Yale. Small wonder that Brainerd remarked that he had refreshing conversation with a Christian friend that night.

After he reached New York City on Tuesday and "waited on the Correspondents for the Indian mission," Brainerd went to Dickinson's home in Elizabethtown on Friday and stayed with Aaron Burr in Newark on Saturday. A son of a Supreme Court judge of Fairfield, Connecticut, and a classmate of Bellamy at Yale, Burr was a slight-built, polished and cheerful bachelor only two years older than Brainerd. Their conversation and praying together no doubt was concerned with something more than David's recent East Hampton experiences and his call to the Indian mission. When, if ever, did two eligible young men entirely refrain from reference to the fairer sex? They may also have reviewed David's fracas with Rector Clap and how only nine months earlier Clap had in an official capacity requested Burr to serve as the associate pastor of New Haven's First Church. Although Burr had declined, the call was a flattering one since the continuing factions in that harassed congregation had thereby acknowledged Burr's brilliant mind and his moderate spirit, and therefore his acceptability to both Old and New Lights in the church. Brainerd preached in the morning and evening at Burr's church on Sunday.

Meeting with his employers for final instructions at nearby Wood-bridge on Monday, March 21, he must have heard with dismay that because of frontier tensions pending settlement of Indian land claims, they had again decided against sending him to Pennsylvania for the present. They had been in touch with a native son of neighboring Newark, the veteran missionary to the Massachusetts Indians, John Sergeant, who had recently visited the Indians on the New York-Pennsylvania border, and they now instructed Brainerd to study the Indian language with Sergeant and to assist him at Stockbridge. (In May they sent Azariah Horton to ascertain more fully the true state of affairs in Pennsylvania.)

In his later letter to Pemberton, David did not fail to mention that he was "speedily dismissed" by the commissioners, perhaps over his strong objections. He was on his way the next day, and after spending Wednesday in New York City, he rode nearly fifty miles to North Castle on Thursday.

Continuing disconsolately at an average of only fifteen miles a day, he bore sharply north between the hills to Danbury and crossed the Housatonic River to New Milford which boasted the only covered bridge north of Derby. On Sunday he re-crossed the river and rode the five or six miles to the Indians at Scaticock, where he and Bellamy had preached in August. He preached to these Indians again and stayed at Kent through Monday because of the spring rains.

During this weekend of March 26-28 he also wrote a letter to Joseph Bellamy in which he noted that the excesses of the revival seemed, for the most part, a thing of the past, but that one of the remaining difficulties at that time arose from the presence of the Moravians in the region. His edited diary is silent about the extreme prejudice of the Connecticut Yankees to the foreign missionaries who had invaded the New York-Connecticut borders at Shekomeko, Scaticock, and Sharon. Like the Quakers, the Moravians had pious convictions against swearing under oath, and when they refused to swear allegiance to King George of England, insinuations were made that they must be Papists in league with the Canadian French and their Indian allies. The fact that some of the missionaries married their Indian converts was also disapproved by the proper, and jittery, English settlers of the new and unprotected frontier towns.

A year later, in the spring of 1744, a formidable persecution broke out against the Moravians, and both English magistrates and ministers arrested them and hustled them into the New Milford court. The Connecticut laws of 1742-43 against vagrant, non-licensed exhorters were enforced against them and they were expelled from the colony. Conditions were no better in New York. After the missions had been abandoned for five years, a more sober and appreciative attitude prevailed, and the Moravians were invited to resume their efforts.

Leaving the Scaticock Indians, Brainerd arrived at the frontier village of Salisbury, the farthest outpost in northwest Connecticut. He lodged in this four-year-old village overnight and spent the next night in Massachusetts, at Sheffield which was first called Skatehook. On Thursday he rode the last twelve miles north through the valley that led to Stockbridge.

It was March 31, 1743, just a year since he had begun the third book of his diary while a recluse at Jedediah Mills in Ripton. He was a recluse no longer. He had visited and re-visited some three dozen towns and must have preached at least three score sermons. His trips from town to town in Connecticut, his travels to New York, Long Island, New Jersey, and back to the west frontier of Massachusetts, amounted to well over twelve hundred miles in the saddle.

There is no indication that he enjoyed any reflections upon his past twelvemonth. The anti-climactic ending to his long anticipated trip to the Delaware River utterly dejected him. He had been tried with briars and thorns, he had given up all for gone, but his elders, he may have brooded, still considered him a probationer. Especially on the last day of his trip to Stockbridge, wrote Edwards, "his mind was overwhelmed with peculiar gloom and melancholy."

8. THE MOST LONELY MELANCHOLY DESERT

THE FIRST ENGLISH SETTLERS had moved into the Upper Valley of the Housatonic River shortly after 1720, and by 1724 they had obtained permission from the Massachusetts government to form two townships. The Indians of the region deeded the land for 460 English pounds, three barrels of cider, and thirty quarts of rum.

The natives, of Algonquian linguistic stock, were Mahicans who had moved *eastward* as the Dutch settled the west bank of the Hudson River. They called themselves Wappingers and Muhekaneoks, or Mahiccondas, "the people of the continually flowing water," River Indians. To the white man they became known as Housatonics and, later, the Stockbridge Indians. The English were pleased to find them mannerly and of generally good moral character and that Konapot, their chief, was favorably disposed to Christianity. Here was opportunity for mission work, and the Commissioners of Indian Affairs at Boston, the colonial agents for the London Society for Propagating the Gospel in Foreign Parts, laid plans toward that endeavor.

In 1734 they found their man. John Sergeant of Newark, New Jersey, the Yale valedictorian of 1729, was tutoring at his *alma mater,* but his long desire had been to devote his life to Indian missions, in spite of his crippled left arm. He responded to the Society's invitation with alacrity and immediately began preaching the Gospel to the natives at Great Barrington, hiring Ebenezer Paupaumunk as interpreter and young Metocsin to call them to worship by blowing on a conch shell. On August 31, 1735, when he was twenty-five, Sergeant was ordained at Deerfield, some fifty miles nearer Boston. The Indians, a large group of ministers, and the Governor of the colony were present for the uncommon ordination of a missionary.

After a year, the General Court set aside six square miles of land at Wnahktutook as a town for the ninety Indians of the area, and granted them full civil rights and self-government based on English law. However, four white families were chosen to settle with them in the town which was incorporated as Stockbridge in May, 1739.

There is no doubt that John Sergeant endured much hardship during his missionary career, especially on his long trips to the western Indians at the headwaters of the Susquehanna River in New York. When at home in the first organized Indian town since the days of old John Eliot in the late 1600's, it would seem that he lived rather comfortably amid the beautiful Berkshire Hills. One of the four English families in Stockbridge, that of Ephraim Williams, a distant, and reportedly, an ambitious and unlovely cousin of Jonathan Edwards, included an equally ambitious but very attractive daughter named Abigail. John Sergeant married this elite young lady in August when she was eighteen. That same year, aided by a government grant, and as his imperious young bride demanded, Sergeant built a handsome miniature mansion with three floors and two chimneys. Although this house now graces the main street of Stockbridge, it originally stood near father Ephraim's stockaded "Castle" on Prospect Hill, well-removed from the Indians along the village street. John's salary was then only a hundred pounds a year, and never again was he without debt. But, although Abigail has been described as a hussy who loved none but herself, one of John's letters to a friend reveals what he thought about his fortunes: "You will forgive me, sir, if I think that a most ingenious woman is not the smallest gift of the Divine bounty that I have received since I undertook a life thought to be so self-denying." And though John left this earthly scene in 1749, long before Abigail who remarried and lived as the queen of the region, it warms the heart of the visitor to Stockbridge to find their graves side by side.

It would seem that Brainerd would tarry with John and Abigail for a few days. Sergeant was a veteran of eight active years among the Indians. Already in 1737 he had baptized the sachem Yokun and fifty of his tribesmen. He knew a great deal about the natives, had devoted much time to the study of their common inter-tribal "Moheekanneew" dialect, and had translated prayers, portions of Scripture and Isaac Watts' *Catechism for Children*. In the village and its environs were four hundred civilized Indians including the baptized sachems Konapot, who held a captain's commission in the Massachusetts militia, and Umpachenee who was a lieutenant. There was much that Brainerd could learn before taking the forest trail to his new station twenty miles west between Stockbridge and the Hudson River.

But he did not tarry. The station assigned to him was in the Schodack-Kinderhook woods, near a mountain from which the Indians imagined they heard *Kau-nau-meek, Kau-nau-meek*, which, they declared, was a voice informing them that the deer were about and that prospects for the hunt were good. He was at "Kaunaumeek" the next day, precisely on Good Friday, April 1. He may have impressed others as to his eagerness to begin his work. Inwardly, however, he was all turmoil. "My heart was sunk. . . . I seemed to have no God to go to. . . . It seemed to me I should never have any success among the Indians. My soul was weary of my life; I longed for death, beyond measure."

Without the stimulation of conversation, circuit preaching, and congenial company, he was utterly lonely, although the Indians received him cordially and were attentive to him. And in his new solitude he now again recalled with revulsion his rash behavior and his censorious spirit — "that I had spent so much time in conversation tending only to promote a party-spirit." He grieved: "I have thought much of having the kingdom of Christ advanced in the world, but now I saw I had enough to do with myself."

In an official report or letter to Pemberton some twenty months later, he appraised the status of the Indians he found at "Cannaumuck," as he spelled it in the fifth volume of his diary. He wrote: "As to the state or temper of mind in which I found these Indians, at my first coming among them, I may justly say, it was much more desirable and encouraging than what appears among those who are altogether uncultivated. Their heathenish jealousies and suspicion, and their prejudices against Christianity, were in a great measure removed by the long-continued labours of the Reverend Mr. Sergeant among a number of the same tribe."

Already on his second Sunday at Kaunaumeek he found two or three Indians who appeared concerned. A squaw told him "that her heart had cried," ever since she had first heard him, and that week he already began to refer to the Indians as "my people." On his third week-end his acute longing for the company of white persons was fulfilled, most distastefully.

"Saturday, April 16. Soon after came an Irishman and a Dutchman, with a design, as they said, to hear me preach the next day; but none can tell how I felt, to hear their *profane talk*. Oh, I longed that some dear Christian knew my distress. I got into a kind of hovel, and there groaned out my complaint to God; and withal felt more sensible gratitude and thankfulness to God, that he had made me to differ from these men, as I knew through grace he had."

He set aside his twenty-fifth birthday for fasting and spent the day alone in the woods in prayer. Ten days later, before leaving to spend the first Sunday of May at Stockbridge, he wrote a frequently underlined letter to his brother John at Yale, his *meo fratri juniori*, as he called John in a diary entry which Edwards omitted.

"The local distance, at which we are held from each other at the present, is a matter of no great moment or importance to either of us. But, alas! the presence of God is what I want. . . . I live in the most lonely melancholy *desert*, about eighteen miles from Albany; for it was not thought best that I should go to Delaware river, as I believe I hinted to you in a letter from New York. I board with a poor Scotchman; his wife can talk scarce any English. *My diet* consists mostly of hasty-pudding, boiled corn, and bread baked in the ashes, and sometimes a little meat and butter. *My lodging* is a little heap of straw, laid upon some boards, a little way from the ground; for it is a log-room, without any floor, that I lodge in. *My work* is exceedingly hard and difficult: I travel on foot a mile and half, the worst of ways, almost daily, and back again; for I live so far from my Indians. I have not seen an English person this month. . . . These and many other circumstances as uncomfortable attend me; and yet my *spiritual conflicts* and *distresses,* so far *exceed* all these, that I scarce think of them, or hardly mind but that I am entertained in the most sumptuous manner. The Lord grant that I may learn to 'endure hardness, as a good soldier of Jesus Christ!' "

At Stockbridge he assisted at the Lord's Supper and preached. Sergeant, who preached two English and two Indian sermons each Sunday, was doubtless delighted with Brainerd's visit. But David stated that he felt poorly in body and soul. "While I was preaching I seemed to be rehearsing idle tales." The gloom and dejection which had settled upon him when he left New York City had stayed with him all through his first month at Kaunaumeek.

But he had no idea of giving up. That same week he began to lay foundation stones for a house of his own on a little knoll west of the winding Kayaderosseras (Kinderhook) Creek. This first hut was located at the intersection of Route 20 and Taconic Parkway, at Brainard, New York, which was named after Jeremiah Brainard, a later member of the clan who settled there. David's loneliness was alleviated somewhat by his interpreter, John Wauwaumpequunnaunt, a Stockbridge Christian who had been taught to read and write English by Stephen Williams, pastor at Long Meadow, and one of the prime movers in the founding of Stockbridge. Stephen was a brother of Solomon Williams, Edwards' cousin, whose conversation Brainerd had enjoyed in Lebanon, and a brother-in-law of James Davenport, having married James' sister Abigail.*

Although his interpreter preferred to live Indian-style with his people, he provided much support, and after several months they had translated simple prayers and Brainerd soon learned to pray with the Indians in their language. "I also translated sundry psalms

---

* When he was 11 years old, Williams had been captured by Indians and held in Canada 21 months. (A cousin, Eunice Williams, captured with her family at Deerfield, when her mother and two children were killed, refused to leave her captors and married an Indian, John de Roger, and lived as a native until her death at ninety.) The Williams, all relatives of Jonathan Edwards, were instrumental in having Edwards succeed Sergeant at the Stockbridge mission in 1751, and Ephraim Williams, Sergeant's father-in-law, made Edwards' position there untenable. Wauwaumpequunnaunt was also Edward's interpreter.

into their language," he wrote, "and soon after we were able to sing in the worship of God."

There is hearsay evidence that when he visited Stockbridge, David did not lodge with John Sergeant and his madam and small children in their fine home with its proud baroque doorway and handsome pine panelling. More likely, he lodged in the village with Joseph Woodbridge or with his married brother Timothy who was Sergeant's assistant from the beginning of the mission and conducted the Indian school in which some forty students were enrolled. Twelve special students who were boarded in Sergeant's original home were supported by Isaac Hollis of London, who had also paid for Wauwaumpequunnaunt's education and had donated nearly a thousand pounds to the mission since 1732.

Brainerd was impressed. He determined that his interpreter should be appointed master of the school he would set up at Kaunaumeek. Before the end of his second month at Kaunaumeek, he was on his way to New Jersey to consult with his employers. After four days of riding he reached Aaron Burr's house in Newark on Thursday, June 3. On Friday he was at Elizabethtown, and by Saturday morning he was again back in New York City. Before night, with permission for the teaching post granted, he retraced his way as far as White Plains.

He had other plans in mind also, for on Monday he prodded his horse for sixty miles to New Haven. There he again sought reconciliation with Rector Clap at Yale. His success was apparently nil, although as he visited friends, perhaps Jedediah Mills and Joseph Bellamy, he felt "pretty comfortable." But, on Saturday, stretching his travel time to the limit, he lost his way between Stockbridge and Kaunaumeek after dark and had to lie all night in the open air. The exposure did not seem to harm him and the next morning he thought that he preached more effectively to his Indians than he had ever done before.

During June he and Wauwaumpequunnaunt set up the "English" school, and the results were gratifying. He observed: "The children . . . and young people, who attended the school, made considerable proficiency (at least some of them) in their learning; so that had they understood the English language well, they would have been able to read somewhat readily in a psalter."

As the summer progressed he continued to build his hut and he left his Scottish host to live in a wigwam among the Indians until he could complete his house. In that way, he explained, he spared himself the inconvenience of walking to their camp almost daily because their site had no pasture for his horse. He also discovered that he could best instruct the Indians in the evenings and mornings, their usual hours at home.

Despite his keen interest and activities for the Indians and his avowed renouncement of the favors of men, the hopelessness of his case at Yale continued to distress him. It kept him in almost constant dejection. His thwarted ambition for scholastic recognition, his desperate longing to obtain his degree, his sense of futility in coping with the Yale authorities, and, above all, his self-accusations, his "ten thousand former sins and follies," overwhelmed him with exasperating confusions. His very preoccupation with the matter set up what he called "a kind of regardless temper of mind." This further dismayed him and filled him with feelings of guilt and shame, so that he wished he could drop out of the sight and memory of anyone who ever knew him, "that I might not be seen or heard of any more."

One can easily suppose that had he been able to disappear beyond the ken of his friends into Pennsylvania, as he had anticipated throughout the past winter, he would not now have been so distraught by the very proximity of Yale and his personal contacts with Sergeant, Bellamy, and other Yale alumni. In the beginning of July, unable to endure further, he again set out for New Haven and Rector Clap.

According to Thomas Brainerd, author of *The Life of John Brainerd,* David kept two diaries while at Kaunaumeek. One contained only the record of his religious experiences and was the volume which Edwards copied verbatim in large part. The other volume (Book Five) from May to November 1743 included the history of his conflict with Yale. Edwards quoted "not more than a fourth part" of this account. Would that Thomas Brainerd had published the 120 pages of this volume which he had in his possession as late as 1865. He wrote: "We may yet give it entire, just as Brainerd wrote it. It is justly severe on the college authorities; they broke his heart."

Jonathan Edwards, however, chose to emphasize how Brainerd abhorred *himself* for the miserable part he had played in the affair, "even to the breaking of his heart." Is that why Edwards omitted the entire record of David's summer trip to Yale between July 2 and July 25, and the following angry bit of his diary which Thomas Brainerd preserved? It exposes another side of David which, one feels, Edwards effectively hid from his readers. It reveals much of the native Yankee spirit which a generation later would oppose the tyranny of the English crown and fight the War of Independence.

"New Haven, July 9, 1743. I was still occupied with some business

depending on certain grandees for performance. Alas! how much
men may lord and tyrannize over their fellow countrymen, yet pretend that all their treatment of them is full of lenity and kindness,
— that they owe them some special regard, — that they would
hardly treat another with so much tenderness, and the like. Like
the Holy Court of Inquisition, when they put a poor innocent to
the rack, they tell him that what they do is all for the benefit of his
soul! Lord, deliver my soul from this temper!"*

His efforts with Rector Clap toward re-instatement again availed
him nothing. There was little hope that he would obtain his degree
at the September Commencement, or at any other time. He is still
not listed as a Yale graduate today, although a house in Yale's Sterling
Divinity Quadrangle is named in his honor and bears the inscription:
"David Brainerd, Class of 1743."

Brainerd's youngest sister Elizabeth was married to Captain David
Miller of Middleton on July 21. It is possible therefore that Brainerd
attended the wedding during this absence from Kaunaumeek. Returning, he completed his hut on the last Saturday of July. He
wrote: "Just at night, moved into my own house, and lodged there
that night; found it much better spending the time alone than in the
wigwam where I was before." After a couple more days of labor
he spent Wednesday, "most of the day," in writing in his new
home. The house, complete with bed-ticking, deer blankets, kettle
and teapot, was a boon to his spirit. "My soul was full of tenderness
and love, even to the most inveterate of my enemies," he reflected.
"I felt peculiarly serious, calm and peaceful."

But on August 15 when he began preparations for winter he
had a bad time when he apparently spent the day in gathering hay
for his horse. The unusual labor and summer heat overtaxed him
so that he thought "that this frail body would soon drop into the dust."
He had also apparently lost congenial contact with his former Scot
host and his wife, for he now explained how he was forced "to go
or send ten or fifteen miles for all the bread I eat." When he got
a supply it would turn moldy and sour before he could eat all of it.
At other times, as when he could not find his horse in the woods, he

* Thomas Brainerd explained: "He wrote in small duodecimo books, about
four by six inches in size, comprehending from forty to one hundred pages
each. Each little manuscript volume is neatly bound in strong paper or
parchment. We have two of these volumes entire. The first contains only
his religious experiences, a great part of which was copied verbatim by
Edwards. It is bound with parchment. On the first page is only written,
David Brainerd's Book."

would go for days without bread and substituted little cakes made from Indian meal. "Yet," he said, "I felt contended with my circumstances . . . and blessed God as much for my present circumstances, as if I had been a king; and thought that I found a disposition to be contented in any circumstances."

Late in April he had written to his brother John that he hardly minded that he was not entertained "in the most sumptuous manner." Here he was as thankful "as if I had been a king." Exactly a year earlier, in August 1742, Count Zinzendorf had declared his bark hut at Shekomeko to be *better than a palace*, and such delectable cliches punctuate the mission annals of the eighteenth and early nineteenth centuries. On August 22, 1831, the saintly Slav missionary priest, Frederic Baraga, wrote from his leaky Arbre Croche hut at the present site of Harbor Springs, Michigan: "I am happier in my little room than all the emperors and kings in their glittering gold palaces." It is invariably the language of the tenderfoot, not that of the veteran. Brainerd, at least, never again expressed himself in this fashion.

He worked hard the remainder of the week to procure fodder for his horse, but he continued so ill that he would gladly have died. On Sunday he felt guilty of "soul-murder" — his preaching was so poor. That night he was very sick. Two days later he thought with pleasure on a ghastly verse: *Come death, shake hands; I'll kiss thy bands: 'Tis happiness for me to die. What! dost thou think, that I will shrink? I'll go to immortality.* And he felt compelled to utilize every moment in study and in labor, else "I find it is impossible to enjoy peace and tranquility of mind."

On the last Sunday of August he was again much annoyed with some irreligious Dutchmen. "O what a hell it would be to spend an eternity with such men!" Here and elsewhere he left no doubt regarding his low estimate of the Hudson River Dutch. Their presence and worldly conversation, he stated, oppressed him more than all the difficulties of his wilderness life. He also felt that they would embitter the Indians against him. Already on May 18 he had written: "The Indians have no land to live on but what the Dutch people lay claim to; and these threaten to drive them off. They have no regard to the *souls* of the poor Indians; and, by what I can learn, they hate me, because I come to preach to them." He also wrote to Pemberton that the Dutch, "although they are called Christians, seem to have no concern for Christ's kingdom, but had rather (as their conduct plainly discovers) that the Indians should remain heathens, that they may with the more ease cheat and so enrich themselves by them." Nor would his attitude toward the Hollanders be softened by the fact that Sergeant's first interpreter, a certain Van Valkenburgh, had been the most troublesome rum-seller at Stockbridge.

Actually, the attitudes of the English and the Dutch to the welfare of the Indian offer striking parallels. John Eliot began his evangelization of the Massachusetts natives in 1645. He established dozens of Christian Indian towns, translated the first Indian Bible, and eventually claimed four thousand converts. But three years before Eliot began his work the Dutch *dominee* Johannes Megapolensis was preaching to the Mohawks at Albany, in their own language. Portions of the Dutch Bible were translated into tribal dialects, and the baptismal records of the Dutch Reformed church at Albany during that period reveal dozens of Indian names. But King Philip's War practically wiped out all of Eliot's accomplishments before his death, and a generation later, in 1723, when Brainerd was five, Solomon Stoddard published his Question: *Whether God is not Angry with the Country for doing so little toward the Conversion of the Indians?* Succeeding generations of the Dutch were also less sensitive than their early leaders. Like his Yankee counterpart, the ordinary Dutchman was crassly indifferent to the spiritual needs of his red brother, and along the entire seaboard there was little room and little love for him.

9. GOD HAS MADE ME WILLING

ON MONDAY, AUGUST 29, the day after his second encounter with profane visitors, David undertook a fourth trip to New York within ten months. The first day, as he detoured south through Bethlehem, he seemed to be engrossed in the analogy of his journey to his seeking the sure road to the heavenly Jerusalem, but he felt dull and dejected on the second day as he rode to Danbury. After perhaps spending Sunday at White Plains, he reached New York on Monday.

Tarrying there only two or three days, presumably with the commissioners, he rode forty miles on his return trip and spent the week-end at Horseneck (West Greenwich). He preached at Stanwich on Saturday to "a considerable assembly," and in the evening moderated "some noisy sort of persons, who appeared to me to be actuated by unseen spiritual pride. Alas, what extremes men incline to run into!" He enlarged upon this theme in his sermon on Sunday, for he recorded: "I think God never helped me more in painting true religion, and in detecting clearly, and tenderly discountenancing false appearances of religion, wild-fire party zeal, spiritual pride, etc., as well as a confident dogmatical spirit, and its spring, *ignorance of the heart.*"

His object in leaving New York so quickly is soon revealed. He aimed to be present at Yale's Commencement. Moreover, it seems reasonable to assume that his sole business in New York had been to enlist the commissioners in a final effort to obtain his college degree, and it is possible that Aaron Burr accompanied him on this trip.

Spending Monday night at Ripton and riding into New Haven on Tuesday, he disclosed that though he had "long feared" the occasion and was "greatly afraid of being overwhelmed," the graduation ceremonies on Wednesday, September 14, did not upset him. He was resigned and calm, despite the awful finality of the day and the futility of trying to change the minds of the implacable authorities of Yale.

In his efforts toward re-instatement Brainerd had never been without allies. Among them were the Hartford ministers and Jonathan Dickinson. Nor was he now without champions in his last ditch try for his degree, for it was at this time that he won the sympathy and aid of the man whose continued interest and subsequent friendship became the avenue by which Brainerd's name has been remembered.

Jonathan Edwards of Northampton Massachusetts, was New England's foremost evangelical and probably the most influential alumnus present at the Yale Commencement of 1743, and Aaron Burr of New Jersey was hardly less distinguished at that time. These two men, doubtless upon Burr's solicitation, now together pleaded Brainerd's cause before the Yale authorities. Burr had been "sent from New Jersey to New-Haven, by the rest of the commissioners, for that end," explained Edwards, and he added: "Many arguments were used, but without success." On Thursday, on the advice of his friends, Brainerd wrote a four-hundred-word apology to the college board: "I humbly ask the forgiveness of the governors of the college, and of the whole society; but of Mr. Whittelsey in particular." He commented in his diary: "God has made me willing to do any thing that I can do, consistent with truth, for the sake of peace, and that I might not be a stumbling block to others."

Rector Clap and his colleagues finally made a concession. Edwards wrote: "[They] appeared willing to admit him again to the college; but not to give him his degree, till he should have remained there at least twelve-months, which being contrary to what the correspondents [Burr, Pemberton and Dickinson] had declared to be their mind, he did not consent to it."

Edwards also related that Brainerd displayed an exemplary Christian spirit during that trying week when he consulted Edwards several times and they had "considerable conversation." Edwards added in a quaint footnote: "His trial was the greater, in that, had it not been for the displeasure of the governors of the college, he would not only on that day have shared with his classmates in the public honours which they then received, but would have appeared at the *head* of that class; which, if he had been with them, would have been the most numerous of any that ever had graduated at that college."

When he met Edwards did David also first meet Jerusha, his betrothed? Did Edwards' second daughter come with her father to the Commencement that year? Edwards was frequently accompanied on his trips abroad by one or another of his girls who would share his horse by sitting behind him on a pillion. His eldest daughter Sarah had ridden with him in that fashion to Boston in May, when he and Rector Clap had met on the road and conversed about Whitefield's alleged threat to import English preachers to replace New England's "unconverted clergy," a conversation which carried over into a pamphlet-letter war between the two men.

And if Jerusha did come with her father to New Haven, where would they have lodged?

When Brainerd rode to New Haven on the day before Commencement, his diary reads: "lodged at ————." Thus did either he or Edwards effectively censor the identity of the place. One cannot but suspect that it was Edwards' redaction and that he did it to avoid ruffling of feathers over bygone days. On his visits to New Haven he himself usually lodged at the home of his wife's brother, James Pierrepont (Yale 1718), a son of New Haven's late first minister and one of the original founders of Yale. James was also a great-grandson of Thomas Hooker who founded Hartford. His brother-in-law was Joseph Noyes, pastor of New Haven's "First" church.

But, despite his lineage and social station, James Pierrepont was a New Light and he had caused raised eyebrows when he had given lodging to George Whitefield. More recently he had participated in the organization of the new "Second" church in New Haven and, worse still, he had opened his home for preaching. This had been brought to public attention a year and a half ago when the County Court tried Benaiah Case, the young man who soon thereafter preached to the Scaticock Indians and was ordained with Buell in November. Case was charged as a transient preacher: "at the now hired dwelling house of James Pierrepont . . . in opposition to that which is openly and publicly dispensed by the approved minister of the place." Brainerd may also have preached at Pierrepont's home when he had sneaked into New Haven a year ago in August. Most recently, Pierrepont had invited the Irish preacher Samuel Finley, but on September 5, on his way to the meeting, Finley was seized by the constable and confined for several days until the Grand Jury decreed that he be carried from constable to constable and town to town until he was placed beyond the boundaries of the colony. That had occurred almost simultaneously with Brainerd's arrival in New Haven on September 13 when quite possibly he had lodged with Edwards and Burr at Pierrepont's home.*

But one searches in vain for a clue to romance or the presence of Jerusha Edwards in her uncle's home during that week of Yale's Commencement. She was then fourteen, not too young for courting. Rector Clap's bride had barely completed her fifteenth year on the day of her marriage, and Jerusha's mother, beautiful Sarah Pierrepont, was only thirteen when her young suitor, Jonathan Edwards, had written to her, "They say there is a young lady in New Haven who has a strange sweetness in her mind. . . ."

Jerusha was her father's favorite, perhaps much like her mother of whom Edwards had further fancifully observed —

"She will sometimes go about from place to place singing sweetly, and seeming to be always full of joy and pleasure, and no one knows for what. She loves to be alone, and walking in the fields and groves, and seems to have some One invisible conversing with her."

Whatever the case, on Friday, the day after he wrote his apology, David went to Derby, and spent Saturday and Sunday, most likely with John Graham, at Southbury. One would imagine that over the week-end he would have been perplexed, despondent, or even bitter. Instead, he said, he felt "serious, kind and tender towards all man-

---

* Finley, an Irish-born Presbyterian, had come from the nearby Milford church which was then desirous of joining the New Brunswick Presbytery in New Jersey. (Rector Clap had fined several scholars for following Gilbert Tennent to this church.) Finley was elected president of the College of New Jersey (Princeton) eighteen years later, in 1761.

kind," and yet, for reasons he did not explain, he experienced "much
of unfixedness and wanderings of mind in religion."

10. O THAT MY SOUL WERE HOLY

WHILE RETURNING from Connecticut to Kaunaumeek for the winter,
David stopped to visit Joseph Bellamy. He rode from Southbury to
Bethlehem on Monday afternoon and preached there in Bellamy's
barn in the evening. Before he could take his leave, the strain of
his summer of worry and work felled him on Tuesday. He apparently suffered an attack of influenza — "a hard pain in my teeth, and
shivering cold . . . a very hard fever, and pains almost over my whole
body."

"I had a sense of the divine goodness in appointing this to be the
place of my sickness, among my friends, who were very kind to me,"
he reflected. His illness abated on Friday but it left him weak and he
stayed with Bellamy another ten days. He returned to Kaunaumeek
on October 4, thankful that God had not suffered one of his bones to
be broken during the past year.

As the riotous colors of the Berkshire's maple forests began to
fade he stated parenthetically that a friend lodged with him. This
person could have been Samuel Hopkins who was then considering
a call from the new North Parish of Sheffield, Massachusetts, a bit
down the Housatonic River near the Connecticut border. Until his
senior year at Yale, Hopkins had been secure and satisfied in
his religious life until Brainerd's earnest persuasions had plunged him
into deep distress, but during his past winter at Northampton he
had emerged spiritually alive under the solicitude of Mrs. Edwards.

While this friend was visiting Brainerd, a runner arrived at Kaunaumeek on Sunday, October 16, with an urgent message from
Stockbridge: "Sir, Just now we received advices from Col. [John]
Stoddard of Northampton, that there is the utmost danger of a rup-
ture with France. He has received the same from his excellency our
governor, ordering him to give notice to all the exposed places, that
they may secure themselves the best they can against any sudden
invasion. We thought best to send directly to Kaunaumeek, that
you may take the prudentest measures for your safety that dwell
there."

David may have been aware of the danger, although he remarked that "for no special reason" he had wondered earlier in the day "whether I could be resigned, if God should let the French Indians come upon me, and deprive me of life, or carry me away captive." His reaction to the message is to be expected: "This news only made me more serious, and taught me that I must not please myself with any of the comforts of life which I had been preparing." He went to Stockbridge on Tuesday, perhaps only to escort his friend through the woods, and returned on Friday. On Saturday he wrote: "The world is a dark, cloudy mansion." He preached to his Indians about "the glories of heaven" on Sunday morning, and in the afternoon he warned them of "the miseries of hell, and the danger of going there."

On Monday, the last day of October, he rode twenty miles to Kinderhook, most likely to procure winter supplies and equipment. Returning home in the chill darkness, he caught what he described as another extremely bad cold, and for the next two days he again had severe pains in his face and teeth. But, disregarding his illness, he observed all day Thursday in fasting and prayer. From early morning to evening candles, he "wrestled with God by prayer" and read the biblical accounts of Elijah and Elisha, of Abraham, Moses and Joseph, and blessed God, he said, for these examples of faith and patience. The next day he made another trip to Kinderhook, "quite to Hudson's river," and again returned home in the evening. "I had rather ride hard and fatigue myself to get home," he said, "than to spend the evening and night amongst those who have no regard for God." But the result of his trip was the same as the week before. He had a relapse of his illness and pains.

As winter came he was ill a good deal of the time, "and yet," stated Edwards, he was "obliged to be at great fatigues in labour and travelling day and night." His most frequent trips were over the twenty miles of forest trails to Stockbridge to study the Indian language with Sergeant as the Commissioners had instructed him to do. But the time he spent there, "in company and conversation which were unprofitable," irked him considerably, and he alternated between spiritual warmth and the dark moods that periodically descended upon him — "I love to live alone in my little cottage, where I can spend much time in prayer. . . . O a barn, or stable; hedge, or any other place, is truly desirable if God is there! . . . If the chariot wheels move with ease and speed at any time, for a short space, yet, by and by, they drive heavily again. 'Oh that I had the wings of a dove. . . .'"

The ennui of his winter idleness distressed him particularly during the long December evenings. He was "perplexed to see the vanity and levity of professed Christians," but "a kind of guilty indolence" overtook him also, so that he seemed "an amazing distance from God; and looking around in the world, to see if there was not some happiness to be derived from it." Could Jerusha Edwards have been involved in those "particular objects" to which he thought himself "most dead"? He dismissed them determinedly, mourning his folly: "God forgive my spiritual idolatry!"

With a degree of freedom he returned to his Kaunaumeek hut for the Sunday Christmas day, and he preached to his Indians with "uncommon plainness." After his return to Stockbridge on Monday, when his horse perhaps slipped and plunged through the ice of a large creek, he noted: "Was very much fatigued with my journey, wherein I underwent great hardships; was much exposed and very wet by falling into a river." A letter of some 350 words which he wrote to his brother John at Yale College on Tuesday plainly reveals his dominant mood.

"I long to see you, and know how you fare in your journey through a world of inexpressible sorrow, where we are compassed about with 'vanity, confusion, and vexation of spirit.' I am more weary of life, I think, than ever I was. The whole *world* appears to me like a huge *vacuum*, a vast empty space, whence nothing desirable, or at least satisfactory, can possibly be derived. . . . *Death* and *eternity* are just before us; a few tossing billows more will waft us into the world of spirits, and we hope, through infinite grace, into endless pleasures, and uninterrupted rest and peace. . . . Dear brother, may the *God of all grace* comfort your heart, and succeed your studies, and make you an instrument of good to his people in your day."

Any sense of rest and peace he may have had were dispelled after he rode from Stockbridge to Sheffield on Wednesday to witness Samuel Hopkins' ordination. After an unsuccessful courtship of a young lady in Northampton (the first of three engagements which provided the basis for Harriet Beecher Stowe's novel, *A Minister's Wooing*), Hopkins had accepted the call to Sheffield, though he considered it to be a dreadful place of "very wicked people" and taverns. His judgment was not without reason. As English civilization crept north up the Housatonic Valley, and west from Boston and Northampton, it met at right angles at Stockbridge. Squeezed between Stockbridge and Sheffield was an area inhabited by disreputable ruffians. However, their presence offended the civil people of the area more on the grounds of respectability than spirituality for it appears that the recent settlers of the region were more concerned with wealth and prestige than godliness. "There seems to be no religion here," Hopkins lamented. His new congregation consisted of only five communicant members.

Brainerd was impressed at the ordination with "a sense of the greatness and importance of the work of a minister of Christ," but the short, six-line excerpt of his diary entry is exasperatingly short. The terse phrase: "Afterwards was grieved to see the vanity of the multitude," is freighted with implication as to the religious-social decorum of that day. Ordinations and the raising of new meeting-houses, especially during this era of Puritanism, were outstanding social events that called for appropriate recognition, such as the ten gallons of rum which five years earlier had climaxed the raising of Edwards' new church at Northampton, after the walls of the old house had given way and the loaded gallery had crashed upon the heads of the worshippers below. Hence, the recent rich and the rough rascals of Hopkins' new parish may well have exceeded the usual merriment of the customary ordination ball and barn dance, and a feast consisting of roast meats, turkeys, gingerbread, cider, punch, rum, grog and specially brewed beers.

David took a dim view of the day's affairs. "Most of the time, I had rather have been alone," he stated flatly. He stayed until the next day, "yet enjoyed little satisfaction, because I could find but few disposed to converse of divine and heavenly things." Returning to Stockbridge, he thanked God that he was "not always exposed to the company and conversation of the world." The next day he continued to wonder how the world "with all its charms" could ever have allured him "in the least degree." As he rode back to Kaunaumeek on Saturday, the last day of 1743, he observed: "The air was clear and calm, but as cold as ever I felt it, or near."

His busy week led to the usual reaction. He felt that he could not face his Indians when he came to preach to them on Sunday. But he was thankful for the blessings of the past year, and reflected that he was able to give "about an hundred pounds New England money" for charitable purposes. On Monday, January 2, 1744, he wrote a letter to Haddam, to his youngest brother Israel. The ordination affair apparently engrossed his thoughts as he wrote the lines that reflected his own strict disciplines.

". . . Most men seem to *live to themselves*, without much regard to the glory of God, or the good of their fellow-creatures. They earnestly desire and eagerly pursue after the riches, the honours, and the pleasures of life, as if they really supposed, that wealth, or greatness, or merriment, could make their immortal souls happy. . . .

"You have no *earthly parents* to be the means of forming your youth to piety and virtue, by their pious examples and seasonable counsels, [hence] observe these few *directions;* though not from a father, yet from a brother who is touched with a tender concern for your present and future happiness. . . .

"Resolve upon, and daily endeavour to practise, a life of *seriousness* and strict *sobriety.* . . . Think of the life of Christ; and when you can find that *he* was pleased with jesting and vain merriment, then you may indulge in it yourself. . . .

"Be careful to make a good *improvement* of precious *time.* . . . We should always look upon ourselves as God's servants, placed in God's world, to do *his* work. . . .

"Never think that you can live to God by *your own* power or strength. . . . Yet nothing but our own *experience* can effectually teach it us. Indeed, we are a long time in learning, that *all* our strength and salvation is in God. . . .

"I long to see you. . ."

January was kind to him, for though he was alone in his little hut in the middle of that winter, he spent some of his happiest hours. "My state of solitude does not make the hours hang heavy on my hands," he wrote. "I find that I do not, and it seems I cannot, lead a *Christian* life when I am abroad. . . . When I return home . . . a new scene opens to my mind." He solemnly rededicated himself to God and observed a strict fast, "neither eating nor drinking from evening to evening." The next day he grieved that his strength failed so that he "could not watch unto prayer the whole night." The first fortnight of the new year was for him "unspeakably blessed." He felt "a measure of that rectitude in which we were first created."

Then, fearful lest he should please himself "with some of the enjoyments of this lower world," he left Kaunaumeek for the last two weeks of the month. Exposed to more frigid weather on his way to Stockbridge on Monday, January 16, he was sick for four days after his arrival there. But on Friday he rode the dozen miles south to Hopkins' home, and on Saturday he rode another dozen to Salisbury, Connecticut. The people at this raw settlement had just called their first pastor, Jonathan Lee, for whose arrival they would wait most of the year.

By Tuesday he had again turned north to the hamlet of Canaan just below the Massachusetts border. Here he was unexpectedly visited by a "considerable number" of people in the evening. He described to them the difference between genuine love for God and self-love. He compared genuine love to the unselfish love between the sexes. Genuine love, he said, is a pleasing passion and produces pleasure to the mind of the one who loves, but it is not that pleasure itself. His theme suggests that he was well aware of the difference between his own ascetic indulgences and his essential commitment.

As he retraced his way that week through Sheffield and Stockbridge the weather still continued cold and stormy. When he arrived home he was again ill and in pain, and the black mood descended upon him for five days and he was "full of shame and self-loathing." When it lifted at the end of the following week, he exclaimed on Friday, February 3: "O how amazing it is that people can talk so much about men's power and goodness; when, if God did not hold us back every moment, we should be devils incarnate! This my bitter experience, for several days last past, has abundantly taught me concerning myself."

Personal sanctification and "the ingathering of God's elect" was his whole desire. He was learning, however, that things physical as well as spiritual contributed to the dark moods that so frequently held him captive. On Sunday he wrote: "Thought myself, after the season of weakness, temptation, and desertion I endured last week, to be somewhat like Samson, when his locks began to grow again."

During these weeks he was also writing a meditation, "something of the native language of spiritual sensation." It was his *Dialogue* of more than 2300 words which he entitled: "A Scheme of a Dialogue between the various powers and affections of the mind, as they are found alternately whispering in the godly soul."

In his outline or scheme he first introduced Understanding who, speaking alternately with Will, Love, and Holy Desire, points out why God cannot be perfectly enjoyed by man because of sin. One after another, new voices or whispers of the Christian heart are heard — Holy Impatience, Tender Conscience, Judgment, Godly Sorrow, Hope or Holy Confidence, Godly Fear, and Reflection. In climax, Spiritual Sensation is awakened and declares how she feels and tastes that the Lord is gracious, that He is the only supreme good and the only soul-satisfying happiness, a complete, self-sufficient, and almighty portion.

He repeated her whispers in his diary for Tuesday, February 7. "O, I feel it is heaven to please him, and to be just what he would have me to be! O that my soul were *holy, as he is holy!* O that it were *pure, even as Christ is pure; and perfect, as my Father in in heaven is perfect!* These, I feel, are the sweetest commands in God's book, comprising all others. And shall I break them! must I break them! am I under the necessity of it as long as I live in the world! . . . . Oh, methinks, if he would punish me for my sins, it would not wound my heart so deep to offend him; but though I sin continually, yet he continually repeats his kindness to me! . . . . O that I could consecrate myself, soul and body, to his service for ever! O that I could give myself to him, so as never more to attempt to be my own. . . . I find I cannot be thus entirely devoted to God; I cannot live, and not sin. . . . When we have done all that we can, to all eternity, we shall not be able to offer the ten thousandth part of the homage which the glorious God deserves!"

He faltered but did not fall as his fervor subsided the next day. He realized that "both mind and body are quickly tired with intenseness and fervour in the things of God." However, his conscience did not allow him to completely escape self-censure, for his "past misconduct" and "misguided zeal" gripped him and again made him "afraid of a shaking leaf." His fear, he disclosed on February 10, was that of the prophet Jeremiah: *Denounce, and we will denounce him, say all my familiar friends, they that watch for my fall.*

When it was March he could see that "nothing had happened but what was best." He felt wholly committed to Christ and at peace with those who had wronged him. Prayer was sweet to him, while worldly allurements, even life itself, seemed "but an empty bubble." And, although the winter had been long and tedious, Kaunaumeek had been only a postponement, a training for his own field of work along the Delaware and Susquehanna rivers in Pennsylvania. Now the month of the maple-sap moon had come, and it would be time of removal, both for himself and for his Indians. Thoughtfully summarizing the results of his year's work with them, he wrote to Pemberton: "And although I cannot say that I have satisfactory evidence of their being 'renewed in the spirit of their mind,' and savingly converted to God . . . their idolatrous sacrifices (of which there was but one or two, that I know of, after my coming among them) were wholly laid aside. And their heathenish custom of dancing, hollooing, etc., they seemed in a considerable measure to have abandoned. And I could not but hope, that they were reformed in some measure from the sin of drunkedness."

As he wrote in his letter to Pemberton, he had already persuaded his small band to move to Stockbridge, where they could be under the tutelage of John Sergeant and Timothy Woodbridge and, he had told his people, he himself would "do more service for Christ among the Indians elsewhere," among the Lenni-Lenape whom the white men called the Delawares. When they first heard of his plans, his Indians appeared very sorrowful, and some of them tried their best to persuade him to stay. They said they had now heard so much about the Christian way that they could never again be willing to live as before, "without a minister, and further instructions in the way to heaven." But he told them that they ought to be willing that others also should hear. They answered, as they had heard, "Those Indians were not willing to become Christians." He then said to them: they might receive further instruction without him, but the Lenni-Lenape could not, there being no minister to teach them.

But on Sunday, March 11, when he preached his last sermon at Kaunaumeek, he found that there was no limit to the instructions which he wanted still to give them. Through the mouth of John Wauwaumpequunnaunt he impressed upon them the Master's own earthly story of the sower who went forth to sow. With seeding time near these Eastern woodland natives would comprehend the beautiful simplicity of the parable, for their own land and their way were rocky. No doubt, he warned them that many would fall by the wayside, though some would perhaps bring forth fruit. He had so much to impart. "Indeed," he wrote that night as he sat in his hut, "I had so much to say to them, that I knew not how to leave off speaking."

11.   NOT FROM NECESSITY

BRAINERD NOW KNEW the exacting realities of his mission to the Indians, and a complete reappraisal of his calling was forced upon him a scant four days after he preached his final Kaunaumeek sermon. He had spent Monday in busy preparation for his fifth trip to the commissioners in New York and, on Tuesday, probably heavily loaded with his belongings, he had left Kaunaumeek at ten o'clock and it was "near night" before he arrived at Stockbridge. On Thursday, March 15, an emissary from Nathaniel Huntting's people found him at Hopkins' home in Sheffield.

His message called for decision: "Here I met a messenger from East Hampton on Long-Island; who by the unanimous vote of that large town, was sent to invite me thither, in order to settle with that people, where I had been before frequently invited. Seemed more at a loss what was my duty than before; when I heard of the great difficulties of that place. I was much concerned and grieved, and felt some desires to comply with their request; but knew not what to do. . . ."

During the next two days of rain he rode to Salisbury where he preached well but was very weak and faint, "so that I could scarce walk" — another variation of that grim phrase which reflected his emotional distress more than his physical plight. While at Salisbury on Palm Sunday, further decision was pressed upon him when a second messenger informed him that another church had voted to invite him "upon probation for settlement."

Edwards wrote that the East Hampton people "for a long time continued in pursuit of what they desired, and were hardly brought to relinquish their endeavours, and give up hopes of obtaining him." The second invitation which he hardly seemed to consider was from Millington, near his former home at Haddam, and, as Edwards remarked, "in the midst of his friends."

Withholding final decision, he continued his trip to New York "under great bodily indisposition." However, urged by friends along the way, he preached several times during the Eastertide, and when he finally arrived in the city on Friday, March 28, he was considerably upset and ill. He stayed with Dickinson at Elizabethtown in New Jersey where he met with the commissioners. On Thursday, April 5, according to Pemberton, the commissioners "at length prevailed with Mr. David Brainerd to refuse several invitations unto places where he had a promising prospect of a comfortable settlement among the English. . . ." David, suffering weakness and headache and his inward dying to two attractive calls, wrote: "Resolved to go on still with the Indian affair, if divine providence permitted; although I had before felt some inclination to go to East Hampton."

On Friday the commissioners instructed him to proceed to Pennsylvania, "as soon as convenient." It was then that he became very ill for three days. Jonathan Dickinson would have displayed more than a fatherly interest in his sick young house guest, for among his many accomplishments Dickinson excelled in the practice of medicine. In 1740 he had written *Observations of that terrible disease, vulgarly called throat distemper.* This treatise is one of the first American documents on the subject of sinus infection, a condition which may have been a chief cause of Brainerd's head pains during his winter in the moist Kaunaumeek forests.

After a fortnight, during which he seemed to have been well entertained in New York City and lamented the distractions of its
pleasures, he arrived at his brother Hezekiah's home in Haddam.
Except that he may have met with some of his brothers and sisters
and their growing families in July at Elizabeth's wedding, this was
his first visit with them since his leaving for Long Island fifteen
months ago. He also visited at East Hampton (Connecticut), and
on Tuesday, April 17, he lectured at Millington where he had been
invited to settle on probation. On the way to the village he felt
very uncertain and therefore contrived to ride alone and in prayer
at a distance from the company that was going. He was soon
greatly strengthened by the words: "If God be for us, who can be
against us?", and as he went on to preach and perhaps to formally
decline the invitation, he confided in his God and feared "nothing
so much as self-confidence."

That evening he seemed to have thoroughly enjoyed a hymn-
sing at his brother's home. George Whitefield's promotion of Isaac
Watts' *Hymns and Psalms* in the American colonies had made hymn-
singing so popular that even Jonathan Edwards complained that for
a time his people "sang nothing else, and neglected the Psalms
entirely."*

Almost any one of Watts' songs would express Brainerd's evangelical
commitment and hope —

'Tis heaven on earth to taste His love, to feel His quickening grace,
    And all the heaven I hope above is but to see His face

—and the weight of his most recent decision to forsake his friends
and kin and the comforts of a home —

    Since I must fight if I would reign, increase my courage, Lord!
    I'll bear the toil, endure the pain, supported by Thy Word.

Or did the company that evening sing the most beautiful of the
grand old man's fervent poems?

When I survey the wondrous cross on which the Prince of Glory died,
My richest gain I count but loss, and pour contempt on all my pride.

Or the more stirring anthems: *O God Our Help in Ages Past; Joy*

---

* *The Bay Psalm Book* (1640) and Tate and Brady's *New Version* (1696)
were being by-passed in favor of Watts' *Hymns* (1711), and his *Psalms of
David Imitated* (1719), which was the first volume (1729) to bear the
imprint of Benjamin Franklin's printery in Philadelphia. Watts wrote
more than 500 hymns before he died in 1748. He was followed by Charles
Wesley who is reported to have written 6000 songs.

to the World; Jesus Shall Reign Where'er the Sun; or, There Is a Land of Pure Delight?

"Eternity appeared very near," he wrote that night, "my nature was very weak, and seemed ready to be dissolved; the sun declining, and the shadows of the evening drawing on apace. I longed to fill up the remaining moments all for God! Though my body was so feeble, and wearied with preaching, and much private conversation, yet I wanted to sit up all night to do something for God. To God, the giver of these refreshments, be glory for ever and ever. Amen."

In his weakness he rode back to Stockbridge, visiting his Connecticut minister friends on the way. If he paid a farewell visit to Jerusha Edwards at Northampton, this week would have been the time for him to do so. Edwards is non-committal and vague about the nine-day interval. When he came to Stockbridge on Friday, April 27, his Indians were "very glad" to see him, and on Sunday, just thirteen months after his arrival among them, he preached in Sergeant's place both parts of the day and took leave of his people. His text was Revelation 14:4, *These were redeemed from among men, being the first fruits unto God and to the Lamb.*

Not much else remained for him to do. He started out for the Delaware, but his illness forced him back to Stockbridge — "Monday, April 30. Rode to Kaunaumeek, but was extremely ill; did not enjoy the comfort I hoped for in my own house. Tuesday, May 1. I this day took all my clothes, books, etc., and disposed of them, and set out for Delaware river: but made it my way to return to Mr. Sergeant's; which I did this day, just at night. Rode several hours in the rain through the howling wilderness, although I was so disordered in body, that little or nothing but blood came from me."

One can only conjecture that he sold his belongings at the Dutch settlement of Kinderhook on his way, as he "set out" for Delaware, but that he then turned back from there and painfully rode some thirty miles of wilderness tracks to Stockbridge. His impatience to be gone is evident. "He continued at Stockbridge the next day," stated Edwards, "and on Thursday he rode to Sheffield, under a great degree of illness; but with encouragement and cheerfulness of mind under his fatigues." From Friday to Monday he again lodged at Salisbury. Seven weeks ago he had received his two calls from the Long Island and Millington churches while he was at Sheffield and Salisbury. He had refused them. It may have seemed to him that he had always been destined to leave all behind — comfortable parishes, friends, an affluent career, and now, too, Separatism, strife, and the bitterness of his New England days. He would leave Congregational Connecticut, travel through the Reformed Dutch country, and proceed to the Presbyterians of the Middle Colonies and the Indians of Pennsylvania.

He was on his own, but not from necessity. The lonely way that lay ahead was his by choice. Yet it was from necessity, for he had been called, and he felt no freedom to choose another way.

Book Three
The Evangelist

He had a very extensive acquaintance with those who have been the subjects of the late religious operations, in places far distant, in people of different nations, education, manners and customs. He had a peculiar opportunity of acquaintance with the false appearances and counterfeits of religion. . . .

—Jonathan Edwards

12. A STRANGER IN THE WILDERNESS

STARTING OUT for the Forks of the Delaware on Monday, May 7 Brainerd left Salisbury, Connecticut. He rode only ten miles to Sharon and was distressed over his "misimprovement of time." Was it because he lodged with Peter Pratt, the Yale graduate of 1736 who was ordained at Sharon on April 30, 1744? Soon after his installation Pratt had fallen into gross intemperance and was silenced in 1747. Or was he disappointed in another way? Close by Sharon lay Wequodnac, an Indian village and a principal Moravian station on the shores of Indian Pond which the missionaries had named Gnadensee, the Lake of Grace. Brainerd may have visited this Indian encampment of seventy wigwams and at least 65 baptized converts. Was he unsuccessful in an attempt to consult the resident missionary David Bruce and to obtain explicit directions to his destination just north of the Moravian headquarters in Pennsylvania?

The principal overland route from New England to Pennsylvania led directly west from Sharon, across the Hudson River, through Esopus or Kingston which Zinzendorf called the Sodom of New York, to the Delaware River near the present juncture of New York, New Jersey and Pennsylvania. Brainerd, however, chose an alternate route. On Tuesday he rode 45 miles southwest from Sharon through the hilly sliver of eastern New York to Fish Kill (fish creek), or Fishkill Landing, now part of the city of Beacon on the east shore of the Hudson. It has been spelled Fishkit in error.

Here, Edwards stated, Brainerd "crossed" the Hudson on Wednesday. It is highly improbable that he forded or swam his horse across the great stream, at this or some lower point where the mountain shores are steeper and the current faster, for crossing the Hudson from Dutch Reformed Fishkill to the Rhenish German colony called the Palatine Parish of Quassaic (Newburgh after 1752) was a routine matter in 1744. Madame Catherine Brett operated a freight service from Fishkill and on May 24, 1743, just a year before Brainerd crossed here, Alexander Colden had obtained a franchise to operate a sail and row boat ferry. The fare allowed for the two-mile ferriage was two shillings, six pence for every man and horse.

After Brainerd reached the west shore he traveled some twenty miles through Goshen where he may have lodged with the Presbyterian minister Silas Leonard, a Yale man and a lively revivalist.

Edwards is all too brief about David's first long journey through the solitary forest where the only sounds were the soft thuds of his horse's hoofs, stating only that he "traveled from the Hudson to the Delaware, about a hundred miles, through a desolate and hideous country above New Jersey, where were very few settlements; in which journey he suffered much fatigue and hardship."

Since he did not travel this route again, it is fortunate that in his letter to Pemberton, Brainerd furnished some details of this trip over the Highlands above New Jersey, apparently to inspect his new field of work while biding his time to be ordained into the ministry of the Presbyterian Church. On Thursday he traveled twenty miles and arrived at the ancient Indian town of Minisink. Here the Esopus Road intersected the trail he had ridden from Goshen. On July 1, 1694, a French trader named Arnout Vielle had reported that he had escorted seven hundred tribesmen, toting seventy thousand pelts of fur, to trade at this present site of Montague on the east shore of the Delaware River in New Jersey. But the Indians whom Brainerd now met at Minisink were conglomerate remnants of various tribes commonly known as Munsees.

"With these Indians I spent some time, and first addressing their king in a friendly manner; and after some discourse, and attempts to contract a friendship with him, I told him I had a desire (for his benefit and happiness) to instruct them in Christianity. At which he laughed, turned his back upon me, and went away. I then addressed another principal man in the same manner, who said he was willing to hear me. After some time, I followed the king into his house, and renewed my discourse to him; but he declined talking, and left the affair to another who appeared to be a rational man. He began, and talked very warmly near a quarter of an hour together; he inquired why I desired the Indians to become Christians, seeing the Christians were so much worse than the Indians are in their present state. The Christians, he said, would lie, steal, and drink, worse than the Indians. It was they first taught the Indians to be drunk; and they stole from one another, to that degree, that their rulers were obliged to hang them for it, and that was not sufficient to deter others from the like practice. But the Indians, he added, were none of them ever hanged for stealing, and yet they did not steal half so much; and he supposed that if the Indians should become Christians, they would then be as bad as these. And hereupon he said, they would live as their fathers lived, and go where their fathers were when they died. . . ."

In his Second Appendix to his Journals, Brainerd emphasized

that many of the Indians' objections were based on facts "too notoriously true." As he left this "rational man," he asked him, "Would you
be my friend?"

"Yes," he replied, "if you don't desire 'em to become Christians."

Brainerd made no mention of his experiences on Friday in the
"hideous and howling woods." Although such quaint phrases meant
little more than great or immense and dreary or dismal, it was true
that between him and his destination lay the rugged Kittatinny
Mountains. He could ford the Delaware River at Minisink and
follow an old Indian trail that led west through Cherry Valley
toward Philadelphia, but it is just as likely that he turned south at
Minisink and traveled the Esopus Road. This 104-mile wagon path
was the first man-made highway of any considerable length in the
colonies. Best known as The Good Esopus Road, it was first recorded as the King's or the Queen's Highway. Later it became The
Trade Path and The Path of the Great Valley and during Brainerd's
day it was known as The Old Mine Road. It had been built by
the Dutch West India Company about 1640 to transport ore to
Esopus from what was known as the Pahaquarry Copper Mines in
New Jersey, some forty miles south of Minisink. The irony of
the story is that the ore, probably pale yellow iron pyrites, was mistaken
for precious metal. This fool's gold deceived many entrepreneurs in
the Middle Colonies and in New England.

All along the road were Dutch settlements and isolated home-
steads. The rich Minisinks Flats were settled by Hollanders, and
long before Brainerd's time Dutch Reformed churches had been
established at Machhackamech (Port Jervis), Minisink and Wallpack.
A scow ferry transported travelers across the Delaware River from
the Pahaquarry Mines to the store which Aaron Depui operated at
Shawnee from 1743 to 1747.

On the other side of the Kittatinny Mountains, some fifteen
miles south of Shawnee, and "about twelve miles above the Forks of
Delaware," said Brainerd, lay his final destination which he reached
before night on Saturday. If he made his way through the mountains
by riding along either side of the river, this final day's travel would
have been through the magnificent Delaware Water Gap where
the river cuts through the mountain ranges. Zinzendorf and his
daughter had come through this gap on their way north from
Bethlehem to Esopus and Shekomeko. Here Brainerd too would
have had to lead his horse along the steep sides of the great notch,
for there was no road through it until 1777. "Melancholy and disconsolate [and] alone in a strange wilderness," he reported that he

"felt very poorly" after his long journey "and after being wet and fatigued."

The place at which he had arrived was Hunter's Settlement, a colony of predominantly Ulster-Scotch or Scotch-Irish folk who had settled north of the confluence of the Delaware River and the Lehigh or West Branch of the Delaware fifteen years earlier. Alexander Hunter, the leader of the group, owned three hundred acres of land and operated a ferry across the Delaware directly east of present Richmond. The "Dutch" people who also lived near here were not likely Hollanders such as lived north of the Gap, but Palatinate Germans who after 1725 immigrated in increasing numbers into the region from their original Hudson River settlements.

The next morning was Sunday, May 13. David arose early. It was Pentecost Sunday, and was he not again in the company of those who had received the gift of the Holy Spirit? What he discovered soon filled him with dismay.

"Have scarcely ever seen such a gloomy morning in my life; there appeared to be no *sabbath;* the children were at play; I a stranger in the wilderness, and knew not where to go; and all circumstances seemed to conspire to render my affairs dark and discouraging. Was disappointed respecting an *interpreter,* and heard that the Indians were much scattered. Oh, I mourned after the presence of God, and seemed like a creature banished from his sight! . . . Rode about three or four miles to the Irish people, where I found some that appeared sober and concerned about religion. My heart then began to be a little encouraged: went and preached, first to the Irish, and then to the Indians; and in the evening, was a little comforted; my soul seemed to rest on God, and take courage. O that the Lord would be my support and comforter in an evil world!"

In his letter to Pemberton, he stated that he had arrived "at a place called by the Indians Lakhauwotung, within the Forks of Delaware in Pennsylvania." Lakhauwotung or Lakhauwootung, or the Moravian spelling, Lechauwekink, "the forks of a stream" or "the mouth of a creek where someone resides," is misspelled Sakhau-wotung in some editions of Brainerd's life.* It encompassed the

---

* K. H. in the first volume of *The Presbyterian Magazine,* edited by C. Van Rensselaer (August 1852) attributes the now prevailing error to S. E. Dwight's edition of 1822, stating that the original diary shows that Brainerd spelled it Lakhauwotung. The modern derivative is the now familiar *Lackawanna,* after a metamorphosis of Lackawaneck, -ick, -ock, -uck, Leghawnny and Lackawanny. The "West Branch" or fork of the Delaware River, was altered from Leche, to Lehi, to its present, *Lehigh.*

area north of and including present Easton at the south apex of the triangle of beautiful land between the rivers. In this favorite abode of the Delaware Indians still remained a few of their small villages including Welagameka and Clistonwackin, "fine land," where Zinzendorf had visited when he recorded in his journal that he prayed for the dying grandchild of the medicine man while his companions preached to the villagers.

"Here also," David wrote to Pemberton, "I saluted their king, and others, in a manner I thought most engaging. And soon after informed the king of my desire to instruct them in the Christian religion. After he had consulted a few minutes with two or three old men, he told me he was willing to hear. I then preached to those few that were present; who appeared very attentive and well disposed. And the king in particular seemed both to wonder, and at the same time to be well pleased with what I taught them, respecting the divine Being. And since that time he has ever shown himself friendly to me, giving me free liberty to preach in his house whenever I think fit."

The fact that he added: "Here therefore I have spent the greater part of the summer past, preaching usually in the king's house," seems to prove that he did not stay some thirty miles up river in the vicinity of Milford for two Sundays, as some have stated, but that he came down to the vicinity of Hunter's Settlement directly from Minisink.

His initial visit to the Forks of Delaware at this time lasted only two weeks. On his first Monday and on Tuesday he was "much engaged" and "very busy in some necessary studies," obviously in preparation for his ordination examination and sermon. On Wednesday and again twice on his second Sunday he preached to the Indians and also addressed the Irish people. At times it seemed impossible for him "to go through with the business" he had undertaken, and as the day approached for him to ride to Newark he became increasingly concerned about his "unworthiness and unfitness for the work of the ministry."

On his third Sunday he attended an Indian funeral and was affected to see their heathenish practices. He did not explain their burial rites and their furnishing of the deceased with supplies and equipment for the spiritual journey that lay ahead. He only exclaimed: "O that they might be 'turned from darkness to light!' "

The next morning, according to his orders, he took leave of his new friends that he might be ordained as a chosen minister of Jesus Christ. And as he rode away he must have rehearsed and prayed the text of his probation sermon — *that they may turn from darkness to light.*

13. I AM WITH YOU ALWAYS

On Monday morning, May 28, 1744 as he left the Forks of Delaware to be ordained at Newark, New Jersey, Brainerd probably crossed the Delaware River on Hunter's scow ferry, and traveled east across the North Jersey hills. He wrote only: "Rode through the wilderness; was much fatigued with the heat; lodged at a place called Blackriver; was exceedingly tired and worn out."

That he spent the night at Black River indicates that he rode the trail that led through Schooley's Mountain and Hackettstown to Black River which is now the town of Chester. On Tuesday his route for the second half of his seventy-mile journey passed through present Mendham, Morristown and South Hanover (Madison), to Newark and Elizabethtown. On Wednesday and Thursday he apparently paid his respects to Dickinson in Elizabethtown and to Pemberton in New York, and then spent eight days at Dickinson's home, "chiefly in studies preparatory to his ordination." He partook of the Lord's Supper at Elizabethtown on June 3 and assisted at this ordinance at Newark on June 10, trembling beforehand at the thought of being left to himself in the duties he had to perform.

In visiting the Elizabethtown cluster of six score houses and the elongated settlement of Newark that stretched for two miles along the Passaic or Second River, Brainerd was in the stronghold of New England Puritanism in the Middle Colonies. Newark was founded in 1666 by Robert Treat who deplored the unification of the New Haven and Connecticut colonies, although later he returned to Connecticut and became its commander-in-chief in King Philip's War, and its governor in 1673. In founding Newark, however, he had established the last Puritan theocracy in Colonial America. It was a virtual extension of the strict New Haven society in the freest of the original thirteen colonies. New Jersey had never been dominated by ecclesiastical authority and, as a result of its liberal climate, Dutch Reformed and Episcopalians, Presbyterians and Congregationalists, Quakers and Baptists, and Finnish and Swedish Lutherans learned early to live together with a considerable degree of tolerance. In this colonial melting pot Newark remained an anachronous religious settlement for half a century, until the ever-increasing number of new arrivals gradually and quietly thawed its exclusiveness.

Chief among the newcomers were the Scotch-Irish or Ulster Protestants who had migrated to and settled in Ireland during the

1600's and were driven out by persecution after the turn of the century. Brainerd had already met some of these hardy souls at the Forks of Delaware. Their Presbyterianism gradually infused the church at Newark, and after Francis Makemie, the North-of-Ireland world trader and missionary, had organized the churches of the Middle Colonies into a Presbytery, the Congregational church of Newark gradually moved toward Presbyterianism and became a member of the Synod of Philadelphia in 1719.

It was neighboring Elizabethtown, however, which enjoyed the life-long services of the outstanding English minister of the Middle Colonies. Jonathan Dickinson, Massachusetts-born, was fifty-six years old in 1744 and had served Elizabethtown since 1710, two years after his graduation from Yale. An extant portrait reveals some resemblance to Jonathan Edwards, his counterpart in New England. Dickinson's white-powdered wig framed a fine-featured face. He had large eyes and heavy black eyebrows and a strong chin, and his mouth was slightly larger and not quite as prim as Edwards'. Dickinson was also more practical. In addition to his medical practice, he worked his glebe or farm with profit and conducted the affairs of his church with efficiency.

Well-educated, tolerant and moderate, and with a Congregational background, Dickinson occupied the middle ground between the Scotch high churchmen or Old Side who advocated an authoritative type of church and strict subscription to the Westminster Confession, and the more "low-church," New Side leaders of revivalism. Thus, though he opposed subscription to the Confession, he advocated the adopting of it, but was most influential in so formulating the Adopting Act of 1729 that it did not apply to "unessential" articles such as that which permitted civil power over the church. He was an evangelical Calvinist, a popular author, and a Christian statesman who keynoted love as the greatest of Christian virtues. One of his most popular books was entitled *The Reasonableness of Christianity*.

Nevertheless, he had to align himself with one side or the other as the issues grew and the atmosphere became charged with feeling. Although some were perturbed by his cordial relations with Edward Vaughn, his cool Anglican townsman and parson of Old St. John's, he warmly espoused and contributed to the Middle Colonies revival of Frelinghuysen, the Tennents, and George Whitefield. In the end his sympathy with the revival helped to precipitate the Great Schism which rent the Presbyterian Church in 1741 after the Old Side Synod of Philadelphia ousted the three-year-old New Side

Presbytery of New Brunswick. Two-thirds of the Presbyterian ministers in the colonies were graduates of the University of Glasgow, while almost all of the ministers of the New Brunswick Presbytery were graduates of the Neshaminy Log College which William Tennent, Sr., Gilbert's father, had founded in 1726.

The Synod's action cannot be evaluated without cognizance of the long controversy which involved rules against itinerant preaching, recognition of proper educational degrees, and the authority of the Synod over-against the presbyteries. At the same time, the action was a desperate effort to halt the revival or at least its unsavory excesses by disowning the New Brunswick men. As the strife had mounted Gilbert Tennent preached his vitriolic Nottingham Sermon in 1740, but many voices and pens coined the cutting jibes and countercharges that were hurled between the "uneducated" New Side and the "unconverted" Old Side. The climax was reached when the New Brunswick Presbytery insisted on the ordination of a young Log College candidate named John Rowland, at the New Jersey churches of Maidenhead (now Lawrenceville) and Hopewell Township near Pennington.

Following the expulsion of the New Brunswick group, the Presbytery of New York, led by Dickinson, Pemberton and John Pierson of Woodbridge, protested the Synod's action without success. Finally, after their efforts to reinstate the ousted men failed in May 1743, the New Yorkers met with them in July. Out of this union was to come the new independent Synod of New York in 1745, but it was in the interim year of 1744 that the Presbytery of New York met on Monday, June 11, to ordain David Brainerd, the New Englander recently expelled from Yale.

Brainerd was "very weak and disordered in body" and apparently very nervous as the time approached for his probation sermon. Spending most of the day alone until three o'clock, he preached from his assigned text, Acts 26:17, 18, part of the apostle Paul's speech when he related to King Agrippa how Christ had appointed him a minister and a witness: *unto whom I send thee, to open their eyes, that they may turn from darkness to light and from the power of Satan unto God.* . . . Afterwards he passed an examination before the Presbytery, and after further interrogation on Tuesday, his ordination took place that morning at ten o'clock.

As Ebenezer Pemberton preached the special sermon for the occasion there doubtless came to Brainerd's mind the day at Yale when he had first heard this forty-year-old New Yorker. He instantly recognized Pemberton's text. It was Luke 14:23 — *And the Lord*

said unto the servant, Go out into the highways and hedges, and com-
pel them to come in, that my house may be filled. Pemberton divided
his sermon under three heads: the melancholy state of the Gentile
world, the compassionate care which the Blessed Redeemer takes of
them, and the duty of the ministers of the Gospel to compel them
to come in and accept of His gracious invitation.

After developing his theme, including the glory of Rome and of
Athens now in dust, he spoke directly to Brainerd.

"And suffer me, dear sir, in the first place to address myself to you,
who are this day coming under a public conversation in the service
of Christ, to bear his name among the Gentiles; to whom the Master
is now sending you forth, to compel them to come in, that his house
may be filled. We trust, you are a chosen vessel, designed for extensive service in this honourable, though difficult employment. . . .

"What heavenly skill is required, to convey the super-natural
mysteries of the gospel into the minds of uninstructed pagans, who
are a people of a strange speech and hard language. . . .

"What deep self denial is necessary, to enable you cheerfully to
forsake the pleasures of your native country, with the agreeable
society of your friends and acquaintances, to dwell among those who
inhabit not indeed the highways and hedges, but uncultivated deserts,
and the remotest recesses of the wilderness. . . .

"Methinks I hear you crying out, Who is sufficient for these
things! . . . You have the divine promise for your security and
consolation: Lo, I am with you always, even to the end of the
world."

Six and a half years had passed since the winter of 1737 when the
son of the Worshipful Hezekiah Brainerd of his Majesty's Council
had decided to dedicate his life to the ministry as his grandfathers,
six great uncles, and a brother and cousin had done before him.
But how different his calling from theirs. They, like the prophet-
priest Ezekiel, had been sent to the house of Israel while he, as
Pemberton's sermon emphasized, was being directed to uninstructed
pagans of strange speech and hard language whose words he could
not understand.

Since his expulsion from Yale, Brainerd's life had also become
almost completely identified with his Presbyterian mentors: Pemberton,
Dickinson, and Aaron Burr. These men who had employed him and
championed his cause at Yale had now also ordained him. He had
identified himself with men of high calibre. Though zealous as himself, they were moderate and irenic, and it was their vision and their

immediate interest in him that led to the founding of Princeton University. Although they and their colleague John Pierson had envisaged a College of New Jersey as early as 1739, the tradition obtains that Brainerd's expulsion from Yale gave impetus to their plan, or, at least, that it greatly persuaded the Log College men to support the school which was opened in Dickinson's home in May 1747. The story of Brainerd is not complete without the following excerpt from President John Maclean's *History of the College of New Jersey*.

Subscribing to the opinion that the college owed its origin to the expulsion of Brainerd from Yale, Maclean quoted from Dr. D. D. Fields' *Genealogy of the Brainerd Family* to the effect that Jonathan Edwards and others in New England and the Middle Colonies sympathized with Brainerd — "Among the former were the Rev. Moses Dickinson, pastor of the church in Norwalk, Connecticut; among the latter, the Rev. Jonathan Dickinson." In conclusion Fields wrote that he had personally learned from Moses' son, the Honorable John Dickinson, Chief Judge of the Middlesex County Court of Connecticut, "that the establishment of Princeton College was owing to the sympathy felt for David Brainerd . . . and that the plan of the college was drawn in his father's house." Archibald Alexander, author of *The Log College*, also quoted an acquaintance who stated she had heard Aaron Burr declare: that if it had not been for the treatment Brainerd received at Yale, "New Jersey College would never have been erected."

Situated comfortably in Jonathan Dickinson's home on Wednesday, David spent considerable time "in writing an account of the Indian affairs to go to Scotland." His writings at this time were not published as part of his Journal, but his Kaunaumeek and other experiences to November 5 were printed in the form of the lengthy letter to Ebenezer Pemberton. On Thursday, ready to return to the Forks of Delaware, he received "some particular kindness from friends." The gift could have been as small as some baked delicacies from Dickinson's daughters, or perhaps it was the famous Brainerd Lexicon preserved at Princeton University.*

As usual, Brainerd "wondered that God should open the hearts of any to treat me with kindness; saw myself to be unworthy of any

---

* *Johannis Buxtorfi Lexicon hebraicum et chaldaicum*, 1645, Basel. This volume which originally belonged to Brainerd was bound by the Indians in otter skin painted with red stripes. It was left at Edwards' home after Brainerd's death and was acquired by the University in 1907 from a descendant of the Edwards' family.

favour from God, or any of my fellowmen." And again his arrival upon the threshold of a new phase of his life seemed to result in physical immobility, as had occurred on Long Island, at Bellamy's in Bethlehem, at Stockbridge, and on his previous visit to Dickinson's home in April when he had decided against the Long Island invitation.

He wrote: "was much exercised with pain in my head; however, I determined to set out on my journey towards Delaware in the afternoon; but when the afternoon came, my pain increased exceedingly, so I was greatly distressed with pain and sickness; was sometimes almost bereaved of the exercise of reason by the extremity of pain."

This time Dickinson's knowledge of medicines and his diagnosis called for the employment of an emetic on Saturday, which afforded some relief. However, David was not able to "walk abroad" until Monday afternoon, and he remained "very feeble." He was again grateful that he was among friends rather than strangers and the next day, Tuesday, June 19, he departed from his benefactors to seek again God's chosen ones in the remote recesses of the wilderness.

14. AS DARK AS MIDNIGHT

After spending most of three days to travel the seventy miles from Dickinson's home in New Jersey, Brainerd arrived at the Forks of Delaware on Thursday, June 21. As he began to apply himself to the task that lay before him, he was still feeble and scarcely able to walk, but his health concerned him less than the burden on his spirit. His assignment to convert the Indians appalled him, and it sent him to his knees in prayer — "My whole dependence and hope of success seemed to be on God." He alone, he said, could make them willing to receive instruction, and he became so engaged in prayer that he found himself sending silent requests to God even while he was speaking to them.

His first week was encouraging and he wrote: "Blessed be God, this has been a comfortable week for me." During the next week he made contact with an interpreter and began to translate prayers into the Indian language. He also surveyed his surroundings and probably made his first inquiries "to see if I could procure any lands for the poor Indians, that they might live together, and be under better advantage for instruction." And, as he stated in his letter to Pemberton, he preached to them in their king's house.

In this letter he also explained: "The number of Indians in this place is but small; most of those that formerly belonged here, are dispersed, and removed to places farther back in the country. There are not more than ten houses hereabouts, that continue to be inhabited; and some of these are several miles distant from others, which makes it difficult for the Indians to meet together so frequently as could be desired. When I first began to preach here, the number of my hearers was very small; often not exceeding twenty or twenty-five persons; but toward the latter part of the summer, their number increased, so that I have frequently had forty persons, or more, at once."

The Delawares or Lenni-Lenapes, "the original people," had once claimed most of New Jersey and the Delaware valleys as their home. Generally of an even-tempered, equable disposition, these were the Algonquians who had made the famous treaty of peace with William Penn. Then they had lived in thriving communities of several hundred persons claiming common descent through maternal lineage, and their societal structure had been characterized by their rectangular bark "long-houses" shared by related familial households. Their chiefs or sachems who represented them in warfare and in councils received their appointment through the matron or "chief-maker" of a lineage. All who claimed common lineage belonged to one of three sibs identified as the Turtles, Wolves, and Turkeys. Their communal life had therefore been rather well defined, as is evidenced also by their prohibition against marriage between members of the same sib.

But after a century of contact with the increasing number of white men their cultural and communal life had largely disintegrated. Continuous mingling with the Delaware Bay Swedes, with the Dutch and English of New Jersey, and with William Penn's Quakers, had led many of the Delawares to adopt the white man's ways, his clothes, his diseases, and his rum. Those who had moved farther west still managed to preserve a semblance of their ancient ways and beliefs in guiding spirits which resided in beasts, birds and reptiles, but those who remained near the white settlements succumbed to such demoralization that even their religious ideas were confused and incoherent. After three years of living and working with them Brainerd concluded: "They seemed not to know what they thought themselves." Some of their leaders advocated adoption of the white man's ways in all respects. Others urged a return to the ways of their fathers. They could do neither.

Equally devastating was the humiliating fact that now some twenty years ago the Delawares had become "women": that once a proud and independent people, they had become the subjects of their haughty "uncles," the strong Iroquois or Five Nations Confederacy of New York State, who in collusion with the Penn government further hastened the dispossession of their lands.

Most of the Delaware lands in New Jersey had been lost to them already before 1700, but until a few years before Brainerd's arrival, a goodly number of these essentially agricultural Indians had continued to live in the choice Forks of Delaware paradise, until the first Germans and Scotch-Irish moved in as squatters. But their presence was not the only reason why, at this late date, Brainerd's chances "to procure any land for the poor Indians" were very slim. Seven years earlier the agents of the proprietory heirs of Pennsylvania, John and Thomas Penn, had brought to its close the peaceful co-existence which their father, the Delawares' great white brother Onas, had guaranteed. It would seem that the Scotch-Irish Quaker, James Logan, was deeply involved. A cousin of Gilbert Tennent's father, Logan was acting-governor and *de facto* superintendent of Indian affairs. He also had large land interests and holdings which included the Durham Furnace ironworks adjacent to Chief Nutimus' forests on the Delaware River, just south of the Lehigh, which were needed to supply charcoal for the furnaces and forges. His scheme, the Walking Purchase of 1737, had forever deprived the Indians of their homes in the Forks of Delaware triangle. Whether deliberate dishonesty was intended is still a debatable subject, but the following story is generally accepted.

Logan had first produced a land deed of 1686 which he claimed included the Forks area north of the Lehigh and west of the Delaware. This the Indians protested as impossible. Recognizing the strength of their counterclaims, Logan resorted to threat. He told Nutimus that he looked upon him as no bigger than a little finger of his left hand and that he, Logan, was "a great, big man." He had stretched his arms wide to demonstrate his bigness.

Nutimus tried to appeal to the great League of the Iroquois, but Logan had already persuaded their chiefs to declare that their Delaware "cousins" had sold the land that lay south of the Blue Mountains. Logan then persuaded the Delawares to sign a deed stating that the northern extension of the land in question was to be measured by a walk of a day and a half north, beginning at Tohiccon Creek, but the illiterate natives understood that the walk would most assuredly *terminate* at that creek. That was not yet the worst.

The Indians' common understanding of the proposed walk included rest periods and an occasional smoke after a few miles, and perhaps the chance shooting of a rabbit or a squirrel. But Logan had a path cleared in readiness for the "walk" and hired three young woodsmen to start out at the first glimmer of dawn. At the end of the first day, September 19, 1737, the three men had advanced well north of Nutimus' land, and by noon of the next day, after two of them had dropped out from exhaustion, the lone survivor of the trio, one Edward Marshall, had passed to the west and north through Lehigh Gap to a point some twenty miles north of the Blue mountain range. He had walked fifty-five miles in eighteen hours, and the Delawares had lost twelve hundred square miles of choice land. Of this vast tract, Logan allowed ten square miles for all the Indians living in the entire Forks area.

Within a couple of years more than a hundred white families had settled within the Forks. Four years later, when Brainerd arrived, hundreds more had moved in, and a tract of five thousand acres, which included the plantation of the Indian chief Captain John at Welagameka, had been taken up by the evangelist-promoter George Whitefield for a Negro college. He began to build it with the help of the Moravian Brethren who had sailed north with him from Georgia, but abandoned his plan and sold the land (Nazareth) to the Moravians who in the meanwhile had settled the town of Bethlehem at the southern limits of the Forks.

Before the end of 1742, Captain John, Nutimus, and other sachems with their people were forced to leave their land and their peach, apple and pear orchards, and to move westward toward the Susquehanna River. The final blow had descended upon them at the Great Treaty held with the Five Nations Confederacy at Philadelphia in July, when the Iroquois chief Canassatego ordered the Delawares to leave the region. Addressing Sassoonan, a Delaware chief of a former Schuylkill River tribe who had sold their lands in 1732 and now lived along the Susquehanna River, and Nutimus who represented the Delaware River residents, Canassatego lashed out with all the sarcasm of his Indian oratory. The capitalization of Boyd's *Treaties* helps preserve its flavor.

"You ought to be taken by the Hair of the Head and shaken severely, till you recover your Senses and become sober. . . . How came you to take upon you to sell Land at all: We conquered you; we made Women of you; you know you are Women, and can no more sell Land than Women; nor is it fit you should have the Power of selling Lands, since you would abuse it. This Land that you

claim is gone through your Guts; you have been furnish'd with
Cloaths, Meat and Drink, by the Goods paid you for it, and now
you want it again, like Children as you are. . . . And for all these
Reasons we charge you to remove instantly; we don't give you the
Liberty to think about it. You are Women. Take the Advice of a
wise Man, and remove immediately. . . . We therefore assign you
two places to go, either to *Wyomen* or *Shamokin*. . . ."

The principal man or king who had greeted Brainerd upon his
initial arrival and had extended to him the use of his house for
preaching must therefore be considered to have wielded little authority, for the former big chiefs such as Tishecunk, Lappawinzoe,
Menakihikon, and the more recent sachems, Nutimus and Captain
John, had already moved out. But there was another sachem who
had not been forced to move away. Brainerd made his first mention
of this man when he wrote on Tuesday, June 26: "Was busy most
of the day in translating prayers into the language of the Delaware
Indians; met with great difficulty, by reason that my interpreter
was altogether unacquainted with the business."

In this middle-aged interpreter lay Brainerd's hope of reaching the
Indians' minds and hearts. Since all of his study of the Mahican
dialect at Stockbridge was valueless among their Delaware cousins,
his sole contact was through this one man whom he identified as
Moses Tinda Tautamy, but whose best known appelation has come
down in history as Moses Tattamy. His name also appears as Moses
Tunda Tatamy, Moses Tonda Tetamy, Tatemi, Titami, Tademe,
Totomy and Totemi. But Moses' name is definitely misspelled when
it appears as Finda, Fonda, or Funda, and Fatuary or Fautaury.

A few facts are known about Tattamy before Brainerd met him.
Moses was about fifty years old and he had moved his family from
the Munsee country at Minisinks before the Walking Purchase took
place. In the negotiations of 1737 and earlier he had served as an
interpreter for the Penn government. In July 1742 when Count
Zinzendorf passed through Tattamy's "plantation" of more than two
hundred acres near the present site of Stockertown and the borough
of Tatamy, Moses entertained the Count's party of fifteen persons
with an unrecorded account of the Delawares' mode of sacrifice. John
Heckewelder, the Moravian missionary-historian, described Tattamy
as the Delawares' "great, good, beloved and peaceful chief Tademe,
(commonly called Tattemi)"; also "their good and highly respected
chief Tademi, a man of such an easy and friendly address, that he
could not but be loved by all who knew him."

When Whitefield had appropriated Captain John's plantation in his large tract of land, John and Tattamy made a formal and vigorous protest to the Penn government. Later, when the Delawares were ordered to leave the Forks, Tattamy and his neighbors petitioned the Governor's Council to permit them to stay, stating that "having embraced the Christian Religion and attained some small Degree of Knowledge therein, they are desirous of living under the same Laws with the English." Governor George Thomas thereupon catechized Captain John and Tattamy, but considered their knowledge of Christianity too meager to substantiate their claims. Tattamy, however, was permitted to remain and to retain possession of his land which the government had previously given him in consideration of his services as messenger and translator.

It is doubtful that Brainerd was immediately aware of his new interpreter's entire background, but that Tattamy was well acquainted with the white man's liquors would hardly have escaped his notice. And, in view of Tattamy's recognized abilities as an interpreter in mundane affairs, Brainerd's very definite judgment more than accentuated Tattamy's woeful lack of knowledge concerning the Christian Way and things spiritual. "Truths of the last importance," said Brainerd, "appeared foolishness to him." He was "altogether unacquainted with the business," and therefore, he explained, Tattamy addressed the Indians in a lifeless, indifferent manner. He was something less than an effective mouthpiece.

So it was that the month of June ended and Brainerd saw that everything that respected the conversion of the Indians was "as dark as midnight." Yet he could not but hope that God intended something glorious among them, and he wrestled with the singleness of his calling and with his God. He sought strength for his seemingly hopeless task by reading his Bible and he turned for encouragement to the stories of how God had assisted Nehemiah and Ezra in rebuilding Jerusalem, in "re-establishing his ancient church," and he concluded: "Though the work of their conversion appeared impossible with man, yet with God I saw all things were possible."

"My heart went up to God in prayer for them; could freely tell God, he knew that the cause was not mine, which I was engaged in; but it was his own cause, and it would be for his own glory to convert the poor Indians; and blessed be God, I felt no desire of their conversion, that I might receive honour from the world, as being the instrument of it."

On the last day of the month, as he continued to read the Scriptures, his soul became most solemn as he read the great ninth prayer chapter of the prophecy of Daniel. "I saw," he said, "how

God had called out his servants to prayer, and made them wrestle with him, when he designed to bestow any great mercy on his church." And he read that while Daniel was speaking and praying and confessing his sin and the sins of his people, and presenting his needs before the Lord his God, that the man Gabriel came, and this messenger of God touched him and talked with him, and said: "I am now come forth to give thee skill and understanding. At the beginning of thy supplications the commandment came forth, and I am come to shew thee, for thou art greatly beloved."

15. FOR GOD AGAINST SATAN

On Sunday, the first day of July, Brainerd sensed a flicker of heart interest among his Delaware Indians. He rejoiced, and after he left them and had ridden two miles, he alighted from his horse to rededicate himself to God who had so effectively helped him to plead with them to "turn from all the vanities of the heathen to the living God." As he was also very weak that day and had felt most inadequate before speaking to them, the intensity of his gratefulness overwhelmed him as he remounted and rode home. His fingers became weak and numb, so that he could hardly straighten them, and when he again dismounted from his horse he could not control his legs. "My joints," he said, "seemed all to be loosed."

Throughout that week he worked and preached and translated, and at times he could write: "I felt abundant strength in the inner man," but he was again tried and filled with "continual distress and and great bitterness of spirit" concerning his spiritual insufficiences. On Friday, however, he felt that he had succeeded in being "most of all concerned for ministerial qualifications, and the conversion of the heathen," and had also achieved "less desire to live for any of the pleasures of the world, than ever I had."

"Last year, I longed to be prepared for a world of glory, and speedily to depart out of this world; but of late all my concern almost is for the conversion of the heathen; and for that end I long to live." And he must have recalled Pemberton's and also the apostle Paul's own admonition when he asserted positively: "I long and love to be a pilgrim; and want grace to imitate the life, labours, and sufferings of St. Paul among the heathen."

But his resolution was short-lived. He was ill and unable to rest quietly Saturday night, and on Sunday, despite a conscious awareness of divine aid, he wrote: "[I] longed to 'depart, and be with Christ,' more than at any time of late." And, although he may not have prayed, "It is enough; now, O Lord, take away my life," he did record: "My soul was exceedingly united to the saints of ancient times, as well as those now living; especially my soul melted for the society of Elijah and Elisha."

He continued ill and weak and accomplished little that month until the third Saturday, July 21, when he learned that his Indians intended to meet on Sunday for "an idolatrous feast and dance." Then, he said, "I began to be in anguish." Prayer was his only weapon, and he prayed for hours. And as he prayed his courage and desire to live surged back, although his prayer wrestling wrung his strength from him as he implored his Maker to vindicate *Himself*.

"Thus I spent the evening praying incessantly for divine assistance, and that I might not be self-dependent, but still have my whole dependence upon God. What I passed through was remarkable, and indeed inexpressible. All things here below vanished; and there appeared to be nothing of any considerable importance to me, but holiness of heart and life, and the conversion of the heathen to God. All my cares, fears, and desires, which might be said to be of a worldly nature, disappeared; and were, in my esteem, of little more importance than a puff of wind. . . . I cared not where or how I lived, or what hardships I went through, so that I could but gain souls to Christ. I continued in this frame all the evening and night. While I was asleep, I dreamed of these things; and when I waked, as I frequently did, the first thing I thought of was this great work of pleading for God against Satan."

The Indians, however, were obstinate in their plans. But, awakening Sunday morning with great expectation that God would display His power and glory among them, Brainerd hurried from his bed, dressed quickly, and again prayed in the woods. Then he rode three miles to the scene of their "frolic" and, he said, "I got them to break up." (This was apparently too much for Sereno E. Dwight's sensitivity for the English language. His edition of 1822 reads: "I persuaded them to desist"!)

The Indians also listened to him as he preached to them and as he must have urged them to decision that morning and again in the afternoon. But their apathy distressed him and, he observed, there appeared nothing of the special power of God among them. Instead, he lamented, Satan took occasion to tempt and to buffet him with the cursed suggestion, "There is no God, or if there be, he is not able to convert the Indians before they have more knowledge." Yet he waited upon God, although the Prince of Darkness tempted him to the contrary.

As noted earlier, Brainerd lived much of the time with the Hunter family who had settled among the rolling hills in the vicinity of Martin's Creek as it enters the Delaware River, farther north than most of the Scotch-Irish who located near Philadelphia and along the south and west frontiers and, later, the Cumberland Valley. Alexander Hunter was an educated and a pious person and became one of the first magistrates of Northampton County. Brainerd had his own lodging room at his home. Five years later John Brainerd occupied this room, "the same as my dear brother David used to lodge in," he wrote. The room is said to have been an addition to the home and was probably built of logs.

Although there was then no church building at Hunter's Settlement, Brainerd was not the first preacher to minister to the people there. Eleazar Wales of the Synod of Philadelphia, but later a charter member of the ousted New Brunswick Presbytery, had served the Forks to Delaware from 1731 to 1734 as the first settled pastor. After its organization in 1738, the New Brunswick Presbytery became the chief source of supply ministers to the region. Gilbert Tennent preached there in 1738-39, and through the years there were other preachers. In 1742 James Campbell spent half of his time at the Forks and half at Greenwich on the high New Jersey side of the Delaware River. Charles Beatty of Neshaminy, north of Philadelphia, had preached there prior to Brainerd's arrival, as had Azariah Horton, William Robinson, and Charles McKnight.

It was in his dual capacity as Indian missionary and supply minister to the whites that Brainerd set out on the Monday morning after his Indians' Sunday dance. One can assume that as he left Hunter's Settlement he headed his horse southwest for five miles to Tattamy's plantation, and continued through Whitefield's Nazareth Tract. After another ten miles he and Tattamy arrived at Craig's Settlement near the Lehigh River, which was both older and larger than that of the Hunter group on the Delaware. "Near night," David wrote, he preached to the settlers from Matthew 5:3, *Blessed are the poor in spirit.* There was no church building at Craig's Settlement either, although Thomas Craig had attended the Synod of Philadelphia as an elder as early as 1731. Tradition states that David preached in a meadow owned by James Craig whose home was the usual lodging place for visiting ministers.

The Irish Settlement, as Craig's group was also called, was located around a fine spring and along the banks of the Hockendauqua and Catasauqua creeks, about three miles north of present Catasauqua. Both James and the older Thomas Craig, who were apparently not related, are recognized as the founders of the original colony of sixteen families who arrived at the location in 1728. Settling first as squatters, most of these pioneers had soon obtained legal title to their lands. Thomas Craig had purchased 590 acres in 1739; James apparently received 250 acres in 1743 as a gift from William Allen, a relative by marriage who had acquired five thousand acres in 1735. Other tracts of land were owned or occupied by the Kerrs, Boyds, Wilsons, Armstrongs, McNairs, Walkers and the other Ulstermen of the colony through which the runners of the infamous Walking Purchase had passed.*

On Tuesday, taking advantage of a respite from illness, Brainerd rode another seventeen miles westward, "over a hideous mountain," to locate some Indians who were camping at a place near present Cherryville called Kauksesauchung. The area was long called the "Indian Land," but the present town of Catasauqua, heir to the name, grew up south of it many years later. His diary entry is short — "Got together near thirty of them; preached to them in the evening, and lodged among them." He did not mention that the hideous mountain over which he had climbed was the most easterly range of the Appalachian chain, some twelve to sixteen hundred feet high. It was rough and rocky, and very steep. Five years later his brother John declared that it was the worst road he had ever seen in his life. David's letter to Pemberton tells more about the visit and reveals the Delawares' simple friendliness and some of their fears.

"While I was preaching, they appeared sober and attentive; and were somewhat surprised, having never heard of these things. There were two or three who suspected that I had some ill design upon them; and urged, that the white people had abused them; and taken their lands from them, and therefore they had no reason to think that they were now concerned for their happiness; but, on the contrary, that they designed to make them slaves, or get them on board their vessels, and make them fight with the people over the water, (as they expressed it), meaning the French and Spaniards. However, the most of them appeared very friendly, and told me, they were then going

* Allentown is named after Wm. Allen who became Chief Justice of the Penn colony from 1750 to 1754. His daughter married John Penn.

directly home to Susquehannah, and desired I would make them a visit there, and manifested a considerable desire of further instruction. This invitation gave me some encouragement in my great work; and made me hope, that God designed to 'open an effectual door to me' for spreading the gospel among the poor heathen farther westward."

"The next day," Edwards stated, "he preached to these Indians again; and then returned to the Irish settlement, and there preached to a numerous congregation. There was a considerable appearance of awakening in the congregation."

Cut off from the traditions and conventions of their homelands and deprived of regular preaching and formal church affiliations, the frontier settlers were always subject to a growing indifference to religion and a lessening of moral standards. It was no different at the Forks of Delaware where the lack of resident pastors, infrequent communication, inclement weather, and the general hardships of travel tended to stultify religious life. And although these same factors made a visiting preacher's arrival a joyful event to the faithful who longed for Christian fellowship and the courts of God, it is no great wonder that Brainerd on his first dismal Sunday in the Forks had bemoaned that "there appeared to be no Sabbath." This state of affairs also makes an entry in the Moravian "Bethlehem Diary" more meaningful. It is dated Sunday, July 1, 1742 (Gregorian Calendar), about the time that Gilbert Tennent in an effort to extricate himself from comparison with them, was denouncing not only the Moravians' antinomianism and pietism, but also their proselyting activities which, it was charged, were not unlike his own. The diary reads: "In future an English preaching service is to be held each Sunday: so that our English neighbors and the Irish may have opportunity to hear our message. . . . The English hymnal is to be used on such occasions."

In contrast to the unorganized religious life of their Scotch-Irish neighbors, the communal life of the Moravians was effective in nurturing both their spiritual and their cultural life. Their *Gemeinhaus* or Community House in their village of Bethlehem on the Lehigh was a massive white oak building, which is still well-preserved. In their chapel they had a London spinet to accompany congregational singing. Their observance of holy days, then still generally unacceptable to Congregationalists and Presbyterians, were highlights of the year. At Christmas time they decorated their village with lighted trees. On Easter morning, 1744, only a month before David's arrival within the Forks, the Bethlehem Diary records that the entire Moravian congregation arose at four o'clock and after singing in their chapel they "proceeded two and two to the graves of our brethren and sisters, accompanied by music, rejoicing in God our Saviour."

However crude Brainerd's preaching service in James Craig's meadow may have appeared to the Moravians, there was among the audience, said Edwards, "a considerable appearance of awakening." And Tattamy was also affected. Perhaps the obvious concern of the Scotch-Irish that day impressed upon him the vital importance of his young employer's message. Brainerd referred to this meeting of July 25, 1744, when in his Journal he later related something of Tattamy's spiritual experiences.

"Near the latter end of July, 1744, I preached to an assembly of white people, with more freedom and fervency that I could possibly address the Indians with, without their having first obtained a greater measure of doctrinal knowledge. At this time he was present, and was somewhat awakened to a concern for his soul; so that the next day he discoursed freely with me about his *spiritual* concerns, and gave me an opportunity to use further endeavours to fasten the impressions of his perishing state upon his mind: and I could plainly perceive for some time after this, that he addressed the Indians with more *concern* and *fervency* than he had formerly done."

"But," he concluded, "these impressions seemed quickly to decline; and he remained in a great measure, careless and secure."

Brainerd also disclosed that Tattamy was one of those who advocated that the Delawares conform to the manners and customs of the white man. "Especially," said David, "he appeared very desirous that the Indians should renounce their heathenish notions and practices, and conform to the customs of the Christian world." And David affirmed that his translator was "well fitted for his work." But, he explained, "he seemed to have little or no impression of religion upon his mind, and in that respect was very *unfit* for his work, being incapable of understanding and communicating to others many things of importance." Assessing Tattamy's character, he observed: "He indeed behaved *soberly* after I employed him, (although before, he had been a *hard drinker*), and seemed honestly engaged as far as he was capable in the performance of his work."

When David returned to Hunter's Settlement on Thursday, he was again "extremely fatigued and spent" and so ill that he could not go out to preach on Sunday. What crude remedies of sulphate of iron, bear's oil or snake root did the good women of the settlement urge upon him? During the week following his condition grew worse. Edwards paraphrased his diary for the latter part of the week: "His mind was as much disordered as his body, seeming to be stupid, and without any kind of affections towards all objects, and yet perplexed to think that he lived for nothing; that precious time rolled away and he could do nothing but trifle; and that it was a season wherein *Satan* buffeted him with some peculiar temptations."

One would suspect that his temptations were two in particular and closely linked, much as he had expressed them on his first Sunday at the Forks. On that day he had stated, and perhaps protested overmuch, "I never entertained any thought of quitting my business among the poor Indians: but was comforted, to think, that death would ere long set me free from these distresses." And now, too, even though he affirmed, "I was not so willing to leave this scene of sorrows as I used to be," he probably was still tormented by his awful doubt: "There is no God, or if there be, he is not able to convert the Indians."

If he did entertain these thoughts his declarations to others did not betray the misgivings of his soul. On Tuesday, July 31, he wrote what Edwards identified as a letter to a special friend. Was it addressed to Jerusha Edwards? In it David enjoined his correspondent to seek happiness only in God, and commented on his own state of affairs. With an inexplicable twist he consigned himself to a pilgrim life in the wilderness as befitting his unworthiness for any higher station, quite below his lofty reach at the beginning of the month when he prayed for grace to follow the example of Paul, the great Doctor to the Gentiles.

"I am in a very poor state of health; I think scarce ever poorer: but through divine goodness I am not discontented under my weakness and confinement to this wilderness. I bless God for this retirement: I never was more thankful for anything than I have been of late for the necessity I am under of self-denial in many respects. I love to be a *pilgrim* and *stranger* in this wilderness: it seems most fit for such a poor, ignorant, worthless, despised creature as I. I would not change my present *mission* for any other business in the whole world. . . . I feel as if my *all* was lost, and I was undone for this world, if the poor heathen may not be converted. . . . It would be very refreshing to me to see you here in this desert; especially in my weak disconsolate hours: but I think I could be content never to see you or any of my friends again in this world, if God would bless my labours here to the conversion of the poor Indians.

"I have much that I could willingly communicate to you, which I must omit, till Providence gives us leave to see each other."

That Edwards quoted only one diary entry, for August 5, is mute evidence that the whole of that month was for Brainerd one of illness and uselessness. During the first week he was still so feeble that although he preached to the Indians twice he was "obliged to sit down the whole time," and was "frequently unable to pray in the family."

"I am obliged to let all my thoughts and concerns run at random; for I have neither strength to read, meditate, or pray. . . . I seem to myself like a man that has all his estate embarked in one small boat, unhappily going adrift, down a swift torrent. The poor owner stands on the shore, and looks, and laments his loss. But, alas! I dare not lament; for this sinks my spirits more, and aggravates my bodily disorders! . . . . O that God would pity my distressed state!"

As his strength returned during the next three weeks he resumed some activity and noticed some response to his preaching among the Indians, and, as Edwards enigmatically observed, he enjoyed the company of some ministers who came to visit him. His visitors may have included young Charles Beatty of Neshaminy, the nearest Presbyterian minister some fifty miles to the south. Or perhaps it was his employers from seventy miles east who, noting the ravages of his fevers, advised a furlough, for soon thereafter he went on a three-weeks journey to New England. His diary for September 1 indicates a definite degree of recovery: "I was able to spend two or three hours in writing on a divine subject."

His last quoted entry before leaving the Forks suggests much of his daily struggles with the Indians.

"Lord's Day, September 2. I perceived that some of them were afraid to hearken to and embrace *Christianity,* lest they should be enchanted and poisoned by some of the *powwows:* but I was enabled to plead with them not to fear these; and confiding in God for safety and deliverance, I bid a challenge to all these *powers of darkness,* to do their worst on *me* first. I told my people that I was a *Christian,* and asked them why the *powwows* did not bewitch and poison me. I scarcely ever felt more sensible of my own unworthiness, than in this action: I saw, that the honour of God was concerned in the affair; and I desired to be preserved not from selfish views, but for a testimony of the divine power and goodness, and of the truth of Christianity, and that God might be glorified. Afterwards I found my soul rejoice in God for his assisting grace."

Brainerd's situation *was* a desperate and dangerous one, for his defiance of the Indian priests could result in serious retaliation and threat to his life. These powwows or conjurers were literally the dreamers or diviners of dreams. They held great power among the Indians and jealously guarded their prestige. Although there were also medical men or *medeu* who exorcised sickness and officiated at funerals, Brainerd seems to make little distinction between the two groups. "These are the sort of persons," he wrote, "who are supposed to have a power of foretelling future events, or recovering the sick, at least oftentimes, and of charming, enchanting, or poisoning persons to death by their magic divinations. . . . Some of these diviners are endowed with the spirit in infancy; others in adult age."

In his Second Appendix, he related the story of how a conjurer believed he had received his powers of divination. In the light of later events, it seems highly probable that the narrator was the same powwow he now defied.

This Indian was admitted into the presence of a "great man" who loved, pitied, and desired his welfare. The meeting took place far above the earth and the great man shone as the brightest day, and in him was reflected the whole creation. His shadow, lovely as himself, stood by his side. After the great man had declared who should be this Indian's mother, he asked him to choose what he should be in life. First to be a great hunter, and afterwards a *powwow*, the Indian replied. He was told it would be so, and that a guardian shadow would return to earth with him, to be with him forever. All the while, no words were spoken, but they had a mutual intelligence of each other's thoughts. The Indian saw the great man no more, but his shadow continued with him and appeared to him in dreams and in other ways to protect and advise him.

Brainerd commented: "What is most astonishing, he imagines all this to have passed before he was born." The powwow had been told also that he would one day murder somebody. To Brainerd it was the work of Satan himself. "These *depths of Satan*," he said, "I leave to others to fathom or dive into as they please, and do not pretend, for my own part, to know what ideas to affix to such terms."

He disclosed later that the conjurer *was* a murderer and a miserable drunkard, and for the sake of gospellizing the Indians he could fervently wish that the wretch were dead.

16. THE POOR HEATHEN FARTHER WESTWARD

EDWARDS BRIEFLY SUMMARIZED Brainerd's trip of three weeks to New England in September 1744. It was a journey of recuperation and pleasure, of visiting home and friends. He seemed to enjoy some

peace of mind, said Edwards, but only toward the end of his trip
did he gain in health and strength.

Perhaps there was little else to comment upon. However, it was
again the time of Yale's Commencement. Eleazar Wheelock attended
the exercises that year in company with his Latin-writing Indian
prodigy, Samson Occom, who, let it be said, had been converted under
James Davenport's notorious preaching. And, should he have gone
to the Yale Library, or had he borrowed a copy of the new *American
Magazine* which made its first appearance that year, Brainerd would
have discovered Rector Clap's *Orrerey* or planetarium or the description of it written by none other than Senior Tutor Chauncey Whittelsey.

Such coincidence would not be his only reminder of his sad experience with those two gentlemen. Perhaps the case of John and
Ebenezer Cleveland was already being discussed. During their
vacation these two brothers had attended a Separatist meeting with
their parents in Canterbury. For this offense they were summarily
expelled from Yale on November 19, although eventually they were
granted their degrees when the tide of public opinion turned against
the high-handedness of the Yale authorities.

Concerning a more immediate matter, Brainerd certainly would have
heard. At their meeting that September the Yale trustees decided to
refuse admittance to freshmen applicants who were more than twenty-
one years old. And it definitely appears, their decision was prompted
by their distasteful experience with two former students who had
entered Yale at that age — the lively preacher-student Samuel Buell,
and the zealous, censorious David Brainerd who had been expelled.

In his travel Brainerd would also have noted signs of the general
prosperity in New England. At Stratford, following the completion
of Samuel Johnson's new Episcopal edifice in 1743, the Congregationalists were finishing their new church with a 130 foot spire, forty
feet higher than any other steeple in the valley. The Second Congregational Church in New Haven had built also. Brainerd's good
friend Bellamy had married Frances Sherman of New Haven in
April and his Bethlehem congregation had moved from their barn
to a newly-erected meetinghouse.

Spiritual life in New England was not as prosperous. Whitefield
who had again left England for America in August would receive a
cool reception upon his arrival. Harvard and Yale were preparing
testimonials against him and, as guest speaker at Harvard's September
Commencement, Rector Clap startled his audience with the accusa-
tion that Edwards had informed him that Whitefield intended to

"turn out" the New England clergy. The exchange of published letters that ensued between Clap and Edwards put the clergy in a dither. Edwards, it seems, had said he was *of the opinion,* that he had merely *supposed* Whitefield *may* have had this *in mind* during his first visit to New England.

And there were other disagreeable situations. Benjamin Pomeroy had been penalized for his outspoken criticisms. He had also disobeyed the law by preaching in an open grove at Colchester after Ephraim Little, Harvard 1728, had refused to give him permission to preach in his parish. Found guilty of disregarding Little's decision, Pomeroy was deprived of his salary for seven years.

There was one very satisfying development, however. After much effort and persuasion, the Lebanon colleagues, Eleazar Wheelock and Solomon Williams, had finally brought James Davenport to his senses. Davenport's "Retraction" had appeared in the July 18th issue of *The Boston Gazette*: "I believe, further, that I have done much hurt to religion . . . ." He confessed his error in encouraging laymen to preach, his "great stiffness" in holding to his errors in spite of Christian admonitions and that, at the book-burning in New London, "that horrid action," he had been "under the powerful influence of the false spirit . . . although I thought, in the time of it, that 'twas the Spirit of God in a high degree." He cited his illness at the time: "I had the long fever on me, and the cankry humour raging at once." He resigned from his church on Long Island and did his best to make amends at various places, including Fish's parish at Stonington. "He came," stated Fish, "with such a mild, meek, pleasant and humble spirit, broken and contrite, as I scarce ever saw excelled or equalled."

Affairs at Stockbridge were normal. Sergeant was still working toward obtaining an adequate building for his Indian boarding school. The Moravian missionaries, however, were being harassed. During that eventful September which Brainerd spent in Connecticut, Brothers Mack, Shaw, and Pyrlaeus were seized as Papists and hustled from one to another of the colony's courts and expelled.

Lastly, if David visited Jerusha Edwards at Northampton — there is no inkling that he did — he must soon have learned of the unhappy state of her father's public relations. Earlier in the year Jonathan Edwards had discovered that some young people in his church had secretly read and circulated a midwifery's book, and, with the consent of a committee, he had publicly and indiscriminately disclosed the names of those involved in this questionable episode. His action, however, greatly offended some of his most prominent and vocal parishioners whose children were implicated in the affair. This sorry incident, the "Bad Book Case," so heightened the feeling of ill will against Edwards that it would culminate in his dismissal six years later.

Happy to arrive "home in the Forks of Delaware" on Wednesday, September 26, Brainerd again expressed his thankfulness in his paraphrase of Psalm 34:20, the song that David sang after he had escaped from Gath: "What reason have I to bless God, who has preserved me in riding more than four hundred and twenty miles, and has 'kept all my bones, that not one of them has been broken!' My health likewise is greatly recovered. O that I could dedicate my all to God! This is all the return I can make to him."

While lamenting the "ill effects of the diversions of his late journey," he immediately began to prepare for his first trip to the Susquehanna River. The Indians he had visited at Kauksesuchung in July had seemed genuinely interested in hearing him again at their Susquehanna homes, and on his way to or from New England he had doubtless visited the commissioners and had received their permission to re-visit these natives. And during his recent trip east, or perhaps already on his first trip to Newark, he may have also met the traveling companion for the journey he had planned to the poor heathen farther westward.

He esteemed this new friend most highly. It was as Emerson would say a century later: "We overestimate the conscience of our friend. His goodness seems better than our goodness, his nature finer, his temptations less." David said it this way: "Towards night rode about four miles, and met brother Byram; who was come, at my desire, to be my companion in travel to the Indians. I rejoiced to see him; and, I trust, God made his conversation profitable to me. I saw him, as I thought, more dead to the world, its anxious cares and alluring objects, than I was; and this made me look within myself, and gave me a greater sense of my guilt, ingratitude, and misery."

Brother Byram, whom he probably met at the river ferry, was Eliab Byram, pastor of the Presbyterian church at Rockciticus, now Mendham, forty miles east of the Delaware. Eliab was the second of five sons of Ebenezer Byram of Bridgewater, Massachusetts, one of the leading settlers of "Mendum" in the hilly limestone country of North Jersey and the reported owner of the Black Horse Tavern which still stands on Mendham's main street. Eliab had graduated from Harvard in 1740 and, arriving with his parents in New Jersey in 1743, became one of an increasing number of young men from Harvard and Yale who affiliated with the New York Presbytery.

He had preached in Rockciticus (also spelled Roxciticus) since October 1743 and became the settled pastor in May 1744, the position he held for some nine or ten years. Local Mendham tradition states that at one time Brainerd preached to the Indians there.

On Tuesday morning, October 2, Brainerd, Byram, Tattamy and two other "chief Indians" started out from the Forks of Delaware and traveled about twenty-five miles. They lodged overnight in one of the last houses on their road, "after which," stated Brainerd, "there was nothing but a hideous and howling wilderness." Since Opeholhaupung, the Indian village to which the party headed on Wednesday, was near the present site of Berwick, they must have traveled an Indian trail west and then followed the Lehigh River northwest through the Blue Mountains and the Lehigh Gap to the beautiful waterway at Mauch Chunk, "sleeping bear."*

Brainerd's route through this picturesque country and mountain pass was very rugged and hazardous, and full of rocks. Zinzendorf had traveled through this region and described it as the wildest he had ever seen and at places so steep that his party linked themselves together to keep from falling over the cliffs. Brainerd's experience and description of the forested ranges corroborated that of the Moravian count. He does not seem to have appreciated natural grandeur as did Emerson and Thoreau and the Transcendentalists who would follow him. Their conception of Nature as representing the spiritual universe and glory of the Creator was perhaps more closely suggested by the Quaker John Woolman who stated in 1763 that he was preserved in safety only "through the kindness of Him whose works in those mountain deserts appeared awful."

Brainerd wrote on Wednesday, October 3, "We went on our way into the wilderness, and found the most difficult and dangerous travelling by far, that ever any of us had seen; we had scarce any thing else but lofty mountains, deep valleys, and hideous rocks, to make our way through. . . . Near night my beast that I rode upon hung one of her legs in the rocks, and fell down under me; but through divine goodness, I was not hurt. However, she broke her leg; and being in such a hideous place, and near thirty miles from any house, I saw nothing that could be done to preserve her life, and so was obliged to kill her, and to prosecute my journey on foot."

"This accident," he continued, "made me admire the divine goodness to me," and, combining his earlier phrases of Psalm 34 with

* The name was suggested by the shape of a mountain at this place. The village formerly called by this name is now Jim Thorpe.

part of Job 33:19, he wrote, "that my bones were not broken, and the multitude of them filled with strong pain. Just at dark, we kindled a fire, cut up a few bushes, and made a shelter over our heads, to save us from frost, which was very hard that night; and committing ourselves to God by prayer, we lay down on the ground, and slept quietly."

The mare which he had to kill had borne him four or five thousand miles, and he may have been very fond of her. But it seems, that having witnessed her last agonized moments, he was forced by inner compulsion and in the best Puritan manner to conceal every trace of affection. Although he had always referred to her as his horse, she was now "my beast." Was she his single luxury, perhaps even a Narragansett pacer, one of Robert Hazard's famous Rhode Island mounts that could cover a hundred miles a day with strength to spare? He later stated that he could not replace her for fifty pounds.

After another day's travel, the party again camped in the woods, and on Friday they reached the "twelve Indian houses and about seventy souls, old and young" that was Opeholhaupung on the east bank of the North Branch of the Susquehanna (Safquahannok, Schechsehiquanunk, Tuschoannah). The name Opeholhaupung seems to be Brainerd's exclusive spelling for Wapwallopen, the Moravian's Wamphallobank, a few miles north of present Berwick and the former Indian village of Niskebeckon at Nescopeck Creek. It was one of many villages inhabited by various tribes along the beautiful stream.

Both David's diary and his letter to Pemberton relate the facts of the visit. The chief man was pliable and inclined to listen, and the men twice deferred the start of their fall hunting until Monday morning so that Brainerd was able to speak freely to them. He also visited them from house to house.

"The men, I think universally (except one), attended my preaching. Only the women, supposing the affair we were upon was of a public nature, belonging only to the men, and not what every individual person should concern himself with, could not readily be persuaded to come and hear; but, after much pains used with them for that purpose, some few ventured to come, and stand at a distance."

After he had preached to the Indians several times, he asked both the king and his people whether they would welcome another visit in the spring. The king replied that he should be heartily willing, for his own part, and he wished the young people would learn. Some of the men also answered that they would be very glad, and none expressed disapproval.

Much to Brainerd's satisfaction the Indians again delayed their hunt to Monday afternoon, to hear him once more. He and Byram spent the rest of the afternoon in reading and prayer, "intending to go homeward very early the next day." The visit, though short, had been an encouraging one, and despite the chill of October, Brainerd felt good. They traveled the approximate seventy miles back to Craig's Settlement in two days. "We rose about four in the morning, and commending ourselves to God by prayer, and asking his special protection, we set out on our journey homewards about five, and travelled with great steadiness till past six at night; and then made us a fire, and a shelter of barks and so rested. . . . In the night the wolves howled around us; but God preserved us."

The picture of the two young ministers alternately riding their one horse and plodding through the autumn mountain forest with the three Indians is an intriguing one. On Thursday both Brainerd and Byram preached to the white people at the Irish Settlement, and here David was furnished with a horse. His health and his spirits continued remarkably strong and in deep thankfulness he poured out his soul to God for His abundant goodness.

When he arrived at his lodgings at Hunter's Settlement and learned that his Indians were absent from their homes, he returned to Craig's Settlement on Saturday. There, on Sunday, October 14, his exhilaration was dissipated and he plunged into confusion and perplexity. He could not pray and even thought that he could never be able to preach anymore. Afterwards, however, he was "much assisted" and felt what he spoke in his sermon, but he added: "Yet I was so sensible of my defects in preaching, that I could not be proud of my performance, as at some times; and blessed be the Lord for this mercy." In the evening he longed to be entirely alone in prayer; and he was awake and again in prayer before sunrise.

That day he returned to Hunter's Settlement and during the next ten days of writing and of visiting his Indians he continued to plead with God for holiness. On Sunday he had used the strongest arguments, as he said, "drawn from the incarnation and suffering of Christ for this very end, that men might be holy." He desired it "that I might show gratitude to God," and "that I might not grieve God," and for that reason he longed for it more than his own happiness. He "thirsted and pleaded" to be as holy as the angels, and he longed to be as lively as they are in God's service.

But gradually a sense of the impossibility to reach such attainment in this life again overtook him and, along with an onset of illness and much pain, he complained of deadness and unprofitableness:

"I seemed to live for nothing and to do no good," he said on the last day of October, and again he wished for death, "my kind friend," to "hasten and deliver me from dull mortality, and make me spiritual and vigorous to eternity."

Before preaching to his Indians on Friday, November 2, he could feel no desires for them, and even dreaded to say anything to them. His entry for that day indicates how far he was removed from the poise of his brief but busy days on Long Island when he was "more refined and weaned from a dependence on my frames and spiritual feelings," or at Kaunaumeek when he wrote that the assurance of God's graciousness is the only soul-satisfying happiness.

"What comforts and enlargements I have felt for these many weeks past, have been only transient and short; and the greater part of my time has been filled up with deadness, or struggles with deadness, and bitter conflicts with corruption. I have found myself exercised sorely with some particular things that I thought myself most of all freed from. And thus I have ever found it, when I have thought the battle was over, and the conquest gained, and so let down my watch, the enemy has risen up and done me the greatest injury."

17. UNSUITABLY DESIROUS

It was probably very early on the first Monday of November that Brainerd finished the account of his first year as a missionary, for the dateline of his lengthy published letter to Ebenezer Pemberton reads, "Forks of Delaware, November 5, 1744." On that Guy Fawkes Day he left the Forks on his borrowed horse to attend a Presbytery meeting in New York City. During his two-day trip to the island of Manhattan he was greatly fatigued and exposed to cold and storms, and when he returned from New York to Aaron Burr's home in Newark on Friday, he became ill. His repeated indisposition each time he visited the commissioners must have given them cause for reflection. They had employed the frailest among them for the most arduous task.

Brainerd spent ten days with Aaron Burr and, despite his illness, he probably thoroughly enjoyed his fellow bachelor's company. Firmly religious, brilliant yet blithe, Burr had an engaging personality, and his winning manners and contagious cheerfulness has often been described in letters and papers of his day. One could wish that Brainerd's physical portrait and outward manners had been preserved as fully as that of his friend. Among other glowing tributes, Burr has been described as "a man of small stature, very handsome, with clear, dark eyes of a soft luster . . . and with the beauty of a prince."*

When he had recovered sufficiently Brainerd began his return trip to Pennsylvania. On the first day he was again almost overcome by the November cold. However, he rode to the Mendham-Morristown region of Rockciticus before evening and dined, not with Brother Byram, but with "dear Mr. Jones." Timothy Johnes, of Welsh extraction, was a year older than David. He was born at Southampton, Long Island, had graduated from Yale in 1737, and had been installed at Morristown in February 1743, the same year that Eliab Byram had moved to Rockciticus. That Brainerd would immediately have recognized Johnes as a kindred spirit can be easily imagined. Johnes had several extensive revivals and added 420 members to his church before he died in 1794 when he was seventy-eight years old. During the Revolutionary War when George Washington made his headquarters at Morristown, Johnes welcomed the Episcopalian general to his church and to the communion table which, said this Presbyterian parson, was the *Lord's* table. In the steeple of the church hung the bell presented to the congregation by England's king. Johnes also ministered much to Washington's sick and mutinous army encamped at nearby Jockey Hollow.

The next morning, Thursday, November 22, Brainerd continued westward across the hill country of North Jersey, and as the early evening darkness descended he strayed from his Pohatcong mountain trail and was lost for three hours.

"Came on my way from Rockciticus to Delaware river. Was very much disordered with a cold and pain in my head. About six at night I lost my way in the wilderness, and wandered over rocks and mountains, down hideous steeps, through swamps, and most dreadful and dangerous places; and the night being dark, so that few stars could be seen, I was greatly exposed. I was much pinched with cold, and distressed with an extreme pain in my head, attended with sickness at my stomach; so that every step I took was distressing to me. I had little hope for several hours together, but

* J. Parton: *The Life and Times of Aaron Burr*, p. 36. As the reader may surmise, a decade later Burr and Jerusha Edwards' next younger sister Esther became the parents of Aaron Burr, Jr., the third vice-president of the United States, who in 1804 killed Alexander Hamilton in a duel atop the Weehawken bluff on the New Jersey shore of the Hudson River.

that I must lie out in the woods all night, in this distressed case. But about nine o'clock I found a house, through the abundant goodness of God, and was kindly entertained."

The course he had taken through the dark mountain country had fortunately led him to Greenwich, three miles east of present Philipsburg and the Delaware River, and eight from Hunter's home. Greenwich was a settlement of Presbyterians who had erected their first log church four years earlier on Pohatcong Creek, a mile from the present Old Greenwich Church. From here Brainerd could descend the steep hill to the river and cross it on the scow ferry operated by David Martin whose home was the only one across the river on the future site of Easton, Pennsylvania.

Before he left New Jersey in the morning, he visited a sick man and prayed with him. Then, as he visited another house, "where one was dead and laid out," he looked on the corpse and longed that his time might come, "that I might be with Christ." It anticipated his mood for the winter. Already the night before, after his hours of wandering, he had written that he frequently thought of his final "journey's end" with great joy, whereas formerly he would have pleased himself with "thoughts of enjoying a comfortable house, a warm fire, and other outward comforts."

Resuming his life and preaching, alternately cheerful and dejected, he began to build a house for himself with the help of others, "to live in by himself through the winter." The Hunter settlers probably had a real house-raising for him, for the substantial building stood intact for more than fifty years. The location has long been marked by a modest granite monument erected by the Brainerd Society of Lafayette College as of December 6, 1884. It is located at Martin's Creek, about two hundred yards from a large bend of the Delaware River, eleven miles south of Mt. Bethel. Tradition states that Brainerd also dug a well that was used for a century. His immense satisfaction on moving into his new quarters prompted him to observe Thursday, December 6, as a day for secret prayer and fasting, "to implore the blessing of God on myself, on my poor people, on my friends, and on the church of God." The opportunity for such an "exercise" had been denied him since he had left Kaunaumeek.

His severe self-examination that day and his candid explanation of his longings for death may well have stemmed from some firm advice tendered him during his recent illness in Newark at the home of sanguine Aaron Burr.

"Especially I saw my sinfulness in this," he wrote, "that . . . I have been disposed . . . to be secretly *froward* and impatient, and unsuitably desirous of death, so that I have sometimes thought I could not bear to think my life must be lengthened out. And that which often drove me to this impatient desire of death, was a despair of doing any good in life; and I chose death, rather than a life spent for nothing."

"Yet this was not all which I wanted," he continued lengthily, "for my soul appeared exceedingly polluted, my heart seemed like a nest of vipers, or," here he borrowed a favorite Puritan metaphor from the Apocalypse, "a cage of unclean and hateful birds." Even though he persevered in prayer into the evening, oblivious of his need for food, he saw so much need of divine help, "in every respect," that he did not know how to quit.

In part, his despair was sorely aggravated by his Indians' current conduct. Two days earlier he had been bitterly disappointed to see most of them going together to another religious feast and dance. Apparently he had been unable "to break them up" as he had done in July. He wrote: "My poor Indians are now *worshipping devils,* nothwithstanding all the pains I have taken with them, which almost overwhelms my spirit." When the Indians returned on Friday, he preached to them despite his utter displeasure: "I had no heart to speak to them, and could not do it but as I forced myself: I knew they must hate to hear me."

By Saturday, however, he felt "uncommonly free" from depression, and on Sunday he rode the eight miles back to Greenwich to preach. He was dull in the first service but in the "intermediate season" he prayed alone among the bushes and afterwards, in the second service, he was more fervent. "The Spirit of God, I think, was there; as the effects were apparent, tears running down many cheeks." After he again preached on Monday he came home at dark. His exertions had tired him, and during the next week and more he was troubled with chest pains.

Tattamy was not in the best of health at this time either, but it was his interpreter's spiritual well-being, and that of three or four other Indians, which primarily concerned Brainerd during the second week of December. Of course, he carefully, or simply out of habit, understated his elation: "Found my interpreter under some concern for his soul; which was some comfort to me." His elation is better gauged by his deep remorse the following day. It would seem that under the stimulus of this exciting evidence of grace for which he had prayed so often, there had quickly arisen within him visions of notable accomplishment and fame, of acknowledgment from the world, and a sense of sweet revenge upon those who had ill-treated him.

Every Christian at one time or another can join in his lament of Thursday, December 13, his second day of fasting at the Forks of Delaware.

"The sins I had most sense of, were pride, and wandering thoughts, whereby I mocked God. The former of these cursed iniquities excited me to think of writing, preaching, or converting heathens, or performing some other great work, that my name might live when I should be dead. My soul was in anguish, and ready to drop into despair, to find so much of that cursed temper. With this, and the other evil I laboured under, viz. wandering thoughts, I was almost overwhelmed, and even ready to give over striving after a spirit of devotion; and oftentimes sunk into a considerable degree of despondency, and thought I was 'more brutish than any man.' "

He was greatly humbled at the knowledge of himself. The language of his short entry for Friday has become familiar to the reader of his diary, but against the background of Thursday's confession it explains much in his past behavior, especially just before he preached. He wrote: "Near noon went to the Indians; but knew not what to say to them, and was ashamed to look them in the face: I felt I had no power to address their conscience, and therefore had no boldness to say anything."

On Sunday he felt totally stripped of all power to reach them. He was so overwhelmed with dejection that, he said, "I knew not how to live." Yet even though he "longed for death exceedingly," and his soul was again "sunk into deep waters," and the floods were ready to drown him, his despair was for them, not for himself. As he went out to preach to them he was in anguish as to what to say and what course to take — "I was driven to my wits' end." At last he resorted to the miracles of Christ as proof for the truth of Christianity, and he felt that he made an effective impact upon all who heard him, and he was then again encouraged to find that God enabled him to be faithful once more.

Later, in his Journal, he related what his interpreter Tattamy experienced at this time. After Tattamy's first impressions in July in James Craig's meadow had seemed quickly to decline, he had remained for the most part careless and secure. But in the autumn when he fell ill for several weeks he became burdened from day to day with the haunting question, "What shall I do to be saved?" He could not sleep and had little rest day or night. He appeared like another man to his neighbors who observed his behavior with wonder.

After some time he seemed to stand before an impassable mountain.

Like Bunyan's "Pilgrim" at the hill Difficulty, he was progressing towards heaven but his way was hedged up with thorns, so that he could not stir an inch farther.   He thought if he could only get through the thorns and briers, and climb up the first steep pitch of the mountain, there might be hope for him; but he saw it was impossible for him to get through without help.   "It signified just nothing at all for me to struggle and strive any more," he said. Paradoxically, when he gave up, as Brainerd had also done, and felt that he was a "gone case," he became more calm and composed than he had been while striving.

After another elapse of time it was borne in upon his mind, as if it had been audibly spoken to him: "There is hope, there is hope." His soul seemed to rest, but he experienced no real joy.   Although this was not quite satisfying to David, he considered Tattamy to be under genuine conviction.   As time went on and Tattamy's conversation and deportment changed greatly, David commented with spirit, "Especially there was a surprising alteration in his public performances.   He now addressed the Indians with admirable fervency, and scarcely knew when to leave off.   Sometimes, when I had concluded my discourse and was returning homeward, he would tarry behind to repeat and inculcate what had been spoken."

The first gratifying results of Tattamy's new earnestness became apparent on Tuesday, December 18.   David had talked to the Indians for almost an hour, "without any power to come close to their hearts."

"But at last I felt some fervency, and God helped me to speak with warmth.   My *interpreter* also was amazingly assisted; and I doubt not but 'the spirit of God was upon him'; (though I had no reason to think he had any true and saving grace, but was only under conviction of his lost state); and presently upon this most of the grown persons were much affected, and the tears ran down their cheeks; and one *old man*, (I suppose a hundred years old) was so affected, that he wept, and seemed convinced of the importance of what I taught them.   I staid with them a considerable time, exhorting and directing them; and came away, lifting up my heart to God in prayer and praise, and encouraged and exhorted my *interpreter* to 'strive to enter in at the strait gate.'"

David apparently felt quite fit during this time of some awakening among the Indians.   He frequently preached at two places, and several of the Indians followed him from one place to the other during the week preceding Christmas which, he said, was a "comfortable week," the best since his return from Opeholhaupung on the Susquehanna.   But his apologetic letter of December 24 to Byram or Burr, judging it to have been addressed to either of these happy reverend gentlemen, is non-commital concerning his great expectations.

"I have little to say to you about spiritual joys . . . . the *present world* has nothing in it to *satisfy* an immortal soul . . . I wish I could be more patient and willing to live in it. . . . It is no virtue I know: but I want that divine hope which you observed, when I saw you last, was the very sinews of vital religion. . . . But, perhaps, these thoughts will appear melancholy and gloomy, and consequently will be very undesirable to you; and therefore I forbear to add. I wish you may not read them in the same circumstances in which I write them. I have little more to *do* and *suffer* in a dark, disconsolate world; and then I hope to be as happy as you are. . . ."

In view of his illness and weakness for more than a half year, Brainerd was not wise in choosing to move to his solitary cottage for the remainder of the winter, even though he regularly attended family prayers at the Hunter home where he had formerly lodged. His testing in the Forks wilderness went far deeper than his fretting in the Kaunaumeek woods over his treatment at Yale College. This winter he faced the innermost secrets of his heart, but that was not the whole of it. His second Christmas day as Indian missionary marked the beginning of a mental depression. It lasted a month and was the worst he ever experienced. As his soul again "sunk down into deep waters," he began to use "vapoury disorders" to designate his hypochondria. He described his despondency as a cloud that would envelop him for hours and days until it was scattered, sometimes almost instantaneously, usually during his family prayers with the Hunter family. At such times, he observed, "those things that of late appeared most difficult and almost impossible, appeared not only possible, but easy."

His morbid introspections fortunately gave way to a more objective assessment of his inherent propensity to melancholy. At the end of January, even when he was "perfectly overwhelmed" and so confused that he would forget what he was "aiming at" while in the middle of a sentence, he was able to reflect: "I know it was a degree of distraction, occasioned by vapoury disorders, melancholy, spiritual desertion, and some other things . . . the principal of which respected my Indians." And though he again expressed his desires to die when he witnessed the death of a man at Greenwich, he gradually became more stable. Nor did he ever again descend into the awful depths he described in his diary during that winter.

It is only fair to the memory of Brainerd that the reader of his private diary remember that it was written as a secret confessional.

Jonathan Edwards said that Brainerd "showed himself almost invincibly averse" to the publishing of any part of it — "he had been persuaded with difficulty not entirely to supress all his private writings." When finally the entire matter was left in his hands, Edwards must have experienced many moments of sore trial as he revealed and concealed what was intrusted to him. He considered it the better part of discretion *not* to keep a diary.

Brainerd's entry for Sunday, February 17, one of the very few events in his life that was recalled by an eyewitness and recorded in print, comes as a refreshing ending to the dreary record of his lonely months on the banks of the Delaware. It definitely indicates that he served the Lord's Supper to the large company of God's people who came together for that purpose after their winter confinement in their scattered frontier homes.

"Lord's Day, February 17, 1745. Preached to the *white* people (my *interpreter* being absent) in the wilderness upon the sunny side of a hill; had a considerable assembly, consisting of people who lived (at least many of them) not less than thirty miles asunder; some of them came near twenty miles.

"I discoursed to them, all day, from John 7:37. "Jesus stood and cried, saying, If any man thirst,' etc. In the afternoon it pleased God to grant me great freedom and fervency in my discourse; and I was enabled to imitate the example of Christ in the text, who *stood and cried*. I think I was scarce ever enabled to offer the free grace of God to perishing sinners with more freedom and plainness in my life. And afterwards I was enabled earnestly to invite the children of God to come renewedly, and drink of this fountain of water of life, from whence they have heretofore derived unspeakable satisfaction. It was a very comfortable time to me. There were many tears in the assembly; and I doubt not but that the Spirit of God was there, convincing poor sinners of their need of Christ.

"In the evening I felt some sweet sense of the excellency and glory of God; and my soul rejoiced, that he was 'God over all blessed forever'; but was too much crowded with company and conversation, and longed to be more alone with God. Oh that I could for ever bless God for the mercy of this day, who 'answered me in the joy of my heart.' "

The *Reminiscenses* of Dr. John C. Clyde recalls the scene of that mild winter day at Hunter's Settlement when Brainerd stood under a large apple tree and the sun warmed the backs of his listeners as they stood on the side of the hill in their rough homespun woolens. The eyewitness who was eighty years old in 1810 knew the exact spot of David's outdoor pulpit. Like the many others who lived not less than thirty miles asunder, Jane Wilson, age fifteen, had come on horseback from Bath, near Craig's Settlement. The green hill, she said, was only a few yards from the old Presbyterian church at Martin's Creek. Perhaps James King and his family were there too that day. It may have been King's last communion service, for he died that spring on April 3, when he was thirty-eight years old. His gravestone is the oldest in the Craig's Settlement graveyard, and that of his son Gabriel is the next oldest. It was recalled that his widow Mary Walker was left with four daughters and that often "she would take a child in her arm and ride to Mt. Bethel to hear Brainerd preach in the open air."

Despite their likely prejudice against his Indians, both Ulstermen and Germans, such as the "Dutchman" who interpreted when Tattamy was still absent the following Sunday, loved the young Yankee missionary who at times was "unduly desirous," who so longed to be perfectly whole, who preached with utmost fervency, and complained of being too much crowded with evening conviviality and conversation after worship services. At the Irish Settlement, stated Dr. Clyde, pious James Craig had a Mr. Congleton build a room or lean-to that David might always have a place of retirement when he desired to be alone. Brainerd had Christian friends at both settlements, and he loved them in turn. Ten days later they were dismayed when he told them that he probably would not permanently return to the Forks of Delaware to minister to them.

"Wednesday, March 6. Spent most of the day in preparing for a journey to New England. . . . Toward night, and in the evening, was visited by some friends, some of whom, I trust, were real Christians; who discovered an affectionate regard to me, and seemed grieved that I was about to leave them; especially seeing I did not expect to make any considerable stay among them, if I should live to return from New England. O how kind has God been to me! how has he raised up friends in every place, where his providence has called me! Friends are a great comfort; and it is God who gives them; it is *he* makes them friendly to me."

The next day, on Thursday, March 7, he left his friends at the Forks of Delaware and was gone for five weeks. It is most interesting to note that when Edwards' "Life of Brainerd" was published in 1749, sixteen copies of the first edition were subscribed for at the Forks of Delaware. The purchasers included the Reverend Daniel Lawrence, James Craig, Thomas Craig, William Craig, Mary Dobbin, James

Horner, William Heslet, Mary Knight, James Kerr, John McNair, James Ralston, Hugh Wilson, John Walker, and William Young.

And, as he turned his horse toward Haddam and left the scene of his dreary winter of distress and depression, did he know that his favorite and loyal sister Jerusha had on January 22 named her eighth child David Brainerd Spencer?

18.   THEY THAT FOLLOW THE LAMB

DURING MARCH AND APRIL, Brainerd rode more than six hundred miles in five weeks as he visited New Jersey, New York and Connecticut. "He seems, for the most part, to have been free from melancholy in this journey," observed Edwards as he explained that David's special reason for his trip was to find a companion after his two years of solitary living. He also wanted to raise some money to help support such a colleague, that "we might be together: as Christ sent out his disciples two and two." The matter had become one of utmost importance to him.

It would seem, too, that he desired a companion because he had decided to move to the Susquehanna River.

Brainerd's observations on his travel in New England during that spring of 1745 would be enlightening. King George's War was in full progress. The northern colonies were feverishly preparing for their final assault against the French fort at Louisbourg on Cape Breton. Watchtowers were being built at Northampton for protection against French-Indian attacks and, on April 4, Edwards preached a sermon, "Fast for Success in the Expedition against Cape Breton." At Boston, Whitefield declined an invitation to be chaplain to the expedition. And, amid the excited fears and false rumors of pro-French sympathies on the part of the Iroquois Confederacy that particularly alarmed the New Yorkers, the Moravian missionaries were caught in desperate straits. Their Shekomeko mission had already been closed in December. In February the missionaries David Zeisberger, then twenty-four, and Frederick Post with his Wampanoag wife Rachel, were intercepted near Albany on their way to the Mohawks at Canajoharie. They had been subsequently arrested, shipped down the Hudson River to New York City, and jailed at the City Hall.

Brainerd did not visit Stockbridge on this trip, but while at Woodbury, Connecticut, he managed to dispatch a letter to John Sergeant.
". . . I am in the greatest hurry, and can but hint at things I would
otherwise be a little more particular in," he wrote. He referred to
Opeholhaupung as "about fifteen or twenty miles down the river"
from a place where Sergeant had visited, and stated that he planned
to visit Opeholhaupung again in the middle of April and to spend most
of the summer along the Susquehanna. The last four paragraphs
of his letter are eloquent of his ready sympathy and directness.

"I long to hear of your affairs; and especially how things are like
to turn out with respect to your plan of a free boarding-school, which
is an affair much upon my heart amidst all my heavy concerns, and I
can learn nothing whether it is likely to succeed or not.

"I fully designed to have given something considerable for promoting that good design; but whether I shall be able to give any thing,
or whether it will be my duty to do so under present circumstances, I
know not. I have met with sundry losses lately, to the value of sixty
or seventy pounds, New England money. In particular, I broke my
mare's leg last fall in my journey to Susquehannah, and was obliged
to kill her on the road, and prosecute my journey on foot, and I
can't get her place supplied for fifty pounds. And I lately moved
to have a colleague or companion with me, my spirits sink with my
solitary circumstances. And I expect to contribute something to his
maintenance, seeing his salary must be raised wholly in this country
and can't be expected from Scotland.

"I sold my tea-kettle to Mr. Jo. Woodbridge, and an iron kettle
to Mr. Timothy Woodbridge, both which amounted to something
more than four pounds, which I ordered them to pay to you for the
school. If that succeed, I hope you will use the money that way; if
not, you are welcome to it for yourself. I desire my teapot and
bed-ticking may be improved to the same purpose.

"As to my blankets, I desired Mr. Woodbridge to take the trouble
of turning them into deer skins. If he has not done it, I wish he
would, and send the skins to Mr. Hopkins, or, if it might be, to Mr.
Bellamy. Please to remember me to Madam and all friends."

His days at Stockbridge, the Woodbridge brothers, and his long
Kaunaumeek winter must have seemed long past. Was the burden
of his kettles and other paraphernalia partly the reason why he had
turned his heavily-packed horse back to Stockbridge at the very outset
of his trip to the Delaware a year ago in May? The letter also
discloses how desperately he desired a companion in his work, even
to the extent of helping to pay his salary. Eight months later he

recalled that his quest "cost me a journey of several hundred miles in length," but he had not yet found anyone "qualified and disposed for this good work," although, he then revealed, "I had some encouragement from ministers and others, that it was hoped a maintenance might be procured for one, when the man should be found."

Leaving Connecticut, he returned to New Jersey. There, in Woodbridge, he met a number of ministers who, he stated, were met to consult about the affairs of Christ's Kingdom, "in some important articles." As the organization of the New York and New Brunswick Presbyteries into the Synod of New York was completed in September, Brainerd's employers were placed in positions of leadership. As the first moderator, Dickinson especially lent dignity to the new synod and to the "uneducated" New Brunswick men.

David returned to the Forks of Delaware just before Easter, on Saturday, April 13, thankful again that none of his bones had been broken. Although he was worn out with the fatigues of his six hundred miles of travel, on Easter morning he cried out the gracious offer of God's love to the large crowd of white people who had "gathered from all parts round about." His text was one he preached at least twice again. It was the eleventh verse of the thirty-third chapter of the prophet Ezekiel: *As I live, saith the Lord Jehovah, I have no pleasure in the death of the wicked: but that the wicked turn from his way and live.* His message was the sweet evangelical note of the Great Awakening: *Seek ye the Lord while he may be found.* Almost lost amid the harsh discordances of 1742, its gracious melody was now again being proclaimed in the forests of the Delaware, and it would continue to swell and reverberate before America's retreating wilderness.

It was now already the middle of April. Brainerd had informed Sergeant that this was the approximate time he had planned to return to the Susquehanna. But he had other matters to attend to first. That week he headed his horse south along the Delaware and Lehigh rivers, probably crossing the latter on the Moravian ferry at Bethlehem, and rode some fifty miles on the road traversed weekly by the Brethren's Bethlehem-Philadelphia post. Edwards explained: "*This week* he went a journey to Philadelphia, in order to engage the governor to use his interest with the chief man of the Six Nations, (with whom he maintained a strict friendship,) that he would give him leave to live at Susquehannah, and instruct the Indians that are within their territories."

The Quaker capital between the bends of the Delaware and Schuylkill rivers had been laid out in geometric design. Its Market

Street was a hundred feet wide and exactly paralleled by "tree" streets such as Pine, Spruce, Locust, Walnut, Chestnut, Cherry, Sassafras and Cedar. These were half the width of Market Street and were intersected by numbered lanes. Among the prominent buildings was the "New-Building," near the corner of Fourth and Mulberry streets. It was the large hall which Benjamin Franklin had initiated for George Whitefield and others so that, declared the thirty-four-year-old Market Street printer in his *Autobiography*, "even if the Mufti of Constantinople were to send a missionary to preach Mohammedanism to us, he would find a pulpit at his service."

The new, first minister of the Second Presbyterian Church of Philadelphia which had been organized in 1743 as a result of Whitefield's work and was even then using the "New-Building," was Gilbert Tennent. Once fondly described by Whitefield as a son of thunder, Tennent had borne unceasing attacks from those who opposed him. He had been made the scapegoat for practically all the excesses and misunderstandings that arose from the Great Revival, and his prestige had fallen considerably. Before he had announced his decision to leave New Brunswick an Anglican church had been organized largely by defectors from his church and Frelinghuysen's Dutch Reformed congregations.

Tennent had become a somewhat more reflective person since the day he had expressed his regret over his "mismanagement" at the height of the Great Awakening, when he had so confidently separated the chaff from the wheat. One of his Philadelphia sermons, published in 1744 and based on I Thessalonians 4:10, 11, was entitled, "The Necessity of Studying to be Quiet and Doing Our Own Business." But the colorful journal of William Black, a young and brash secretary of Governor William Gooch of Virginia, reveals that Tennent still entranced his auditory. Having stepped into the large hall for a little while on Sunday, June 3, 1744, Black wrote: "[I] found him Delivering his Doctrine with very Good Grace, Split his Text as Judiciously, turn'd up the whites of his Eyes as Theologically, Cuff'd his Cushion as Orthodoxly, and twist'd his Band as Primitively as his Master Whitefield could have done, had he been there himself. . . ."

Concerning the content of Brainerd's conversation with Deputy Governor George Thomas about the Susquehanna tribes, nothing has been preserved. The frontier Indians and the French were a matter of constant and grave concern to the governor, especially in view of the New England campaign against Fort Louisbourg. The Quakers' passivism also constituted a problem at that time when the frontier settlers feared and demanded action against possible Indian attacks. In that year of 1745 the issue was so touchy that two men elected to be mayor of Philadelphia flatly refused to serve, and a third left town rather than pay the fine levied against him for his refusal to accept the difficult position.

Edwards made only a single comment about Brainerd's visit to the city. He said, "In his way to and from thence, he lodged with Mr. Beaty, a young presbyterian minister. He speaks of seasons of sweet spiritual refreshment that he enjoyed at his lodgings."

Although "Old Buttonwood," the First Presbyterian Church of Philadelphia, had been built in 1704, after its people had shared the Barbadoes Store with Baptists since 1695, Presbyterianism was most lively and burgeoning in the churches some dozen miles north and east of the city, at Bensalem, at Abington, and at Neshaminy, the home of the Log College. The "Mr. Beaty" whom Brainerd lodged with was young Charles Clinton Beatty, a well-born immigrant peddler of Scotch-Irish and English descent who had graduated from the College in 1742 and a year later had succeeded the school's founder, William Tennent Sr., as pastor of the New Side congregation at Neshaminy. Gilbert Tennent had preached Beatty's ordination sermon in the new stone edifice which had been erected a stone's throw from the Old Side church.*

Four years older than David, Beatty was an excellent preacher, and his lively mind and warmth marked him as a man destined to play an almost romantic role in the affairs of his church and country during his twenty-nine years at Neshaminy. He has been compared to St. Paul's partner Barnabas. If for no other reason, his name will long be recalled as the army chaplain who rationed the daily gill of rum to his troops to insure their presence at prayers, as related in Franklin's *Autobiography* account of the French and Indian War in 1756. Beatty's career included Indian mission work near Pittsburgh and in Ohio, several trips to the Southern Colonies, Scotland and Holland, and to England to raise funds for the Presbyterian Ministers' Fund, the first modern life insurance company still in existence. He also raised eleven children. He died of yellow fever in 1772 on

---

* The well-known story of Beatty's introduction to the Log College is to the effect that Beatty surprised Wm. Tennent Sr. and his scholars by offering them his merchandise in Latin. Their subsequent conversation (in Latin) revealed such evidence of learning and piety on the part of the young mercantile peddler that Tennent ordered him to sell what he had and to study at the Log College in preparation for the ministry.

Barbadoes in the West Indies where he had sailed to solicit funds for Princeton University, the College of New Jersey.

Although the Log College had closed when the ailing senior Tennent retired in 1742, the old teacher still resided in Neshaminy, and it is therefore likely that Beatty would accompany Brainerd in paying respects to this former Episcopal minister who had left Ireland and joined the Synod of Philadelphia in 1716. After an unsuccessful attempt to become the rector of Yale College, he had come to Neshaminy when he was about fifty-nine years old. Here he ministered to the Neshaminy church and his "upper congregation" at Deep Run and founded his "college," primarily to instruct his four sons, but also because he saw the dire need for ministers on the rapidly expanding frontier. The influx of immigrants was so heavy that already in 1729 James Logan, Tennent's cousin, had written to Thomas Penn: "It looks as if Ireland is to send all its inhabitants hither for last week not less than six ships arrived and every day two or three arrive also." After the 1740-41 Irish famine, twelve thousand Irish and Scotch-Irish began to arrive in Pennsylvania on a hundred ships each year.

No description of Tennent's rustic school where some forty New Side ministers were trained can surpass Whitefield's journal for November 22, 1739, when he preached to three thousand people in Tennent's meetinghouse yard. Whitefield called Tennent an old gray-haired Disciple and Soldier of Jesus Christ who entertained him, he said, like one of the ancient patriarchs. But in describing Tennent and his wife personally, he thought of the aged parents of John the Baptist — "His wife to me seemed like Elizabeth, and he like Zachary."

Of the college itself, Whitefield wrote: "The place where the young men study now is, in contempt, called 'the college.' It is a log house about twenty feet long and nearly as many broad; and to me it seemed to resemble the school of the old prophets, for their habitations were mean; and that they sought not great things for themselves is plain from those passages of Scripture wherein we are told that each of them took them a beam to build them a house, and that at the feast of the sons of the prophets one of them put on the pot whilst the others went to fetch some herbs out of the field."

After lodging for the night with Charles Beatty, Brainerd rode south with him to the Abington Presbyterian church between Neshaminy and Philadelphia. Although it had been recently organized, in 1741, it already was a prominent church. Its preacher was Richard Treat who was Connecticut-born and a relative of that colony's Governor

Robert Treat who had founded Newark. He was a Yale graduate and had been ordained at Abington in 1740 when he was twenty-three. Three years later he was "reconverted" through the preaching of Whitefield and became identified with the Tennent group. He was a personal friend of Whitefield and entertained him several times in his home.

It was Saturday, April 20, Brainerd's twenty-seventh birthday, when he and Beatty arrived at Abington to aid Treat in the administration of the Lord's Supper, "according to the method of the Church of Scotland," Edwards explained. When they arrived Treat was preaching the Saturday preparatory sermon. Especially on the scattered frontier, the serving of the multitudes who came from miles around required the assistance of visiting ministers. The lengthy forms of worship usually began with a prayer and fast service on Thursday when communion tokens in the form of small distinctive discs, usually metal, were distributed to approved participants. On Saturday the final preparatory services were held and the season was ended with a thanksgiving on Monday.

Beatty and Brainerd participated in the services on each of the three days they spent at Abington. On Saturday, when Treat had finished preaching, David delivered his "Blessed are the poor in spirit" sermon. He did well. "Scores were in tears," he said, and he conversed with many after the service until he was so tired that he could "scarcely speak loud."

Sunday was literally the great day of the feast as the partakers surrendered their tokens and shared in the wine and specially baked sacramental bread at tables covered with spotless linen. Unlike the English Independents who were accustomed to pew communion, the Scots insisted that communicants must be actually seated at the table and served in relays if necessary to accommodate any great number. The Westminster Confession was phrased to recognize this conviction. As the communicants filed to and from each serving amid the singing of Psalms (the 103rd was a great favorite), the ministers in charge would alternate in dispensing the elements. Some services are known to have thus continued for seven or eight hours and were sometimes carried over to another day. An alternative was to set out long rows of tables in groves outside the church to permit larger servings.

Brainerd wrote in his diary for that Sunday: "Mr. Beatty preached to the multitude abroad, who could not half have crowded into the meeting-house. In the season of the communion, I had comfortable and sweet apprehensions of the blissful communion of God's people, when they shall meet at their Father's table in his kingdom, in a

state of perfection. In the afternoon I preached abroad, to the whole
assembly, from Revelation 14:4, These are they that follow the Lamb.
God was pleased again to give me very great freedom and clearness,
but not so much warmth as before. However, there was a most
amazing attention in the whole assembly; and, as I was informed
afterwards, this was a sweet season to many."

At eleven o'clock on Monday morning, Beatty again preached,
"with freedom and life"; and Brainerd spoke, with less freedom, from
John 7:37, *Jesus stood and cried, saying, If any man thirst, let him
come unto me and drink,* the same he had preached on the green hill
at Martin's Creek. When they rode back together to Neshaminy for
the night, David enjoyed the time "very agreeably on divine things."
After he spent Tuesday in riding back to the Forks of Delaware, he
also observed on Wednesday, "Just in the evening, was visited by a
dear Christian friend, with whom I spent an hour or two in conversation, on the very soul of religion." He added: "There are many with
whom I can talk about religion; but alas! I find few with whom I
can talk religion itself: but, blessed be the Lord, there are some that
love to feed on the kernel, rather than the shell."

He preached at Craig's Settlement on Sunday and returned, but on
Monday (the day James King died at Craig's Settlement), he was
ill and confined to bed, "being neither able to read, meditate, nor
pray, and had none to converse with in that wilderness." He complained about his weakness, but his fretting was tempered by a new
appreciation of human limitation and the need for periods of relaxation: "Of late, I have seen it my duty to *divert* myself by all lawful
means, that I may be fit, at least some small part of my time, to
labour for God. . . . I see now, more than ever, that they are
absolutely necessary." And, "blessed be the Lord," he added on
Thursday, "my mind is not gloomy, as at some other times."

After two months' absence from the Indians he would again
set out, if his health permitted, to spend the month of May at
the Susquehanna. That week his thoughts "ran upon" Psalm 17:15,
I shall be satisfied, and Isaiah 53:10, *yet it pleased the Lord to bruise
him.* After forty days he would use both these texts at his next
wonderful Supper of the Lord at Neshaminy. "I longed to preach
to the whole world, and it seemed to me," he exclaimed, "they must
needs all be melted in hearing such divine truths, as I then had a
view and relish of."

One may wonder concerning the identity of the "dear Christian
friend" with whom he had conversed with such genuine satisfaction
on Wednesday. Was it Eliab Byram who had come to confer

about their second Susquehanna trip and had returned to his own
church in New Jersey, and for whose re-appearance David delayed
his departure another full week, leaving finally on the following
Wednesday instead of Monday as he usually did? A later reference to *two* ministers at Susquehanna will recall this possibility.

19. SCARCE EVER SO MUCH DAMPED

WEAK AND CONCERNED how to manage the difficult journey, and too
ill to devote the day to prayer and fasting, Brainerd made final
preparation on Tuesday, May 7, for his first major trip to the interior
Indians. The next morning he and Tattamy mounted their horses
and started out for the Susquehanna River.

They apparently did not return to the Indian village where they had
visited with Eliab Byram and the two chiefs in October. Their
reason for by-passing it may have encouraged Brainerd but it may
also have given him cause for other reflections because, unlike himself, the Moravians had recently been successful in their missionary
efforts there. Only a fortnight ago they had baptized their first
Delaware converts. They were a chief and his squaw from Wamp-
hollabank, Brainerd's Opeholhaupung. "Their baptism caused such
a sensation among their kindred," reported De Schweinitz in his
Life of David Zeisberger, "that thirty-six warriors marched to the
settlement [Bethlehem], in order to carry them off by force. But the
testimony of the converts, and the friendly welcome of the inhabitants,
disarmed them of their design."

Jonathan Edwards reported David's and Tattamy's twenty-four days
of travel in a mere fifty lines, omitting all of Brainerd's diary between
May 7 and June 4, but he wrote a good description of their first
rugged forty-eight hours on the difficult trails through the Blue
Mountains.

"He set out on his journey to Susquehannah with his interpreter.
He endured great hardships and fatigues in his way thither through
a hideous wilderness; where after having lodged one night in the open
woods, he was overtaken with a north-easterly storm, in which he was
almost ready to perish. Having no manner of shelter, and not being
able to make a fire in so great a rain, he could have no comfort if
he stopt; therefore he determined to go forward in hopes of meeting

with some shelter, without which he thought it impossible to live the night through; but their horses — happening to have eat poison (for the want of other food) at a place where they lodged the night before — were so sick that they could neither ride nor lead them, but were obliged to drive them and travel on foot; until, through the mercy of God, just at dusk they came to a bark-hut, where they lodged that night."

"After he came to Susquehannah," Edwards continued, "he travelled about a hundred miles on the river, and visited many towns and settlements of the Indians; saw some seven or eight distinct tribes; and preached to different nations by different interpreters." At times Brainerd was greatly discouraged by the natives' opposition to Christianity; at other times their willingness to listen gave him new hope. And he must have been truly excited to discover the Indians whom he had first lived with and taught in New York —

"He here met with some that had formerly been his hearers at Kaunaumeek, and had removed hither; who saw and heard him again with great joy. He spent a fortnight among the Indians on this river, and passed through considerable labours and hardships, frequently lodging on the ground, and sometimes in the open air."

The new abode of the former Kaunaumeek natives is not divulged. Most likely, however, David met them at Shamokin, southwest of Opeholhaupung. This Indian town which had enticed Brainerd was on the site of present Sunbury, strategically located below the junction of the West and North Branches of the Susquehanna River. It should not be confused with the present city of Shamokin. Brainerd may also have been dismayed to find his first Indian friends here, for they would be in bad company at this place. This is obvious from his Journal four months later. At that time he identified the town as "Shaumoking," — "one of the places and the largest of those which I visited last May." Actually, this cluster of three Indian villages comprised one of the four largest, if not the greatest, Indian town in Pennsylvania at that time.

Brainerd wrote: "This town (as I observed in my Journal of May last) lies partly on the east side of the river, partly on the west, and partly on a large island in it, and contains upwards of fifty houses, and they tell me, near three hundred persons, though I never saw much more than half that number in it; but of three different tribes of Indians, speaking three languages wholly *unintelligible* to each other. About one half of its inhabitants are Delawares, the others called Senakes and Tutelas. The Indians of this place are accounted the most drunken, mischievous, and *ruffianly fellows* of any in these parts: and *Satan* seems to have his *seat* in this *town* in an eminent manner."

The Susquehanna was the last important Indian river before the Pennsylvania tribes were forced west to the waters of the Allegheny and the Ohio, and it meant much more to the Indians than merely a peaceful stream on which to live. Its course of 450 miles from New York to Maryland was one of their great highways and the key to the control which the Iroquois Confederacy exercised far to the south. It was part of their Catawba War Trail that extended for five hundred miles from their capital Onondaga in Central New York to North Carolina, where they engaged the Catawbas in Perennial warfare. And, in Brainerd's times especially, the entire length of the Susquehanna was the home of the many migrant tribes forced from their original lands in the white man's colonies.

The "Senakes" which David mentioned first were not migrants but belonged to the Five Nations, or Iroquois Confederacy, consisting of the Senecas, Mohawks, Oneidas, Onondagas, and Cayugas. These were the "United People" who had made "women" of the Leni-Lenape, the "Original People." In mentioning the "Tutelas" Brainerd left singular confirmation as to the remarkable diversity of the many tribes on the river. Just how and when the Tutelo tribe had come to the eastern coast is a mystery. They were Siouan people, related to the Sioux of the Dakotas and far Northwest. Before coming to Pennsylvania about 1722, they had been living in North Carolina and in Virginia. When Captain John Smith met them in 1609 he had described them as particularly barbarous.

Beside the numerous Delawares who had left New Jersey and, more recently, the Forks of Delaware, there were other tribes. The Tuscaroras, an Iroquoian linquistic group, had been forced out of North Carolina in 1712 by the pressure of the Catawbas and the white settlers. In 1722 they had joined the Five Nations Confederacy and during Brainerd's time they were still in the process of gradual migration through Pennsylvania to the lands of the now Six Nations in New York. There were also the Susquehannas whom Captain Smith had first discovered in Virginia. The Dutch called this tribe the Minquas, and in 1756 when the Scotch-Irish "Paxton Boys" exterminated them at Lancaster, they were known as Conestogas. There were the Canay, probably from West Virginia, who were also called Ganawese or Piscataways. The Nanticokes, held in dread by other tribes because of their reputed skill in witchcraft, were from Maryland. They had the unique custom of removing the bones of their dead from place to place during their migrations, a custom which Brainerd noted. Lastly, there were the Shawnees who were originally from the Ohio Valley but had lived in the South, and at the Forks of Delaware prior to 1728-30.

Shamokin was the principal headquarters of these many tribes. It was the home of kings. The former Schuylkill Delaware chief was Sassoonan, also known as Allumpapees, Allummapees, Allumapis, Alomipies, Olumapies, and Swantane. He kept his fires at Shamokin on the far or west side of the river. It was he and Nutimus who had borne the scathing sarcasm of the Iroquois chief Canassatego at the Great Treaty in Philadelphia in 1742. Brainerd referred to Sassoonan as "the Delaware king who was supposed to be at the point of death when I was here in May." The Moravian bishop Jacob Spangenberg, who also visited Shamokin that same month, revealed a bit more: "He is very old, almost blind, and very poor, but withal has still power over and is beloved by his people; and he is a friend of the English." Two years later Conrad Weiser, Pennsylvania's veteran Indian agent, wrote: "[He] has been drunk for these two or three years almost constantly."

Yet, despite his faults and special weakness for liquor, Sassoonan was an intelligent and loyal chief as far as the white man was concerned. Through the years he had attended many of the important conferences between the Indians and the Penn government. In 1731, after he killed his nephew Sam Shakatawein in a drunken brawl, he had petitioned the Penn officials to curtail the flow of liquor to the Indians. But, pathetically, and in common with his subjects, Sassoonan stressed that he had no desire to prohibit the whiskey trade entirely. His desire was only that "no Christian should carry any rum to Shamokin where he lives, to sell; when they want any, they will send for it themselves; they would not be wholly deprived of it, but they would not have it brought by the Christians."

Another interesting person at Shamokin was Madame Montour. She was about sixty years old and with her son Andrew she had but recently moved to the town from Ostonwackin, or "French Town" (now Montoursville), on the West Branch of the river where the Moravian missionary David Bruce and his wife had lived during 1743. Madame Montour was an official interpreter at Albany as early as 1711, and at Philadelphia in 1727. Despite her secret hostility to Zinzendorf when he visited her in 1742 she shed many tears when she once again heard the Gospel which she had faintly remembered from her childhood. As a child, she said, she had been told that Christ was born in France and that He had been crucified by the English.

The principal power, living at "East" Shamokin, was Shikellamy, "he who causes it to be light." An Oneida chieftain, either a native Cayuga or a Frenchman, he had been captured and adopted by the Oneidas when he was two years old and had been baptized by a Jesuit priest in Canada. Having now resided at Shamokin since 1728, he had been this same year (1745) promoted to executive deputy of the Grand Council of the Six Nations. As overlord of all tributary tribes on the Susquehanna, he had supported Sassoonan in his liquor control petition of 1731 by delivery of an ultimatum to the Penn government that if the liquor trade were not better regulated, friendly relations with the Confederacy would cease. Three generations removed from the devilish Iroquois who burned the magnificent Catholic Jean de Brèbeuf in 1649, he was the man of whom Zinzendorf wrote after his visit to Shamokin: "He was truly an excellent and good man, possessed of many noble qualities of mind, that could do honor to many white men, laying claims to refinement and intelligence. He was possessed of great dignity, sobriety and prudence, [and] extreme kindness."

The Penn government had a most faithful liaison chief in wise Shikellamy, whose name appears in colonial documents as Shick Calamy, Shickellima, Shehellemus, Shillemy, and other variations. He was a person of sagacity and dignity and, unlike Sassoonan, he maintained strict sobriety and abstained and absented himself from the wild drunken orgies at Shamokin. During his lifetime Shikellamy had also attended most of the important government conferences and had accompanied Conrad Weiser on several long and hazardous peace missions to the Iroquois in New York.

Weiser and Shikellamy were thus close friends and, in a providential way, held the safety of the American colonies between them. In 1737, Weiser had secured an armistice between the Iroquois and the Catawbas and Cherokees, and had thus spared Virginia from invasion in 1738. Most lately, in the spring of 1743, he had negotiated the vital treaty between the Six Nations and the English against the French. And, to keep Shikellamy happy, he had employed eight young Germans to build a house for him at Shamokin. Built in seventeen days, it was "49½ feet long, 17½ feet wide, and covered with shingles."

Shikellamy's friendship was of continuing vital importance in this spring of 1745. With King George's War at its height at this very time that Brainerd was at Shamokin (the New England expedition sailed against doomed Louisbourg on May 15), the Six Nations had to be kept aligned with the English at all costs. Should the Iroquois join the Canadian French, the English colonies would be in great peril.

To cement relations and, specifically, to execute a permanent treaty of peace between the Six Nations and the Catawbas, Conrad Weiser and several Moravians arrived at Shamokin only a few days after Brainerd and Tattamy left the town. Weiser was born in Germany and had grown up in the faith of the Reformed Church, but for two years he had served as a minister with Conrad Beissel's Seventh Day Baptists who founded the Ephrata Cloisters, America's first Protestant monastery. He was now, however, on intimate terms and in the service of the Moravians, much to the perturbation of Governor Thomas who misunderstood and therefore mistrusted them. Weiser's companions were young David Zeisberger, John Joseph Schebosh a former Quaker, and Bishop Jacob Spangenberg — the same who had revitalized John Wesley in his faith with the questions, "Have you the witness within yourself? Does the Spirit of God bear witness with your spirit that you are a child of God?" They had left Bethlehem six days after Brainerd started on his journey, but had traveled the route south of the Blue Mountains through Heidelberg and the Lutheran settlement of Tulpelhocken, "the land of turtles," where Weiser now lived. There they had waited until he could guide them directly northwest over the mountains to Shamokin.

After spending a week with Shikellamy and treating his fifteen-year-old daughter for fever and ague, the Moravians with Weiser, Shikellamy and one of his three sons, and Madame Montour's son Andrew, left on the ten-day trip to Onondaga, where they obtained permission from the Iroquois to move their Shekomeko mission to the Wyoming Valley northeast of Shamokin. On the way, Zeisberger, Schebosh, and Spangenberg were adopted into Iroquois tribes. Conrad Weiser had been adopted thirty-two years earlier.*

All had not gone as well with the lone Yankee and his interpreter Tattamy. Since Brainerd was ill when he left the Forks of Delaware, his physical condition was greatly below the good health he had enjoyed on his first trip to the Susquehanna with Eliab Byram. Edwards reported: "At length he fell extremely ill, as he was riding in the wilderness. But at last coming to an Indian trader's hut, he got leave and extreme pains in his head and bowels, attended with a great evacuation of blood; so that he thought he must have perished in the

---

* Weiser's party was at Shamokin from Tuesday, May 21, to Monday, May 27. Accounts based on Moravian Journals and the "New Style" calendar state that the party arrived on June 1 and left on June 7.

wilderness. But at last coming to an Indian trader's hut, he got leave to stay there; and though without physic or food proper for him, it pleased God, after about a week's distress, to relieve him so far that he was able to ride."

Happily, Bishop Spangenberg's journal of his trip to Shamokin and Onondaga comments on Brainerd's activities, his aspirations, and his dubious success. Upon his arrival at Shamokin, Spangenberg wrote the following account — and made the puzzling reference to *two* ministers. It seems rather idle to suppose that Spangenberg may have been confused by a reference to Byram's presence with Brainerd on the North Branch of the river in October. It may be significant that only on his third Susquehanna trip did Brainerd remark that he had "no other companion" than his interpreter.

"We were told," Spangenberg wrote, "that two ministers and an Indian had been lately here — probably it was the Presbyterian Brainerd and his interpreter Tatami. He had assembled the Delawares in Shikellmy's house, and (as Shikellmy's people told us) informed them that on Sundays they should assemble as the whites do, and pray as they do. Hence he would build a house for that purpose, and stay with them two years. That the Governor had given him orders to that effect, and he would be glad to see the Indians hearken to him. To this Shikellmy said: 'We are Indians, and don't wish to be transformed into white men. The English are our Brethren, but we never promised to become what they are. As little as we desire the preacher to become an Indian, so little ought he to desire the Indians to become preachers. He should *not* build a house here; they don't want one.'

"They departed for Philadelphia the next day."

In view of Conrad Weiser's high estimate of his long-time friend and his strong intimations that Shikellamy professed some form of personal faith in the white man's God, these remarks of the old chief defy exact interpretation.* His declarations at this time, however, may have been the particular basis for the ideas which Brainerd enlarged upon in his Appendix Two, that many of the Indians "look upon it as disgraceful for them to become Christians, as it would be esteemed among Christians to become pagans." The Indians, he further ex-

---

* Late in 1748, Shikellamy was touched by the preaching of the Moravian bishop, Baron John de Watteville, and David Zeisberger. He journeyed to Bethlehem for further instruction and on his return journey fell ill at Weiser's home at Tulpelhocken. It is affirmed that he died in the Christian faith, at Shamokin, on December 6, 1748, Moravian calendar. Zeisberger was present at his death and burial.

plained, fancied that their creator "gained some special skill by seeing the white people made, and so made *them* better," and that the Indians would frequently sit and laugh at the white men as being good for nothing else but to plough and fatigue themselves with hard labor, and could not enjoy the easy way of life which the Indians' god had expressly prescribed for them.

During his third week along the Susquehanna Brainerd traveled south for about thirty-five miles to the mouth of the Juniata (Choniata) River, where the trader John Harris had cleared land and built a house as early as 1732-33. Here where the Blue Mountains cross the Susquehanna, he probably came to Duncan's Island near the present city of Duncannon. Brainerd rightly referred to the locality as Juniatta, but Dwight's edition erroneously spelled it as Juncauta. It also appears as Juneauta and Invocanta. The island was the home of some Shawanese whom Conrad Weiser despised and whom Shikel-lamy found most difficult of all his Susquehanna tribes to control against the constant and mounting enticements of the French. It was also the home of the Nanticokes, the people who claimed extra-ordinary skill in witchcraft and who transported the bones of their deceased. Brainerd's impression of these Indians, at this time, was quite favorable. They "appeared more free from prejudices against Christianity, than most of the other Indians," he said. "They appeared friendly, and gave me encouragement to come and see them again."

It was also here and at this time that Brainerd met the Indian reformer. In many respects this man foreshadowed the Delaware and Shawnee prophets who had many followers after 1760 and gave impetus to Pontiac's uprising and conspiracy at Detroit. Brainerd's succinct account is one of the earliest records of a religious reformer, or, as Brainerd described him, "a restorer of what he supposed was the ancient religion of the Indians."*

When this man came toward him, dancing with all his might and rattling corn within a dry tortoise shell attached to a wooden handle, Brainerd shrank away, "although it was then noonday," and he knew who it was. "His appearance and gestures were so prodigiously frightful," stated David, "that no one would have imagined that he could be human." Every part of his body, including his fingers, was covered by his "pontifical garb" — a great coat of undressed boar skins

---

* Brainerd's skepticism is understandable. In his Appendix Two he wrote: "Before the coming of the English they had a belief in four deities, occupying the four corners of the earth, but when they saw the pale faces they reduced the number to three, one creating English, another Negroes, and the third themselves."

that reached his toes, bearskin stockings, and a half black, half
tawny wooden face, "with an extravagant mouth, cut very much awry,"
fastened below a bearskin hood. No sight Brainerd had ever seen
appeared as frightful, "or so near akin to what is usually imagined of
infernal powers."

In the reformer's ceremonial lodge Brainerd found the ground
beat "almost as hard as a rock" from repeated dancing. The man
seemed to appreciate some parts of Brainerd's explanation of Christianity, but some of it he disliked extremely — "He told me that
God had taught him his religion, and that he never would turn from
it, but wanted to find some that would join heartily with him in it;
for the Indians, he said, were grown very degenerate and corrupt."
When on this account about four or five years earlier his heart had
become very distressed, he could not bear to stay among his fellows
but went away to live alone for some months in the woods. Finally,
God comforted him and showed him what to do. "Since that time,"
he said, "he had known God and tried to serve him; and loved all
men, be they who they would, so as he never did before."

He treated Brainerd with uncommon courtesy. Other Indians told
David that he vehemently opposed their drinking strong liquor and
would "go crying into the woods" when he could not dissuade them
from their drink. "It was manifest," observed Brainerd, "he had a
set of religious notions that he had looked into *for himself*, and not
taken for *granted* upon bare tradition." While Brainerd talked to
him, he would say, "Now that I like," or "So God has taught me."
He utterly denied the existence of a devil and stated there was no
such creature known to the Indians of former days. He rather believed
that departed souls all went southward. The good souls, however,
were admitted into a beautiful town with spiritual walls, while the
evil ones would forever hover around the walls in vain attempts to
enter.

Though he could hardly be delighted, Brainerd was quite impressed
by this man whom he considered to be devout and zealous. "He
seemed to be sincere, honest, and conscientious in his *own way*, and
according to his own religious notions, which was more than I ever
saw in any other pagan. I perceived that he was looked upon and
derided amongst most of the Indians as a *precise zealot*, that made a
needless noise about religious matters; but I must say, there was something in his temper and disposition that looked more like true religion
than anything I ever observed amongst other heathens."

But, whatever encouragement he may have received from his
encounter with the reformer and from the Indians' invitation that he

return to them, Brainerd later stated that he was "scarce ever so much damped and discouraged" in his concern for the conversion of the Indians, as he was at this time. He made no distinction between Susquehanna and the Forks of Delaware. He was a lone voice crying in the wilderness, and the passers-by, though curious, gave scant heed to his crying. His year in Penn's Woods seemed a complete failure.

Since Juniata was only a few miles above Harris Ferry (now Harrisburg), it would seem that he and Tattamy (and the other minister?) returned to the Forks of Delaware by traveling south of the Blue Mountains, toward Philadelphia as Spangenberg stated in his journal. There is no record. When they arrived home they had been gone twenty-three days.

Edwards finished his account of the trip by saying, "He arrived at the Forks of Delaware on *Thursday,* May 30, having rode in this journey about three hundred and forty miles. He came home in a very weak state, and under dejection of mind. However, on the sabbath, after having preached to the Indians, he preached to the white people with some success, from Isaiah 53:10, 'Yet it pleased the Lord to bruise him,' etc., some being awakened by his preaching. The next day, he was much exercised for want of spiritual life and fervency."

Book Four

The Apostle

We are now come to that part of Mr. Brainerd's life, wherein he had his greatest success, in his labours for the good of souls, and in his particular business as a missionary to the Indians. . . . He went forth weeping, bearing precious seed, and now he comes rejoicing, bringing his sheaves with him.

—Jonathan Edwards

20. LIKE THE WOMEN OF SAMARIA

I SHALL BE SATISFIED, WHEN I AWAKE, WITH THY LIKENESS. Brainerd's mind had dwelt upon this line of Psalm 17 while he had prepared for his second trip to Susquehanna, and it was again his meditation on Wednesday, June 5, as he prepared to participate in Charles Beatty's great communion service at Neshaminy. Hoping for conversions at Susquehanna might be unreal as a dream, but "divine things opened with clearness and certainty." "Lord, give me more of thy likeness," he prayed, "I shall be satisfied, when I awake, with it."

The weather was unseasonably warm, a portent of the hot, dry summer ahead. When he arrived within the Forks of Neshaminy on Friday, he was very fatigued after his day's ride in the heat. But on Saturday afternoon "being desired," he preached effectively to a crowded audience in the 40 by 30 foot Warwick church which is still cherished, preserved and used by an appreciative congregation. His text was Isaiah 40:1, *Comfort ye, comfort ye, my people.* On Sunday he preached one of his favorite sermons, the same he had delivered a week earlier at the Forks of Delaware after his return from the Susquehanna. As he spoke "extempore" under the Penn Oaks on the banks of Little Neshaminy Creek it most powerfully moved the thousands who had gathered at Beatty's church in that season of Pentecost.

"In the forenoon Mr. Beatty preached; and there appeared some warmth in the assembly. Afterwards I assisted in the administration of the Lord's Supper: and towards the close of it, I discoursed to the multitude *extempore,* with some reference to that sacred passage, Isaiah 53:10, 'Yet it pleased the Lord to bruise him.' Here God gave me great assistance in addressing sinners: and the word was attended with amazing power; many scores, if not hundreds, in that great assembly, consisting of three or four thousand, were much affected; so that there was a 'very great mourning, like the mourning of Hadadrimmon.' In the evening, I could hardly look any body in the face, because of the imperfections I saw in my performance in the day past."

Brainerd loved to read and meditate among the biblical prophets of Israel, but he chose most of his Old Testament preaching texts from Isaiah and the Psalms. Of 39 identified sermons on 26 Old Testament texts, 25 are from these two books. But he was even more, and literally, a Gospel preacher, for 111 of the 150 sermons identified in his diaries and Journals are based on 96 New Testament texts, and 64 of these are from the four Gospels. Eleven are from the Acts of the Apostles, four from Revelation, and only seventeen are from nine epistles.

His sermon on Monday also elicited "great solemnity and attention" as the assembly sensed his personal hope: "I shall be satisfied. . . ." Here, above all else, was his delight — to find and to be among the members of the Body of Christ, to "discourse" about the things of God, to feel the responsiveness and sympathy of God's people, and to await the day when he would spend eternity with them before the throne of Christ.

"O how desirable it is, to keep company with God's dear children! These are the 'excellent ones of the earth, in whom,' I can truly say, 'is all my delight.' O what delight will it afford, to meet them all in a state of perfection! Lord, prepare me for that state."

With that expression of sentiment on Tuesday, June 11, Jonathan Edwards ended the first part of David's diaries. Except for some supplemental excerpts, he left it to his readers to read Brainerd's Journals from June 19, 1745 to June 19, 1746. When he edited the diaries, the Journals had already been published.

As for his mission at this juncture, Brainerd hardly knew what to think. He was "exceedingly depressed" and disillusioned about his prospects among the Indians along the Susquehanna, and except for Tattamy and his wife, he also counted his year at the Forks of Delaware as loss. His once high hopes for an early and sudden display of God's power among the Indians had *never* been reduced "to so low an ebb." He did not have "the least hope" or "the least rational prospect" of seeing a work of grace among them, and he was "almost resolved" to quit at the end of the year if he had "no better prospect of special success." He considered himself a burden to the Society in Scotland that paid him.

However, "hearing that there was a number of Indians at a place called Crossweeksung, in New Jersey, near eighty miles southeast from the Forks of Delaware," he determined it his duty, "though in the midst of darkness and discouragement," to visit them. With this intention in mind he crossed the Delaware River into West Jersey on Wednesday. About this same time Daniel Lawrence took his place as supply preacher at the Forks of Delaware.

All of Brainerd's earlier visits to New Jersey had been to the northern or the "East Jersey" section. He had not been south of the route from the Forks of Delaware to Newark and Elizabethtown. As he

visited several ministers during the next seven days, he was in strange
territory. But he was not a total stranger. He had met most of the
ministers in those parts at Presbytery meetings. Also, Pemberton's
Sermon at Ordination of David Brainerd had been printed in Boston
by Roger & Fowles late in 1744. Dedicated to the Scottish Society
and its president, the Marquis of Lothian, it had been advertised as
"just published" in the Boston *News Letter* for Thursday, January
17. Brainerd's "Letter to Pemberton" appears to have accompanied it
as a separate appendix.

He went first to Maidenhead (Lawrenceville) and likely also
visited the two New Side churches in the old Hopewell and Amwell
Townships to the south and north of the Sourland Hills. These
churches had recently experienced revival under John Rowland
whose *Narrative of the Revival and Progress of Religion in the Towns
of Hopewell, Amwell, and Maidenhead* was advertised in the
Pennsylvania Journal of May 23.*

On Tuesday, June 18, Brainerd completed his trip to the north and
east, and headed south from the area where Frelinghuysen and Gilbert
Tennent had launched the New Jersey revival — "Set out from New
Brunswick with a design to visit some Indians at a place called
Crossweeksung in New Jersey, towards the sea. In the afternoon,
came to a place called *Cranberry,* and meeting with a serious minister, Mr. Macknight, I lodged there with him. Had some enlargement
and freedom in prayer with a number of people."

Cranberry (now Cranbury) is some fifteen miles south of New
Brunswick, half-way between that city and Crossweeksung (now
Crosswicks) which is seven to eight miles southeast of Trenton.
These locations are worth noting, for it was here that Brainerd
climaxed his missionary career. Today the New Jersey Turnpike
skirts Cranbury on the east and Crosswicks on the west. Just below
Cranbury the great road intersects the original dividing line between
"East Jersey" which was settled by Dutch Reformed, Episcopalians,
and Presbyterians, and "West Jersey" which was predominantly
Quaker country.

Unlike the Forks of Delaware, West Jersey had been colonized
by Europeans for almost a century. First had come the Dutch
after they conquered the Delaware Bay Swedes in 1655. They had

---

* Rowland's ordination at these churches had precipitated the schism in
the Presbyterian Church. The present town of Hopewell was then called
Columbia. It was a Baptist hamlet. The old Presbyterian "Hopewell" church
stood near Queenstown or Penny Town, named Pennington in 1747.

pushed up the river and built a fort as far north as Trenton at the rapids or Falls of Delaware. Then, in 1677, four years before William Penn founded Philadelphia, five shiploads of Quakers had settled south of Trenton at Burlington. But since Trenton was at the head of navigable tidewater, it became the principal point for passenger and cargo boats to and from Philadelphia. Daily wagons also plied the roads from Trenton through Crossweeksung and north to New Brunswick and New York. A 1730 journal stated that "the whole way it is almost a continual lane of fences and good farmer's houses, and the whole country is there settled or settling very quickly." By 1748, "Trent-town" was described by Peter Kalm, a Swedish professor, as "a long narrow town" of some one hundred houses.

Crossweeksung had been settled by Quakers in 1681, the same year as Philadelphia. It was the nearest town to Trenton. Its original name was probably Closswicks or Criswicks, signifying "separation," most likely in reference to the forks of Crosswicks Creek. It was the site of an iron ore bog that was extensively worked and, when Brainerd arrived, four mills and a tannery had been in operation in the village and township for many years.

Cranberry had been settled in 1698, chiefly by Calvinistic Scotch settlers who apparently named their town Cranborough or Cranbury, its present name, after the emblem of the Grant clan. Here, it seems, Brainerd lodged most frequently, if not daily, with Charles McKnight, and rode to and from the Indians at Crossweeksung. McKnight had arrived from Ireland about 1740, had attended the Log College, and had preached for a time at the Forks of Delaware. He had been installed as the pastor of both Cranberry and Allentown only a year ago. His opposition to the British in the Revolutionary War is indicative of his calibre and temperament. His church was burned and he was imprisoned and died in 1778 as a result of the suffering he endured.* One of his sons, Captain Richard McKnight, died a prison-ship martyr.

After a century of white occupation, few Indians lingered in New Jersey, especially after the veritable flood of immigrants arrived between 1700 and 1745. Only a few remnant Delawares lived as beggars on the fringes of the white man's villages. Decimated by epidemics of smallpox and the flow of firewater, they eked out their

---

* Not his church at Cranbury which was built in 1740, but probably at or near Shrewsbury, New Jersey. Cranbury's present Presbyterian church was built about 1790. McKnight is buried in the Trinity Church Yard, New York City.

livelihood from the fields and woods by making baskets, brooms, and wooden utensils to sell to their white neighbors. In varying degrees they understood or spoke English, and intermarriage with runaway Negro slaves was not uncommon. However, they maintained some contact with the Forks of Delaware and interior Indians. "Some of them, not many months before," stated Brainerd, "were enraged with my interpreter, because he attempted to teach them something of Christianity." They "had been as much opposed to anything of that nature, as any Indians whatsoever."

No wonder, then, that Brainerd must have steeled himself against disappointment as he related the experiences of his first hopeful day at Crossweeksung in the opening paragraphs of his "public" journal which became famous on both sides of the Atlantic Ocean. The date of his first account was Wednesday, June 19, the same day a year ago when as an ordained missionary he had left Elizabethtown to begin his work at the Forks of Delaware. He later explained that the few women whom he met were exactly four.

"I found very few persons at the place I visited, and perceived that the Indians in these parts were very much scattered, there being not more than two or three families in a place, and these small settlements six, ten, fifteen, twenty, and thirty miles, and some more, from the place I was then at. However, I preached to those few I found, who appeared well disposed, and not inclined to object and cavil, as the Indians had frequently done elsewhere.

"When I had concluded my discourse, I informed them (there being none but a few women and children) that I would willingly visit them again the next day. Whereupon they readily set out, and travelled ten or fifteen miles, in order to give notice to some of their friends at that distance. These women, like the women of Samaria, seemed desirous that others might 'see the man that told them what they had done' in their lives past, and the misery that attended their *idolatrous* ways."

From Edwards' diary excerpts which supplement the period covered by the Journal, the reader learns that, at the close of his first day at Crossweeksung, Brainerd was worn out. He was again hardly able to walk or to even sit up. On Thursday afternoon, however, and in the evening, he preached again. There were more Indians in attendance each time, and all were attentive and well-disposed to hear him.

On Friday, apparently to keep a previously-made appointment, he rode some twenty miles northeast to Freehold, to the largest Presbyterian church in the area, and spent the day with William Tennent, Jr., a younger brother of Gilbert Tennent who had installed McKnight.

It is not surprising that he went to Freehold, rather than to Trenton which was closer to Crossweeksung. Freehold was a New Side town where Whitefield had preached on May 1, 1740, to an audience of some seven thousand persons. But a half year earlier at Trenton, the great evangelist had to be content to address a crowd which had gathered to see the execution of a criminal. This was because David Cowell, the Old Side minister of Trenton, refused his pulpit to Whitefield, even as he had also vigorously opposed John Rowland's preaching in his presbytery. Cowell was nevertheless a sincere and capable Christian. A Harvard graduate, a bachelor and a skilled physician, he later served as acting president of the College of New Jersey. But there is no record that Brainerd ever visited Cowell or that Cowell ever supported or entered into Brainerd's effort.

Brainerd returned to Crossweeksung at Saturday noon, and when he preached to nearly thirty Indians in the evening, several were "made to shed tears, and to wish for Christ to save them"! Elated, "then willing to live," yet death still appeared pleasant to him, as he recorded in his diary, he preached to the Indians again on Sunday and on Monday, until he became practically exhausted. By Thursday he had forty listeners, and he exclaimed: "O how heart-reviving and soul-refreshing it is to me to see the fruit of my labours!" On Friday there were even more in attendance, "from their several and distant habitations," and they asked Brainerd to preach twice a day. He "cheerfully complied" that day and on Saturday, and thought it a remarkable evidence of God's providence on both days that the Indians were able "with only walking a little way" to kill three deer, which made it possible for their entire company to remain together to hear him.

That night he rode back to McKnight's home in Cranberry in joyous prayer, and though "exceedingly worn out," he preached twice on both Sunday and Monday to the forty or fifty persons, old and young, who had "now learned to attend the worship of God with Christian decency in all respects." He talked to them individually and was amazed at the knowledge they had absorbed and retained in the ten days he had taught them. One "wished God would change her heart"; another "wanted to find Christ"; and an old ex-chief wept bitterly with concern for his soul.

As a matter of self-preservation, Brainerd left the Crossweeksungs two weeks after he found them. Edwards stated: "He was so fatigued by constant preaching to these Indians, yielding to their earnest and importunate desires, that he found it necessary to give himself some relaxation." Brainerd remarked that his trip to the Susquehanna had left him in very poor health and that he wished to re-visit the Indians at the Forks of Delaware. Although he was apprehensive that the good impressions that had been made would "decline and wear off," he left Crossweeksung with a prospect that was actually most encouraging.

"Tuesday, July 2. When I came to take leave of them, and spoke something particularly to each of them, they all earnestly inquired when I would come again, and expressed a great desire of being further instructed. And of their own accord agreed, that when I should come again, they would all meet and live together during my continuance with them; and that they would do their utmost endeavours to gather all the Indians in these parts that were yet farther remote."

He promised to return as soon as his health and business elsewhere would permit and, admonishing them to "apply for direction" from William Tennent at Freehold, he set out for New Brunswick.

As he rode the forty miles northward to the small neat town of Dutch brick houses set on the banks above the tidewaters of the Raritan River he wondered and reflected on what he had learned about these amazingly "attentive, orderly and well disposed" Indians. He had learned that one or two of the Crossweeksung natives on a visit to the Forks of Delaware had apparently been touched by his preaching there. Returning to Crossweeksung, they had tried to convince their friends of the evil of idolatry. "Although the other Indians seemed but little to regard, and rather to deride them, yet this, perhaps, has put them into a *thinking* posture of mind, or at least, given them some thoughts about Christianity, and excited in some of them a *curiosity to hear*," he mused. After he went to bed that night, he prayed until sleep overtook him.

He spent about a week in New Jersey, "performing some necessary business," and in "visiting several ministers" who must have included his employers Burr and Dickinson to whom he would relate his sudden and encouraging prospects at Crossweeksung. At the Dickinsons he would have missed the mother of that home, Joanne Melyne Dickinson, who had died in her sixty-third year on April 20, his birthday, when he and Beatty had participated in Treat's communion service at Abington. On Friday, July 12, he arrived at his own house in the Forks of Delaware.

Although his remarks from Sunday to Sunday indicate no amazement or elation, his Indians at the Forks were now also unusually receptive to his preaching. Several of them appeared concerned:

"they wept much the whole time of divine service," and attended diligently beyond what had been common among them. "Divine truth," he said, "seemed to make very considerable impressions upon several of them, and caused the tears to flow freely."

The real reason for Brainerd's return to the Forks, as well as the Indians' heightened concern, is soon disclosed. On this second Sunday at the Forks, on July 21, just a year and four days after his interpreter was "somewhat awakened" in Craig's meadow, Brainerd baptized Moses Tinda Tattamy and his wife — "the first whom I baptized among the Indians." Having gone their separate ways for a few days, David and his faithful companion had returned "home" for this great and joyful event. "I think," said Brainerd earnestly, "that I have reason to hope that he is 'created anew in Christ Jesus to good works.'

"His change is *abiding*, and his life, so far as I know, *unblemished* to this day, though it is now more than six months since he experienced this change; in which space of time he has been as much exposed to *strong* drink, as possible, in divers places where it has been moving free as water; and yet has never, that I know of, discovered any hankering desire after it. . . . He has been a great comfort to me [and] he has, I am persuaded, already been, and I trust will yet be, a blessing to the other Indians."

On Friday Brainerd also baptized Tattamy's children. Again no names or numbers are given, but according to Brainerd's later tallies, Tattamy must have had five children. One son was most probably Peter who may have been about twelve years old. On October 22, 1753, John Brainerd wrote of the death of Peter *Tottony*: "He had been a member of New Jersey College near two years, was much beloved of his classmates and the other scholars, and made a decent handsome appearance among them. He died of a quick consumption."

Another son was Bill, perhaps under ten years of age, of whom it is pointedly recorded at the Easton Treaty in July 1756 that he was the son of old Moses Tattamy, Teedyuscung's counsellor, with whom he had come to the conference. It is also noted that he was a Christian convert of the Brainerds. Bill was shot in the thigh by an irresponsible Scotch-Irish youth. The wound festered for five weeks until Bill died on August 9, 1756, despite the best efforts of the government doctor who kept Governor Denny notified of the daily condition of the young man. The governor in turn consoled Tattamy and demonstrated much concern, for the attack had so incensed the Indians under Teedyuscung, the new King of the Delawares who had cast off the Iroquois yoke, that the entire negotiations at the conference were for a time jeopardized.*

Brainerd's private diary for that wonderful baptismal day reveals the tenderness of his joy. His body was "weak and worn out," but he was filled with thankful praise. "I could not but cry," he wrote. "I had some lively taste of heaven." His thoughts of death were still sweet, but he was far from his dire melancholy of the past winter. He longed to fill up the rest of his life in his Master's work, "willing to stay awhile on earth," yet his best success was but weakness and only a foretaste of the life to come — "How I longed to be with Christ, to be employed in the glorious work of angels, and with an angel's vigour and delight!"

He also spent the third Sunday, July 28, at the Forks of Delaware. On that day some of his Indians told him that the baptisms "had made them more concerned than any thing they had ever seen or heard before."

The troublesome old medicine man, "a murderer, a powwow or conjurer, and a notorious drunkard," possibly the same whom David had challenged ten months ago to do his worst, was among those "excited" by the events. He had, even frequently, attended Brainerd's preaching from time to time, but like many others, he had remained extremely attached to strong drink and "in no degree reformed." And, although sometime during the past year he had been thrown into "some kind of horror and desperation," after he had murdered "a likely young Indian," he had continued to thwart Brainerd's influence among the Indians who were somewhat disposed to consider the Gospel seriously.

Brainerd elucidated in a special case history: "That which was the worst of all his conduct, was his *conjuration* . . . he still followed his old *charms* and juggling tricks, 'giving out that he himself was some great one, and to him they gave heed,' supposing him to be possessed of a *great power*. So that when I have instructed them respecting the *miracles* wrought by Christ in healing the sick, etc., and mentioned them as evidences of his *divine* mission, and the truths of his doctrines, they have quickly observed the wonders of that kind which this man had performed by his *magic charms*. . . . I have often thought that it would be a great favour to the

* In the spring of 1760 when Tattamy was still in the service of the Penn government, "The Friendly Association" offered to board his *daughter*. (Anthony F. C. Wallace, *King of the Delawares: Teedyuscung*, Philadelphia: University of Pennsylvania Press, 1949, p. 213)

design of gospellizing these Indians, if God would take that wretch out of the world; for I had scarce any hope of his ever becoming good."

But now, on Wednesday, July 31, as Brainerd and Tattamy began their return to New Jersey, the old conjurer, "with the invitation of an Indian who was a friend to Christianity," followed them.

Only his diary discloses Brainerd's tension of expectation. As he arrived at Crossweeksung he could hardly trust his hope that the encouraging appearances there would not "prove wholly abortive" after his month of absence.

"It seemed to me I had no care, or hardly any desire, to be the instrument of so glorious a work, as I wished and prayed for among the Indians: if the blessed work might be accomplished to the honour of God, and the enlargement of the dear Redeemer's kingdom, this was all my desire and care; and for this mercy I hoped, but with trembling; for I felt what Job expresses, 'If I had called, and he had answered me, yet would I not believe that he had hearkened unto my voice.' My rising hopes, respecting the conversion of the Indians, have been so often dashed, that my spirit is as it were broken, and my courage wasted, and I hardly dare hope."

21. LIKE A MIGHTY RUSHING WIND

Brainerd had left the Crossweeksung Indians on July 2. The first day after his return, on Friday, August 2, he sent word that the Indians should gather on Saturday that he might preach to them. Although he had instructed them with some assurance "to apply for direction" from William Tennent, the evangelical pastor of Freehold, he had wondered and feared whether his initial contacts with them had made any lasting impression on their minds and hearts.

He found them still serious in demeanor. Indeed, a number of them were "under deep concern for an interest in Christ," as he expressed it. And he gave full credit for their concern to Tennent. Their convictions of their sinful and perishing state, he said, were in his absence much promoted by the labors and endeavors of Tennent whose house they had frequented. This was more than he had dared hope for as he had ridden from the Forks of Delaware.

Only about twenty Indians were present at first, but "not above two" could Brainerd see who had dry eyes as he preached to them, "with some view to Revelation 22:17," *And whosoever will, let him take of the water of life freely.* His elementary exposition of the free offer of the gospel seemed to take hold: "Some were much concerned, and discovered vehement longings of soul after Christ, to save them from the misery they felt and feared."

On Sunday he helped Charles McKnight administrate the Lord's Supper, and the Indians, now "nearly fifty in all, old and young," and some who could understand English, went to the Cranberry church with him, and were much affected.

"Now a change in their manners began to appear very visible. In the evening, when they came to sup together, they would not taste a morsel till they had sent to me to come and ask a blessing on their food; at which time sundry of them wept; especially when I reminded them how they had in times past eaten their feasts in *honour* to *devils*, and neglected to thank God for them."

He doubtless repeated his plea to take of the water of life when he concluded the services on Monday with the text he had expounded at Abington in April: *If any man thirst, let him come unto me and drink.* He particularly addressed the Indians "who sat by themselves in a part of the house," and, as he later learned, several more were strongly stirred. In the evening most of them came to the house where he lodged, inquiring "what they should do to be saved." Tattamy also worked with them. He was with them day and night, stated David. And, at least one woman, Brainerd was convinced, "obtained comfort . . . solid and well-grounded."

"This day there was one woman, who had been much concerned for her soul, ever since she first heard me preach in June last, who obtained comfort, I trust, solid and well grounded: she seemed to be filled with love to Christ, at the same time behaved humbly and tenderly, and appeared afraid of nothing so much as grieving and offending him whom her soul loved."

"Afraid of nothing so much"! A hundred and twenty years later an echo to this quite ordinary phrase appeared in print — "*the first convert to Christianity* under David Brainerd's preaching after he went amongst the Indians . . . said that he was the first white man she could ever love, having suffered so much from them, for she had always been *afraid of them.*" Her fear of the white man had also been "well grounded," for this first-fruit of David's preaching at Crossweeksung was the ill-treated daughter of a king — a wealthy king who though he had been great in the sight of both Christians and Indians, had fallen upon evil days and had come to an ignoble end. The story of his only surviving daughter came to light more than a century later when in 1865 Thomas Brainerd published his book, *The Life of John Brainerd,* a biography of David's brother and successor.

Thomas Brainerd had written to several friends, including a missionary by the name of Cutting Marsh at Waupaca, Wisconsin, inquiring whether they could learn anything at all about any memories which the surviving Delaware Indians had retained about David and John. Did any Indians in 1864 remember aught that their fathers had told them? Cutting Marsh wrote to a Delaware woman of his acquaintance who lived with the descendants of the Stockbridge Indians in Wisconsin. Had she ever heard of the Brainerds? She had! Bartholemew S. Calvin, her father, had told his children much about both David and John. Indeed, it was Bartholemew's mother, the wife of Stephen Calvin, who was David's first convert at Crossweeksung.

The story begins with Weequehela (Wukqely, Weequahela, Wequehalak, Wequalia). He was the last great sachem among the Delawares in New Jersey in the early 1700's and owned much land, many horses and cattle, much silverware and negro slaves. Documented sources confirm that he lived the life of an English squire on a vast plantation and frequently entertained governors and great white men in his home which was fully furnished with English furniture, calico curtains and featherbeds. But in 1727 a land dispute developed between him and his English neighbor, Captain John Leonard, who wilfully trespassed on the king's land, a cedar swamp which Leonard claimed was his. Weequehela's great-granddaughter stated in her story to Cutting Marsh that Leonard had extorted large tracts of land from Weequehela after getting him drunk. According to the Lenape code of honor, Weequehela shot Leonard through the heart. Great sachem that he was, Weequehela made no attempt to escape for, he said, it was not right for a man of his status to do so and, according to the beliefs of his fathers, he had done no wrong. He said, "If I suffer the white people to hang me, the Great Spirit will receive me to the good hunting ground; but if I run away, he will not suffer me to go there." He did, however, advise his people to move west, and asked that he might be shot by the white man's gun, but his request was denied, and he was hanged at Perth Amboy before the Governor's reprieve could halt the execution.

The American Weekly Mercury for July 6-13, 1727, reported the story in less sympathetic tones: "*Perth Amboy, July 8.* On the 30th of the last Month *Wequalia* (the Indian King) was Executed according to Sentence passed against him, for the Murder of Capt. *John Leonard*. And as said *Wequalia* had lived a base Inhuman Life, and Murdered his own Brother and other Indians formerly, so he died a hardened and impenitent Wretch, not shewing the least Remorse for any [of] the Actions of his Vile Life; nor would he own the Murder of said Capt. John Leonard, of which he was Notoriously Convicted, for and deservedly suffer'd Death. He saved us the Labour of Writing his Confession, having made none; he only bid *Adieu* to the *few Indians* that Attended him to the Gallows, which were only his near Relatives, all the other Indians refused to shew him the least Regard."

But, and perhaps significantly, the report stated in conclusion, "There was a great Concourse of people at the Execution, together with two Companies of the Militia in Arms, in Order to Protect the Sheriff and Officers from any Insult of the Mob or Indians." These precautionary measures seem rather out of place for the execution of a wretch without friends. His death, as a matter of record, troubled the hearts of both the Indians and the English in Pennsylvania and New Jersey for many years, and even a generation later in the Indian Wars of 1755-56, Weequehela's kinsmen among the Munsees claimed blood vengeance in his name.

After Weequehela's death, according to Cutting Marsh's informant, his widow and four or five children, "one of them being only a few days old," were badly mistreated and deprived of all their property and possessions. Soon all had died except only a three-year-old daughter. Before she grew up she saw her aunt killed by a white man, and she suffered almost everything but death so that she was always afraid of white men, until Brainerd came into her life. "She loved David Brainerd very much," explained her granddaughter more than a century later, "because he loved his heavenly Father so much that he was willing to endure hardships, travelling over mountains, suffering hunger, and lying on the ground that he might do her people good; and she did every thing she could for his comfort."

When Brainerd came to Crossweeksung this daughter of Weequehela would have been a young woman in her twenties and, one can presume, she was already married to Stephen Calvin, an Indian of high intelligence and good will whom their granddaughter in 1864 described as a teacher or interpreter for Brainerd. The story itself suggests much concerning the "well disposed, serious and attentive" Indians of Crossweeksung whose late pagan king had greatly admired the white man and his ways, and had exhorted his people to live in peace with their pale-face neighbors.*

That week of August 4, 1745, which had begun with such encouraging signs at Charles McKnight's church on Sunday, was indeed the most thrilling and glorious week of David Brainerd's life. On Tuesday morning the Indians returned again to his lodgings in Cranberry, and they appeared "surprisingly tender." When they returned to Crossweeksung, Brainerd rejoined them there in the afternoon and had fifty-five listeners, "about forty that were capable of attending divine services with understanding." Before he finished his urgent appeal based on I John 4:10 — *not that we loved God, but that he loved us* — "scarcely three in forty" he said "could refrain from tears and bitter cries."

"The more I invited them to come and partake of his love, the more their distress was aggravated, because they felt themselves unable to come. It was surprising to see how their hearts seemed to be pierced with the tender and melting invitations of the gospel, when there was not a word of terror spoken to them.

"There was this day two persons that obtained relief and comfort, which (when I came to discourse with them particularly) appeared solid, rational and scriptural . . . 'they wanted Christ should wipe their hearts quite clean.' "

On Wednesday he told them of the Suffering Servant who was bruised in their stead. More than two years ago Azariah Horton's people on Long Island had listened quietly when he preached this message from Isaiah to them. This day it was different. Although only a few were as strongly affected as on the day before, several were affected even more powerfully.

"Some few could neither go nor stand, but lay flat on the ground as if pierced at heart, crying incessantly for mercy. Several were newly awakened; and it was remarkable that, as fast as they came from re-

---

* Although the granddaughter's intelligent account of Weequehela is remarkably true to other accounts as they were recorded 150 years before her time, one can only conjecture about the actual status and fate of the widow and children. Since the Governor's Council referred to Weequehela (Wukqely) as a full sachem as early as 1709, he may have been quite old when he was executed in 1727. His widow and very young children whom the granddaughter mentioned may have been a second family occupying a lower status than his true or first wife and children. One cannot ignore "Sarah Stores widow of Quaquahela" who claimed extensive land given her by her husband and was therefore the only female signer among the Cranberry Indians at the Crosswicks Conference of 1758.

mote places round about, the Spirit of God seemed to seize them with concern for their souls."

That day two more "newly met with comfort." Another case which "did not appear so clear," said Brainerd, was that of "a principal man among the Indians." He was "most secure and self-righteous, and thought his state good, because he knew more than the generality of the Indians." In addition, he told Brainerd with a great deal of confidence, "he had been a Christian more than ten years." But there were now five Indians whose experience satisfied Brainerd as being genuine conversions. These had been already deeply affected when he had preached to them in June.

Charles McKnight accompanied David when he preached to about sixty-five persons, men, women, and children, on Thursday afternoon. It was August 8. The text he used was *his* text and his theme, the same he had heard from the lips of Ebenezer Pemberton in the Newark church — *Go out into the highways and hedges, and compel them to come in, that my house may be filled.* He preached with "uncommon freedom" and power, he said, and what followed never ceased to astound him. It was the day for which he had so fervently and repeatedly prayed — "that God would make this the day of his power and grace amongst the poor Indians."

"There was much visible concern among them while I was discoursing publicly; but afterwards when I spoke to one and another more particularly, whom I perceived under much concern, the power of God seemed to descend upon the assembly 'like a mighty rushing wind,' and with an astonishing energy bore down all before it.

"I stood amazed at the influence, that seized the audience almost universally, and could compare it to nothing more aptly than the irresistible force of a mighty torrent or swelling deluge, that with its insupportable weight and pressure bears down and sweeps before it whatever is in its way. . . . Old men and women who had been drunken wretches for many years, and some little children not more than six or seven years of age, appeared in distress for their souls, as well as persons of middle age. . . .

"They were almost universally praying and crying for mercy in every part of the house, and many out of doors, and numbers could neither go nor stand. Their concern was so great, each one for himself, that none seemed to take notice of those about them, but each prayed freely for himself. . . . I must say, I never saw *any day like it* in all respects: it was a day wherein I am persuaded the Lord did much to destroy the kingdom of darkness among this people. . . . This was indeed a surprising day of God's power, and seemed enough to convince an Atheist of the truth, importance, and power of God's word."

"Nay," echoed Charles McKnight a full year later, as if recalling their excited conversation at his home that night, "so very extraordinary was the concern which appeared among these poor Indians in general, that I am ready to conclude, it might have been sufficient to have convinced an Atheist, that the Lord was indeed in the place."

The secure, self-righteous headman whose case had not appeared clear the day before now wept bitterly, and the ancient powwow who had followed Brainerd and Tattamy from the Forks of Delaware "cried for mercy with many tears." Brainerd explained in his lengthy case history: "my preaching pricked his heart and made him very *uneasy*, but did not bring him to so *great* distress, because he hoped he could do *something* for his own relief . . . [nevertheless] his spirit of conjuration left him entirely; that he had no more power of that nature since, than any other man living."

The sudden and unexpected seizures that overcame the Indians are not better described by Brainerd than in his account of the derisive young woman.

"A young Indian woman, who I believe never knew before she had a soul, nor ever thought of any such thing, hearing that there was something strange among the Indians, came to see what was the matter. In her way to the Indians she called at my lodgings, and when I told her I designed presently to preach to the Indians, laughed and seemed to mock; but went however to them. I had not proceeded far in my public discourse before she felt *effectually* that she had a soul; and before I had concluded my discourse, was so convinced of her sin and misery, and so distressed with concern for her soul's salvation, that she seemed like one pierced through with a dart, and cried out incessantly. She could neither go nor stand, nor sit on her seat without being held up. After public service was over, she lay flat on the ground praying earnestly, and would take no notice of, nor give any answer to, any who spoke to her. I hearkened to know what she said, and perceived the burden of her prayer to be, *Guttummaukalummeh wechaumeh kmeleh Nolah*, i.e., 'Have mercy on me, and help me to give you my heart.' And thus she continued praying incessantly for many hours together."

There were "seventy persons, old and young," when Brainerd exhorted them twice on Friday about the parable of the sower and "all ye that labour." Near night when he talked to them individually and in small groups, two or three were again powerfully shaken. Soon all the other Indians "immediately gathered round" and practically all were deeply affected, "near as prevalent as it was the day before . . . everyone seemed to *mourn apart* . . . *Guttummaukalummeh, guttummaukalummeh* was the common cry." And on Saturday another murderer and notorious drunkard of about fifty years of age "seemed to be pierced at heart with distress."

This was the sweet answer to his prayers, these were the souls for whom he had agonized. It was as when Christ had breathed on his disciples and said, "Receive ye the Holy Spirit." These were genuine conversions.

What then of the ugly hysteria and patently false manifestations of the Great Awakening in New England, especially in Connecticut?

Neither he nor anyone else recorded how he sweated and prayed: "God my Father, magnify Thyself and Thyself alone. Keep *me* from the deceits of the Evil One and keep *them* from false zeal and extravagance. My Father, let him not have dominion over them. These are they to whom Thou didst send me. Keep them, O keep them in Thy hand."

22. I HAVE FOUND MY SHEEP

The summer of the Great Awakening among the Crossweeksung Indians of New Jersey was both hot and dry. The archives of the state reveal that a severe drought prevailed throughout that summer of 1745. And it would seem that one can reasonably assume that Brainerd readily adapted his discourses to the situation. On August 3 he had preached on "the water of life." On August 5 he had called out: "If any man thirst." Before that great, dry month of August would end he would shout: "Ho, everyone that thirsteth! Come ye to the waters!" Still later he would report that his people still thirsted, that spiritual blessings appeared as gentle showers, and that his flock was as a wet fleece when all else was comparatively dry.

The news of the exciting events at Crossweeksung had soon spread abroad so that some Indians came "more than forty miles" to hear the young white preacher, but many came without an inkling of what was taking place. These natives, it would seem, would have been those from the Indian village of Nescochogue, just about forty miles south on Nescochogue Lake at Sweetwater, now Pleasant Mills, where they had egress to the Atlantic Ocean by way of the Mullica River. Local tradition there claims that all the Nescochogue tribal leaders were eventually converted to Christianity through Brainerd's preaching. Living closer to Crossweeksung were a few more Indians along the Rancocas Creek near Mount Holly, about fifteen miles south.

Brainerd wrote in his General Remarks: "Many came without any intelligence of what was going on here, and consequently without any design of *theirs*, so much as to gratify their curiosity; so that it seemed as if God had summoned them together from all quarters for nothing else but to deliver his message to them." In his later Appendix he observed: "Like Saul and his messengers coming among the prophets, they no sooner came but they prophesied."

The news had spread also into the white villages. "Numbers of careless spectators of the white people, some Quakers and others," he said, came out of curiosity on Sunday, August 11, as they already did during the week before, "to hear what 'this babbler would say' to the poor ignorant Indians. . . . Several of the white heathen were awakened, and could not longer be idle spectators."

The personal conduct of the Indians soon disclosed radical changes. One mother became grief-stricken for fear that she had displayed "an inordinate and sinful" anger toward her child. This is the more interesting in that it was generally observed that the Delawares rarely punished their children. The Moravians described the Delawares' child-training in some detail. Heckewelder wrote that it was done "in the gentlest and most persuasive manner," and explained: "nor is the parent's authority ever supported by harsh or compulsive means; no whips, no punishments, no threats are ever used to enforce commands or compel obedience." Others have observed that the parents' attitude was not at all based on indifference but was distinctly religious, involving concepts of recognition and respectful deference to the idea that each person, each child, had a personal guardian spirit who directed his life.

Had Brainerd learned these ways of life among these people who had grown from childhood practically devoid of the concept of a father or father-god who would punish them for their wrongs? Was that his important discovery that led him to repeatedly emphasize that he spoke no word of terror to them, and that their great concern was "never excited by any harangues of terror"? Did he preach only the Amiable Jesus?

He seems to partly support the "romantic" view of the Delawares' parent-child relationship when he stated in an appendix: "While I have been preaching, their children have frequently cried to such a degree, that I could scarcely be heard, and their pagan mothers would take no manner of care to quiet them." But in another context when he related that the children generally misbehaved, fought and struck their mothers and were given to much lying, he squelched the idea when he stated that some of the parents were "very severe" in punishing their children for such misconduct. In fact, he used the parent-child relationship to illustrate God's manner of viewing men's wickedness and His punishment of them.

Marital affairs also came under close scrutiny among the former dissolute Indians. In one case, a man publicly renounced his second wife and returned to his first spouse whom he had left without just cause. Since both husbands and wives had been commonly forsaking their conjugal relationships at the slightest whim or provocation, Brainerd was concerned that the man's commendable action might discourage the other Indians as making too great demands on them. "I suppose a few weeks before," he said, "the whole world could not have persuaded this man to a compliance with Christian rules in this affair. I was not without fears that this proceeding might be like putting 'new wine into old bottles,' and that some might be prejudiced against Christianity, when they saw the demands made by it."

However, the man was determined, and his action seemed rather to have a salutary effect. Three or four other couples were subsequently rejoined to their first mates as they "generally owned that the laws of Christ were good and right, respecting the affairs of marriage."

On Saturday, August 17, Brainerd told his converts how Philip had baptized the Ethiopian, and he began to prepare them "to partake of that ordinance." Strange Indians continued to arrive and "Presbyterians, Baptists, Quakers, etc." were present on Sunday morning as he proclaimed the Word of God to all who would hear. Afterward he preached to the Indians on Christ, the Bread of Life, and they "were yet hungry and thirsty for the word of God, and appeared *unwearied* in their attendance upon it."

"I never saw the work of God appear so independent of means as at this time," he said again. "I seemed to do nothing, and indeed to have nothing to do, but to 'stand still, and see the salvation of God.'"

But he preached, and he must have preached effectively. What would a recording of Tattamy's interpretation have disclosed when on Monday morning they pursued their theme from the fifty-fifth chapter of Isaiah?

Ho, every one that thirsteth, come ye to the waters. . . .

Wherefore do ye spend money for that which is not bread? . . .

Hearken diligently unto me. . . . Incline your ear, and come unto me: hear, and your soul shall live.

Ye shall go out with joy, and be led forth with peace: the mountains and the hills shall break forth before you into singing, and all the trees of the field shall clap their hands. . . .

"There were numbers of poor impotent souls that waited at the pool for healing," concluded Brainerd that day, "and the angel seemed, as at other times of late, to trouble the waters. . . ."

Since the beginning of the month he had been with his converts almost constantly, but now he left them for four days and went to William Tennent's church at Freehold where he preached to a "considerable assembly" who probably were concluding their celebration of the Lord's Supper. Although he repeated his familiar sermon, *Blessed are the poor in spirit,* he did it poorly — "I do not remember to have been so straightened for a whole twelvemonth past." However, he accepted it as God's will for him and he remained "composed and comfortable," despite his "very dry and barren" performance before the Freehold people who doubtless had expected a lively and inspiring sermon from the young New Englander who had brought revival to the Indians.

Founded in 1682-85 by prior New England settlers and by refugee Scots under the capable leadership of Walter Ker, the Freehold church was the first regularly constituted Presbyterian church in America. William Tennent wrote that Elder Ker "in the year 1685, for his faithful and conscientious adherence to God and His truth, as professed by the Church of Scotland, was there apprehended and sent to this country, under a sentence of perpetual banishment . . . by which it appears that the Devil and his instruments lost their aim in sending him from home, where it is unlikely he could ever have been so serviceable to Christ's kingdom as he has been here." Now in his eighty-ninth year, Ker had come ashore near New Jersey's pine country from the stranded sailship *Caledonia.* Other members of the congregation had survived the wreck of the *Henry and Francis* on the Jersey coast after a hundred days at sea and an epidemic of fever that claimed the lives of sixty of its two hundred passengers.

Brainerd was refreshed to meet his new friends among the staunch believers of Freehold and at Elizabethtown where he visited Jonathan Dickinson and other friends on Tuesday. He told them what God

had done for the Indians and broached his ideas toward contriving
something for their settlement together. He also wrote a letter to
his brother John at Yale, "but grieved that time slid away, while I did
so little for God." By Friday afternoon, after a morning of weakness,
he was back at Crossweeksung to resume his instructions preparatory
to the Indians' baptism, and to give "further exhortations" that they
might be fitted to "ascend up and meet him in the air" when He
shall "descend with a shout, and the voice of the archangel."

More newcomers had arrived during his absence. Some of them
had lived with Quakers "under gospel light" and had learned to
read and were civil, but, said Brainerd, they "appeared utter strangers
to their hearts." He was surprised to see their "self-righteous disposition" and the high value they put on their "supposed attainments."
Yet even one of these was deeply affected and cried, much to the
satisfaction of the recent converts who were "grieved with the conversation and conduct of these newcomers who boasted of their
knowledge."

Second only to the great day of revival on August 8, the most
wonderful day in the lives of David Brainerd and of his Crossweeksung converts was the day of their baptism. It was Sunday,
August 25, two months and a week after Weequehelah's daughter
and the others, like the women of Samaria, had run to tell their
people to come and see the man who had told them what they had
done in their past lives. News of the unprecedented mass baptism
had spread and hundreds of curious whites were on hand to
witness the event. In recent memory it had happened only once
before when a year earlier the Anglican minister Colin Campbell of
St. Andrews Church in Burlington had baptized two Indian adults.

In the morning Brainerd preached from Luke 15:3-7, the parable
of the lost sheep and the joyful shepherd who called together his
neighbors, saying, *Rejoice with me, for I have found my sheep which
was lost.* But Brainerd's neighbors were less than joyful or even
sympathetic. Predominantly Quakers, they had little affection for
New Englanders who had once persecuted Friends. Moreover, they
believed in the sufficiency of "inward light" and claimed no need for
the outward rite of baptism or the visible Table of Communion between man and God. "There being a multitude of *white* people
present," said Brainerd, "I made an address to *them,* at the close of
my discourse to the Indians: but could not so much as keep them
orderly; for scores of them kept walking and gazing about, and behaved more indecently than *any Indians* I have ever addressed; and

a view of their abusive conduct so sunk my spirits, that I could scarce go on with my work."

In the afternoon when he preached from Revelation 3:20, *Behold, I stand at the door and knock*, the Indians "behaved seriously, though many others were vain." Afterwards he baptized twenty-five neglected, despised, riff-raff Indians in the name of Jesus Christ and *his* Father, and *his* Spirit, for, he later explained: "Their language does not admit of their speaking any word denoting relation, such as father, son, etc., absolutely." Fifteen of the initiates were adults; ten were their children. And was there not among them the daughter of King Weequehela and her husband, Stephen Calvin, whom she had brought to hear of the Jew who had died also for the Lenni-Lenape? It was, said Brainerd, "a desirable and sweet season indeed!"

"They rejoiced that they had in a public and solemn manner dedicated themselves to God. Love seemed to reign among them! They took each other by the hand with tenderness and affection, as if their hearts were knit together, while I was discoursing to them: and all their deportment towards each other was such, that a *serious spectator* might justly be excited to cry out with admiration, 'Behold how they love one another.'"

Many of the still unbaptized, he said, "wept bitterly, longing to be partakers of the same joy and comfort."

The next day he disclosed to them "the persevering nature of those consolations which Christ gives his people," and his converts received his assurances with joy. He recorded: "This was a tender, affectionate, humble, delightful melting, and appeared to be the genuine effect of a Spirit of *adoption,* and very far from that spirit of *bondage* that they not long since laboured under. . . . It was indeed a lovely and very interesting assembly. Their number was now about *ninety-five* persons, old and young." Before the day was over an aged idolator voluntarily gave up his feast and dance rattles to the other Indians who quickly destroyed them.

Three busy, glorious months had brought blessings untold and unexpected, not in Pennsylvania, but in New Jersey, probably the last place that Brainerd had considered as the place for his mission endeavors. Whether his success had obliterated his sense of past failure or had stimulated him to greater hope, his compelling concern now again fastened on the Indians "far back." He was now fully convinced, he said, that his duty was to return quickly to the lost tribes on the Susquehanna River. September and the hunting season were close at hand. If he were to find them at home he would have to hurry. He would therefore leave Crossweeksung in the

morning, and, in anticipation of this undertaking, he asked his people
if they would be willing to spend the close of Monday in prayer that
the spirit of God would go with him and bless his endeavors with
"their brethren far remote."

"They cheerfully complied with the motion, and soon after I
left them (the sun being about an hour and a half high at night)
they began and continued praying all night till *break of day*, or very
near, never mistrusting, they tell me, till they went out and viewed
the stars, and saw the *morning-star* a considerable height, that it was
later than common bed time."

23. THE DARK CORNERS OF THE EARTH

Although Brainerd was absent from Crossweeksung for five weeks
and four days in the fall of 1745, he spent only ten days along the
Susquehanna. On this third trip he and Tattamy did not go directly
to the river, but first visited Philadelphia and the Forks of Delaware.
Edwards explained: "it was five days from his departure from Crossweeksung before he reached the Forks; going round by the way of
Philadelphia, and waiting on the Governor of Pennsylvania, to get
a recommendation from him to the chief of the Indians; which he
obtained."

David preached at both Hunter's and Craig's settlements on
Wednesday, September 4, and that week as he also addressed the
Indians of the Forks for the first time since Tattamy's baptism,
although some had visited Crossweeksung, he appreciated the "considerable concern" among them, especially as it applied to "two
stupid creatures whom I could scarce ever before keep awake." At
the same time he feared that their interest might evaporate like the
morning cloud of the prophet-poet Hosea, "as something of that
nature had formerly done in these parts." And although there were
other hopeful signs, his diary reveals that on Friday night he
wished he could die and quit the scene of sin and darkness. During
this journey, said Edwards, he was much engaged in spiritual thoughts.

Sunday brought an even livelier response from the Indians, "not
unlike what has been of late at Crossweeksung," and some white
people were also jarred out of their complacency. But, Brainerd
explained, some Indians who had always refused to hear him and

raged against those who did, were of late more bitter than ever and
scoffed at Christianity and now asked the others, "How often they
have cried," and "Whether they have not now cried enough to do
the turn." "So that," he observed from Hebrews 11:36, "they have
already 'trial of cruel mockings.'" That night in prayer with the
Hunter's and alone for an hour, he was so engaged for all his
needs and hopes and friends that he "knew not how to leave the
mercy seat" — "O how I delighted to pray and cry to God."

When he and Tattamy set out on their journey of 120 miles
on Monday, they stayed at Craig's Settlement the first night. They
then camped out for three nights and arrived at Shamokin on
Friday, September 13, without incident. His diary for the following
week along the river was illegible because his ink was not serviceable,
and he wrote it with the juice of some berry.

His Journal reports, however, that he was kindly received at
Shamokin but a "heathenish dance and revel" in the house where he
lodged robbed him of the satisfaction he had received from the natives'
cordial greetings. He repeatedly asked them to stop their noises for
the sake of a sick Indian in the house, but their racket continued
unabated through the night. "Alas!" he exclaimed, "how destitute
of natural affections are these poor uncultivated pagans! although
they seem somewhat kind in their own way." Then, borrowing a
phrase from Psalm 74, he added, "Of a truth 'the dark corners of the
earth are full of the habitations of cruelty.'"

The Delaware king Sassoonan had recovered from his sickness of
last spring and "appeared kindly disposed, and willing to be instructed" when Brainerd visited him on Saturday. Receiving more
encouragement than he had expected, David was refreshed. His only
legible diary entry for that week reveals how he yearned for the
conversion of this town "where the devil now reigns in the most
eminent manner." As the natives were dancing and reveling, "as if
possessed by the devil," he prayed: "Lord, set up thy kingdom; for
thine own glory. Glorify thyself, and I shall rejoice. Get honour to
thy blessed name; and this is all I desire. Do with me just what thou
wilt. Blessed be thy name for ever, that thou art God, and that thou
wilt glorify thyself. O that the whole world might glorify thee!
O let these poor people be brought to know thee, and love thee, for
the glory of thy dear ever-blessed name."

David Zeisberger who in love for the Delawares spent his octo-
genarian life, nevertheless agreed with Brainerd: the Eastern Indians
of the eighteenth century were a miserable lot, the vilest of savages,
universally given to lying, cheating and theft. Sexual promiscuity

was rampant, and drunkedness, which Brainerd several times called "their darling vice," aggravated their other vices. The women were not exempt. Rushed by a large group of inebriated squaws, Zeisberger at one time had to bowl them over with his fists and barely escaped their disgusting ambitions toward him.

Zeisberger's biographer Edmund De Schweinitz summed it mildly when he wrote: "The rum-shop of an Indian village was its bane and curse. Drunkedness prevailed to a fearful extent, and manifested itself in outrageous forms. It was a common occurrence to see almost the entire population in a state of wild intoxication, brawling, fighting, and giving full sway to the worst propensities of their untamed nature. At such times the Indians were little better than fiends, and it is not an extravagance to say that their towns became outlets of hell."

Although many of the Indians were so drunk from day to day that Brainerd could not speak to them, he was free from melancholy at Shamokin. He visited Sassoonan again on Sunday afternoon and made contact with an Iroquois. Had he lived longer, his course would most probably have been what he intimated that day — "Towards night, discoursed with one who understood the languages of the Six Nations, as they are usually called; who discovered an inclination to hearken to Christianity, which gave me some hopes that the gospel might hereafter be sent to those nations far remote."

However, the factors blocking peaceful progress among the Pennsylvania Indians were practically insurmountable. The English had taken the calculated risk of alienating the Delawares by courting the friendship and influence of the Iroquois and their lordship over the Delawares. Hence, the Delaware-Shawnese War which flared along the frontiers in 1755-56 had long been considered almost inevitable, but it was preferred to a conflict with the Six Nations allied with the French. The demoralized Delawares had therefore virtually started on their trail which never ended until they reached the forks of the Kansas and Missouri rivers almost a century later. Already they knew they had no abiding places and referred to their houses as mere night lodges.

But Brainerd applied himself to the job at hand as he saw it on Monday, September 16, 1745. It would be his last opportunity before the Shamokin natives began their autumn hunting on Tuesday. More than likely his best success toward night in the one part of the tri-village where they were sober was in that area controlled by Shikellamy. There, "having first obtained the king's cheerful consent," Brainerd and Tattamy rounded up about fifty

Indians and talked to them. They were surprisingly attentive. David's spirits were then again "much refreshed," and he and Tattamy returned to their "poor hard lodgings," rejoicing in hopes that God designed to set up His Kingdom there.

They did not remain at Shamokin, however, but left at Tuesday noon, apparently to hurry to Juniata, where they arrived on Thursday. Here Tattamy left, "being obliged to attend upon some important business elsewhere [perhaps on an errand for the governor], and knowing that he could neither speak or understand the language of these Indians."

On this second visit to the island where he had met the reformer in the spring, Brainerd was terribly disappointed with the Nanticokes who had invited him to return. By this time he had gained a deeper insight into their background, character, and customs, and he devoted considerable linage to their ways. He explained that many of them understood English "considerably well." They had formerly lived in Maryland among or near white people and were generally not "as savage," but they were therefore perhaps even more "very drunken, vicious, and profane" than their more primitive fellows. He also explained how their customs differed from other Indians on the river — "They do not bury their dead in a common form, but let their flesh consume above-ground, in close cribs made for that purpose; and at the end of the year, or sometimes a longer space of time, they take the bones, when the flesh is all consumed, and wash and scrape them, and afterwards bury them with some ceremony."

Like the motley crowd at Shamokin, these Nanticokes at Juniata were preparing for a great sacrifice and dance, probably as the prelude to their hunting season. They were much too busy to listen to the lone white visitor and their fellow pagan whom Brainerd had induced to interpret for him. In fact, as Brainerd said, "They now seemed resolved to retain their pagan notions and persist in their idolatrous practices." His attempts to contact some individuals on Friday were also futile.

"In the evening they met together, near a hundred of them, and danced round a large fire, having prepared ten fat deer for the sacrifice, the fat of whose inwards they burnt in the fire while they were dancing, and sometimes raised the flame to a prodigious height, at the same time yelling and shouting in such a manner, that they might easily have been heard two miles or more. They continued their *sacred dance* all night, or near the matter, after which they ate the *flesh of the sacrifice,* and so retired each one to his lodging."

Alone on the island, "as to any Christian company," Brainerd stated he enjoyed little satisfaction. "Having walked to and fro till body and mind were pained and much oppressed, I at length crept into a little crib made for corn, and there slept on the poles." On Saturday morning he again tried to contact a few individuals, but the situation was hopeless. He quickly learned they had something else to do, he said. "Near noon they gathered together all their *powwows*, or conjurers, and set about half a dozen of them playing their juggling tricks, and acting their frantic distracted postures, in order to find out why they were then so sickly upon the island, numbers of them being at that time disordered with a *fever*, and bloody *flux*.

"In this exercise they were engaged for several hours, making all the wild, ridiculous and distracted motions imaginable; sometimes singing; sometimes howling; sometimes extending their hands to the utmost stretch, spreading all their fingers; and they seemed to push with them, as if they designed to fight something away, or at least keep it off at arm's-end; sometimes stroking their faces with their hands, then spurting water as fine as mist; sometimes sitting flat on the earth, then bowing down their faces to the ground; wringing their sides, as if in pain and anguish, twisting their faces, turning up their eyes, grunting, puffing, etc."

"Their monstrous actions," he said "tended to excite ideas of horror, and seemed to have something in them, as I thought, peculiarly suited to raise the devil, *if he could* be raised by any thing odd, ridiculous, and frightful." As he sat not thirty feet from them, he could observe that some of them were "much more fervent and devout in the business than others." They seemed "to *chant, peep,* and *mutter* with a great degree of warmth and vigour, as if determined to awaken and engage the powers below." As he sat unobserved, he held his Bible in his hand, "resolving," he explained, "if possible, to spoil their sport, and prevent their receiving any answers from the *infernal* world." The Indians carried on for more than three hours with several intervals of rest. He observed with tongue in cheek: they "at length broke up, I apprehended, without receiving any answer at all."

At the time, however, he could feel no humor in his predicament. This, his third mission to the Susquehanna, seemed doomed to certain failure. Although he still persisted in his attempts to speak to them, they soon scattered, he said, and did not give him a chance. Alone without the company of Tattamy, his spirits sank and gave him "the most gloomy turn of mind imaginable," and "the most burdensome and disagreeable Sabbath" of his life. He was again practically stripped of all hope and resolve for their conversion and he said, "I

seemed to have nothing to do on earth, if this failed." Their conversion was his only desire, and nothing less could console him. "A
prospect of the greatest success in the saving conversion of souls
under *gospel-light*," he said, "would have done little or nothing towards
compensating for the loss of my hope in this respect."

He made still further attempts on Monday, but had no success,
and he left them that day, complaining bitterly of the evil effects
of the close proximity of the white man and of his rum, even as
Sassoonan and Shikellamy had been doing for ten years. "The
great difficulty," he wrote in a report to Scotland, "is that the people
who live back in the country nearest them, and the *traders* that go
among them, are generally of the most irreligious and vicious sort."

He took most of four days to ride back to the Forks of Delaware.
He rode slowly because he was ill and dejected, and he had failed in
his most cherished hope for success on the Susquehanna. As he approached Craig's Settlement on Thursday, September 26, he "could
not think that any of God's children made so poor a hand of living
to God as he did." However, comforts and friendly visits at the settlement soon helped to restore him. He was thankful that God had
accounted him faithful and he was encouraged to continue His work.
When he went to his own house for three days on Monday some of
the Forks of Delaware Indians "cheerfully accepted" his invitation
that they accompany or follow him to New Jersey. And when he
arrived at Crossweeksung on Saturday, October 5, his gratitude
overflowed.

"O what a difference is there between these and the Indians I had
lately treated with upon Susquehannah! To be with *those* seemed
like being banished from God, and all his people; to be with *these*
like being admitted into his family, and to the enjoyment of his
divine presence!"

24. A STAFF TO WALK WITH

ON THE SUNDAY after his return from the Susquehanna, Brainerd
preached to his Crossweeksung Indians in the morning, in the afternoon, and at night. His sermons were *I am the door of the sheep*;
the conversion of Paul's and Silas' jailer; and Paul's discourse at
Troas, when Paul, *intending to depart on the morrow*, prolonged his

speech until midnight. Brainerd had nicely fitted his evening text to the occasion for, after only two days with them, he too would again depart on the morrow. However, he was not long preaching for, "being much tired with the labours of the day," he retired early. The Indians, however, continued to pray for nearly two hours more.

In his diary for Monday, October 7, Brainerd explained the brevity of his stay: "Being called by the church and people of East Hampton on Long Island, as a member of a council, to assist and advise in affairs of difficulty in that church, I set out on my journey this morning, before it was well light, and travelled to Elizabeth-town, and there lodged. Enjoyed some comfort on the road, in conversation with Mr. Wm. Tennent, who was sent for on the same business."

If as they rode side by side Tennent related the events of his life, Brainerd must have marvelled about this tall, personable parson of the Freehold church. In 1723, when he was preparing for his ministerial examinations, he had become ill and had fallen into a trance. Everyone considered him dead, until he awoke at his own funeral service three days later. After he was able to speak he declared that he had been in heaven. His trance, he later explained, had been to him as ten or twenty minutes, but "the ravishing sounds of songs and hallelujahs" remained in his mind for three years thereafter. Later he had lost a toe while asleep at night and the excised member had never been found.

Now, after a dozen years at Freehold, William was a highly respected and loved pastor, a sound and sprightly preacher, and a lover of fine horses. The second son of the remarkable Tennent family of Neshaminy and the Log College, he had succeeded his younger brother John as the pastor at Freehold. Although they were quieter than their elder brother Gilbert, both John and William were revivalists of note. John had died in 1732 at the age of twenty-five years after he had served the Freehold congregation a scant seventeen months, but in that short time it was he who had ignited the initial spark of the English awakening in the Middle Colonies. Succeeding him, William brought this revival to its full power among the Scotch Covenanters of Freehold while Gilbert did the same farther north at New Brunswick. A fourth brother was a minister in Delaware until he fell victim to alcoholism.

For the past seven years William had lived comfortably with the widow Noble whom he had married a week after he met her in New York City, but one incident had marred the even tenor of his recent years. In 1742, John Rowland whose ordination had been one of the particular bones of contention in the Synod of Philadelphia, had been impersonated by a rogue who stole the horse of a leading citizen who was on his way to church. Posing as Rowland, the thief had "borrowed" the horse on the ruse of fetching a sermon he had forgotten. The culprit was the notorious Thomas Bell, a Harvard graduate of 1734 who, according to one account, excelled in low art and cunning: "In all the arts of theft, robbery, fraud, deception and defamation, he was so deeply skilled, and so thoroughly practiced that it is believed he never had his equal in this country."

Charged with Bell's crime, Rowland was hailed into court, where Tennent and two other men testified that he had been in Pennsylvania at the time of the crime. Although acquitted, Rowland left New Jersey because of the high degree of feeling against him. Then, at the instigation of Chief Justice Robert Hunter Morris, an Anglican who was unfriendly to New Side Presbyterian preachers in particular, the witnesses were tried for perjury in Supreme Court at Trenton. Amid the great hullabaloo that ensued, Tennent declined to defend himself. Only because three prominent lawyers were engaged from Philadelphia and New York by his brother Gilbert and other friends, was he finally acquitted and spared the humiliation of pillory or standing as a public spectacle on the courthouse steps.

As to the difficulties at the Long Island church since Brainerd had declined its call two years ago and towards which he and Tennent were now traveling, Edwards shed no light, except as it personally affected Brainerd. He said only, "The importance of the business lay with such weight on his mind that he slept but little for several nights successively." Brainerd perhaps knew that he was still a very acceptable choice to the people of East Hampton.

Aaron Burr was also a member of the council and since, as other records disclose, he preached the sermon at the ordination of New Englander David Bostwick at Jamaica, Long Island, on Wednesday, it is likely that Brainerd and the entire ministerial party accompanied Burr to that place before proceeding to East Hampton. There they found that the illness of Nathaniel Huntting and the people's ineffectual attempts to agree upon a new minister had strained and further divided that congregation.

Sprague's *Annals* tells how East Hampton's problem was temporarily solved.

"A majority [had] at length agreed upon a candidate, and they went so far as to convoke an ecclesiastical council for the purpose of ordaining him. But when the council convened, they found so formidable an opposition, that they did not feel justified in proceeding to the ordination. Many of the people complained of their decision, for this among other reasons, — that they could not afford to incur the additional expense of looking for another minister — but to this objection it was answered by Mr. Burr and some other members of the council from New Jersey — that they should be at no additional expense in the matter, as they would themselves undertake to furnish them a minister who should be acceptable."

On his return to Crossweeksung on October 24, Brainerd found his Indians as eager for the Gospel as before, and he remarked: "I have oftentimes thought that they would cheerfully and diligently attend divine worship twenty-four hours together, if they had an opportunity to do so." On the first week-end after his return, as he prepared to ride to a neighboring congregation to help administrate the Lord's Supper, he invited them to go with him, since, he explained, most of his Indians now understood something of the English language. The church was probably McKnight's Cranberry congregation where the Indians had first witnessed the ordinance twelve weeks earlier. There, as he preached on Sunday to a vast assembly of people out of doors who, he said, "appeared generally easy and secure enough," one of several newly-arrived strange Indians, a woman who had never heard him before and who had been persuaded to come by her friends, "much against her will," was seized with distressing concern and soon expressed the desire to travel forty miles to bring her husband, that he might also hear.

After preaching again to another great assembly on Monday afternoon, Brainerd returned to Crossweeksung. There he said, "I know not how," he was enabled to open the Scriptures concerning the wedding feast as related in Matthew 22 to the capacities of his Indians "in a plain, easy, and familiar manner, beyond all that I could have done by the utmost study." The results were sweet and gratifying. "If ever there was among my people an appearance of the New Jerusalem," he said, "'as a bride adorned for her husband,' there was much of it at this time." He reveled in it and was loath to leave at day's end.

In his diary for Tuesday, October 29, he mentioned for the first time the contemplated site for his Indians' new village. He wrote: "About noon, rode and viewed the Indians lands at Cranberry. . . ." The same sentence reveals that he would at times still suddenly sink into his black moods. On that dismal Tuesday after his blessed experiences on Monday, he continued: "Was much dejected, and greatly perplexed in mind; knew not how to see anybody again, my soul was sunk within me." But he also sounded a new note, for he added:

"Oh that God would keep me from giving way to sinful dejection, which may hinder my usefulness."

On the next Sunday, November 3, he baptized six more adults and eight children. The group included a woman of eighty years, the former self-righteous headman, and the man of fifty years — "one of them had been a murderer, and both notorious drunkards, as well as excessively quarrelsome." David had deferred their baptism for many weeks, and still withheld the rite from the chief Forks of Delaware powwow. On Monday a squaw who had formerly attempted to disturb worship services when she was intoxicated was brought under concern for her soul, and Brainerd baptized still another child. It was November 4, probably marking the completion of the third year since his appointment as a missionary, and he took count and ended the first part of his Journal. He had baptized an equal number of adults and children, but today's child had increased the number of the children to twenty-four.

In his remarks to this part of his Journal, Brainerd praised Tattamy who interpreted with accuracy and zeal and "took pains day and night" to repeat and inculcate the truths of the Gospel. Realist that he was, he spoke circumspectly as to the practical effects in the daily behavior of his converts. They "appear" regularly disposed in the affairs of marriage, he observed; "they seem generally divorced from drunkedness, their darling vice"; "a principle of honesty and justice appears in many of them"; "they seem concerned to discharge their old debts, which they have neglected, and perhaps scarcely thought of for years past." Unlike his brother John, David never described how occasionally it was necessary to tie a drunk Indian to a tree until he became sober. In his Appendix Two, however, he explained that their "wandering to and fro," was perhaps their greatest hindrance to progress.

"This has often deprived me of opportunities to discourse to them; and it has thrown them in the way of temptation; either among pagans farther remote, where they have gone to hunt, who have laughed at them for hearkening to Christianity; or among white people more horribly wicked, who have often made them drunk, and then got their commodities — such as skins, baskets, brooms, shovels, and the like, with which they designed to have bought corn, and other necessaries of life, for themselves and families."

Old ways and habits and associates contributed to the constant struggle of his converts against reverting to their former state also in later days. In May 1760, shortly before he is no longer mentioned in government documents, Tattamy is reported to have forgotten to take along some essential articles on an official mission, while "in one of his drunken Fits." There is no evidence, however, that he rejected the faith he professed. His continued services as interpreter at most of the important government councils and his close association with hard-drinking Teedyuscung, the apostate Moravian proselyte Gideon and new "King of the Delawares," apparently provided temptations too strong for old Moses to withstand.

There are other traces, however, that underscore the effectiveness of Brainerd's labor of love and the genuineness of his Indians' conversions. That their sympathies continued for the Englishman is attested by John Brainerd who reported that at least twenty Christian Indians died in battle at Lake George, New York, in the French War of 1757; and, at the height of Pontiac's War in 1763, the following notice, signed by John, appeared in *The Pennsylvania Journal* for September 5.

"Whereas a report has been spreading that the Christian Indians in New Jersey, under my care, were many of them gone back to join the murdering Indians on the frontiers; this is to inform and assure the public that such report is wholly without foundation; that these Indians evidently discover a great abhorrence of the perfidious and inhuman proceedings of their remote Savage brethren, and that there is not one of them missing, or that discover a contrary temper."

Many of the Christian Indians joined the Moravians as the Indian population moved west. Such were the aged Tepiscowahand and his sister who had been present at Brainerd's revival, as they told Charles Beatty in 1767 in Ohio, when they asked Beatty and John Brainerd "to talk to them about religion." Such were also the Moravian elders Samuel Moore and Tobias, both former members of David's congregation, who were wantonly murdered by white men in the methodical slaughter of the entire Moravian Indian congregation of ninety-six men, women and children at Gnadenhutten, Ohio, in March 1782. And, as late as 1834, the *Missionary Herald* reported the conversation of a mission worker with two Christian Delaware sisters who lived among the Shawnees near the Kansas River, six hundred miles west of the Mississippi. Their grandmother, their mother, and their father Jacob Stakit had all been members of David Brainerd's congregation in New Jersey. Their grandmother, they said, had often told them about their beloved Yankee.

"He was a young man, — he was a lovely man; he was a staff to walk with. . . . He slept on a deer-skin or a bear-skin. He ate bear-meat and samp: then we knew he was not proud. He would come to my grandmother and say, 'I am hungry, — make haste!' Then she would take down the kettle, and he would eat. But some of the people did not like him, and said, 'What has this white man come here for? we don't want him here!' and they told him to go off. . . . After a while they found he was an honest man and then they would do any thing he said."

25. IN LABORS ABUNDANT

SINCE MARCH 1, when he went to New England, Brainerd had ridden more than three thousand miles. His average of eighty to a hundred miles a week is better appreciated today in terms of twenty hours in the saddle. On Tuesday, Guy Fawkes Day, and during the next three weeks, his diary discloses that he increased this mileage as he traveled to various places to raise money through collections in the churches to pay "a schoolmaster" for his Indians. On Sunday he occupied Dickinson's pulpit twice. On Monday he sailed to Long Island for a Presbytery meeting at the Dutch Reformed town of Newtown (Queens Borough). There a thief stole his horse. The loss did not seem to upset him and even on Friday, November 15, when the violence of the wind forced him to spend the night in profane and drinking company at the ferry-house, he remained calm and composed, and spent the evening in writing.

He sailed back to New Jersey about ten o'clock on Saturday morning, presumably across the Narrows below New York's Upper Bay and through the Kill van Kull to old Elizabeth Point, and arrived at Elizabethtown near night. Here he apparently held a series of meetings. While riding to the town, he had longings "that God would pour out his Spirit" upon the people of the town "and revive his work among them," and Edwards further remarked that he was "intensely engaged in the service of God" for four days. The results may have disappointed him for he had little freedom in meditation on Thursday as he rode to Tennent's house at Freehold and returned to Crossweeksung.

Back with his Indians on Sunday, November 24, the beginning of the second part of his published Journal, his preaching produced no "boisterous commotions" but "seemed like the gentle but steady showers which effectually water the earth, without violently beating upon the surface." There were several effective impressions among his people, however, and he remarked that they always appeared much more affected with the comfortable truths of God's Word than with the dreadful truths, "the terrors of hell." He warned them to be careful in their behavior, especially among the white people who "waited for their halting, and were ready to draw them into temptations of every kind."

His diary then reveals that he again left his Indians during the first week of December to attend a meeting of the Presbytery at Connecticut Farms. This hamlet which is now the city of Union was settled in 1667 close by Elizabethtown. With Rahway, Westfield and Springfield it was included in Dickinson's large parish. On his return to Crossweeksung, Brainerd spent several days in procuring provisions and in settling his third little house. He did not enjoy the business and was "very much out of his element." (More realistic than Brainerd, who had felt "as if I had been a king," in his first Kaunaumeek cottage, Edwards later described this cabin as "a miserable hut" which the Indians had built.)

Soon, however, David was busily engaged in a more congenial but equally laborious task. His earlier ambitions to write were more than fulfilled, as he indicated in the following diary excerpts which Edwards preserved.

"December 13. Spent the day mainly in labour about my house. In the evening, spent some time in writing; but was very weary, and much outdone with the labour of the day.

"December 14. Rose early, and wrote by candle-light some considerable time; spent most of the day in writing; but was somewhat dejected. In the evening was exercised with a pain in my head."

That he wrote voluminously and that only part of his writings appeared in print is clearly evident. His Appendix Two mentions that the Scottish Society in a letter dated March 2, 1743, reminded him of their "express instructions" that he report fully on the methods used for instructing the Indians, the progress made, the methods presently employed to teach the principles of religion, and, particularly, the difficulties encountered and how he coped with them. The Society also requested a full report on his method of learning the Indian language.

Brainerd fulfilled their requests, with some reservations. He informed the Society that he would appear immodest if he told them all his difficulties and how he coped with them, and he added laconically, "Some of the causes of my difficulties I thought more fit to be concealed than divulged."

More startling is the information that since his ordination, Brainerd had transcribed three separate copies of his Journals. And, alas! Most of the two copies he had repeatedly sent to Scotland had been lost in passage, presumably captured on the high seas by the enemy, the French. With all his other duties, he said, his obligation to write hardly allowed him two free hours a week and robbed him of his sleeping time. He concluded: "This has caused me not a little labour, and so straitened me for time . . . that I have been obliged to write twelve to thirteen hours in a day; till my spirits have been extremely wasted, and my life almost spent, to get these writings accomplished."

Within a month after his death the minutes of the Edinburgh society reported on November 5, 1747: "Mr. David Brainerd sends word that he has materials for a large journal, but the state of his health prevented his being able to methodize and transcribe it." As the society met together on that Guy Fawkes Day they did not know that he had already died. It seems obvious, however, that in that last letter to them David was referring to other materials than the two Journals which had then already been published.*

As for his private diaries, it generally has been considered that Jonathan Edwards destroyed them but, as mentioned earlier, Thomas Brainerd stated that he had 120 pages of David's diary as late as 1865. However, this descendant of David's uncle James also stated that about 1825 the bulk of David's papers were destroyed by John Brainerd's descendants — that when she was a young girl "it was the office" of a relative of the family of Major John Ross (husband of John Brainerd's daughter Mary), to "innocently, but in our view most disastrously . . . aid in consigning the manuscripts of David and John Brainerd, which had long reposed in a garret at Mount Holly, to the flames, about forty years ago. *Hinc illae lacrymae!*"

Late in November David had noted that the influence of the Spirit among his Indians produced no "boisterous commotions." But

---

* An advertisement in the March 16, 1747 *Boston Evening Post* read: "Just published and Sold by Kneeland and Green in Queen Street, and J. Edwards in Cornhil, *Mirabilia Dei inter Indicos,* Or the Rise and Progress of a Remarkable WORK of GRACE amongst a Number of INDIANS in the Provinces of New-Jersey and Pennsylvania. Justly represented in a JOURNAL kept by Order of the Honourable Society, in Scotland, *for promoting Christian Knowledge.* With some general Remarks. By David Brainerd, Minister of the Gospel, and Missionary from the said Society. Published by the Reverend and Worthy *Correspondents* of the said Society. With a Preface by them." Similar copy ("Printed and Sold by Wm. Bradford on Second Street") appeared in *The Pennsylvania Journal* for July 16.

on Sunday, December 15, as he preached on striving to enter in by the narrow door and on the separation of the sheep from the goats, there appeared another "amazing season of grace," and Brainerd remarked: "None can form a just idea of the appearance of our assembly at this time but those who have seen a congregation solemnly awed, and deeply impressed by the special power and influence of divine truths delivered to them in the name of God." He expressed the same idea when he wrote to Eleazar Wheelock: "When I consider the doings of the Lord among the Indians, and then take a view of my journal, I must say 'tis a faint representation I have given of them."

That week he began a Saturday evening "catechetical lecture" based on the Westminster Shorter Catechism. His Indians thereby revealed a doctrinal knowledge that exceeded his expectations. He continued to lecture and to preach and to write, so that he became "much wearied" and "extremely spent" and "could do no more." But he was not satisfied. "I am conscious to myself," he wrote, "that my labours are as great and constant as my nature will bear, and that ordinarily I go to the extent of my strength, so that I do all I can; but the misery is that I do not labour with that *heavenly* temper, that single eye to the *glory* of God, that I long for."

On Sunday he again dealt with the insufficiency of the good life to earn salvation, directing his remarks to several recent arrivals who had lived among Quakers. Among other "errors," he said, they had "imbibed" the Quaker teaching of "the light within," and he concluded: "These persons I found much worse to deal with than those who are wholly under pagan darkness."

On December 22, the Sunday before Christmas, he seems to have thoroughly enjoyed the humor of the conversation of a woman who came to see him. Ludicrous in contrast to his consistent seriousness, it is a reminder that to judge him wholly by his edited diaries is to do injustice to his personality which Edwards so frankly admired as remarkably sociable, pleasant and entertaining, and far from any stiffness, moroseness, or false modesty. He was also aware of his readers as he recorded in his Journal that the woman loved the good people of Scotland and had prayed for them all night. At the same time, the incident reveals something of the distortions against which he constantly had to protect his Indians.

He had dealt personally with the woman for some weeks before she came and told him: "Me try, me try, save myself, last my strength be all gone, could not me stir bit further. Den last, me forced let Jesus Christ alone, send me hell if he please."

"I said, 'But you was not willing to go to hell, was you?'

"She replied, 'Could not me help it. My heart he would wicked for all. Could not me make him good.'

"I asked her, how she got out of this case? She answered still in the same broken language, 'By by my heart be grad desperately.'

"I asked her why her heart was glad? She replied, 'Grad my heart Jesus Christ do what he please with me. Den me tink, grad my heart Jesus Christ send me hell. Did not me care where he put me, me lobe him for all.'

"She could not readily be convinced," concluded Brainerd, "but that she was willing to go to hell if Christ was pleased to send her there."

He spent the next two days in writing with "utmost diligence" — and then it was Christmas. Neither the Quakers nor the New England Puritans observed Christmas, but this year Brainerd took the day into full account. His "word in season," however, was not the Manger of Bethlehem nor the Star in the East.

"The Indians having been used on Christmas days to drink and revel among some of the *white* people in these parts, I thought it proper this day to call them together and discourse to them upon divine things; which I accordingly did from the parable of the barren fig-tree, Luke 13:6-9. A divine influence, I am persuaded, accompanied the word at this season."

A couple of years earlier, at Mount Holly, fifteen miles south of Crossweeksung, a compassionate young Quaker had noted the same deplorable conditions against which Brainerd guarded his Indians. Two years younger than Brainerd, John Woolman had recorded in his journal: "About the time called Christmas, I observed that many people from the country, and dwellers in town, resorting to public houses, spent their time in drinking and vain sports, tending to corrupt one another; on which account I was much troubled."

But at Crossweeksung, never had the Indians, nor their Christian shepherd, experienced a Christmas as they did in 1745.

"The power attending divine truths seemed to have the influence of the *earthquake* rather than of the *whirlwind*. . . . God was in the midst of us of a truth, bowing and melting stubborn hearts! . . . . They seemed to watch and wait for the dropping of God's word, as the thirsty earth for the 'former and latter rain.' Afterwards I discoursed to them on the duty of husbands and wives, from Ephesians 5:22, 23, and have reason to think this was a word in season."

The day after Christmas he encountered a still more remarkable instance of grace. It was a unique instance in all he had ever seen. An old squaw, "much broken" and more than eighty years old, was led by the hand into his hut. She was very childish and utterly incapable of intellectual comprehension. However, having overheard some Christians conversing about the Narrow Way, she had been suddenly struck down and, she thought, she had a dream of a very broad and crooked path and a straight and very narrow path which she followed uphill. Instead of the briers and thorns of Tattamy's vision, she came to a bar or gate. But, just as she was ready to climb over it, she awoke from her dream. Now she was in utmost distress, not knowing how to come to Christ.

Brainerd was instantly on guard. Always watchful for the appearance of "visions, trances and imaginations" among his converts, he carefully questioned the woman and was amazed at her spiritual understanding and deep anguish. When he perceived that her convictions and devotion were "abiding and constant," he concluded: "Whether this exercise be from a divine influence, I shall leave others to judge." He could not account for the transformation of the woman on any rational basis, but only from "the influence of some spirit either good or evil." "The woman, I am sure," he averred, "never heard divine things in the *manner* she now viewed them in. . . ."

As the nights continued long through the slow winter, Brainerd's strength weakened, and signs of dejection again began to appear as his fatigues mounted. On the Friday after Christmas he complained, "My heart seemed barren, though my head and hands were full of labour," and on Saturday, December 28, he unburdened himself in a letter to his brother John.

"I am in one continued, perpetual, and uninterrupted hurry; and Divine Providence throws so much upon me that I do not see it will ever be otherwise. May I 'obtain mercy of God to be faithful to the death!' I cannot say I am weary of my hurry; I only want strength and grace to do more for God than I have ever yet done.

"My dear brother, *The Lord of heaven*, that has carried me through many trials, *bless you* for time, and eternity; and fit you to do service for him in his church below, and to enjoy his blissful presence in his church triumphant. My brother, 'the time is short': oh let us fill it up for God; let us 'count the sufferings of this present time' as nothing, if we can but 'run our race, and finish our course with joy,' Oh, let us strive to live to God. I bless the Lord, I have nothing to do with *earth*, but only to labour honestly in it for God, till I shall 'accomplish as an hireling my day.' I think I do not desire to live one minute for any thing that earth can afford. Oh, that I could live for none but God, till my dying moment!"

He carried on. The next morning, after he had preached on being born again, both his Indians and the white people who were present, "as is usual upon the Sabbath," were deeply affected. Many came to his house during intermission to know "what they should do to be saved," and he remarked: "I was ready to think *then,* that I should never again despair of the conversion of any man or woman living, be they *who* or *what* they would."

There was "a mixture of heaven and hell," he said, "of joy and anguish inexpressible. . . . I could scarcely have *half an hour's* rest from speaking from about half an hour before twelve o'clock (at which time I began public worship) till after *seven* at night."

26. THE NECESSITY OF WATCHFULNESS

During the first fortnight of 1746, David rode for the sake of his health, thought on death, and was troubled with "vapoury disorders." On Friday, January 10, near night, he visited and conversed agreeably with "a serious Baptist minister" and remarked: "I found that I could taste Christ in friends." He continued preaching, and his Indians rewarded him with rapt attention. On Sunday night as he sat by his candle, he ended his daily diary: "They are so frequently and repeatedly roused, that they seem unable at present to lull themselves asleep."

His people had settled near his hut, and "strangers from remote parts" almost continually visited them. "The Indians are now gathered together from all quarters to this place," he explained, "and have built them little cottages, so that more than *twenty* families live within a quarter of a mile from me. A very convenient situation in regard both of public and private instruction."

However, the situation was perhaps too convenient for despite his winter loneliness he was harassed by his converts proximity. "As we are never to 'be weary in well doing,'" he wrote on January 13, "so the obligation seems to be peculiarly strong when the work is so very desirable. And yet I must say, my health is so much impaired, and my spirits so wasted with my labours, and solitary manner of living, (there being no human creature in the house with me), that their repeated and almost incessant application to me for help and direction, are sometimes exceeding burdensome, and so exhaust my spirits, that I become fit for nothing at all, entirely unable to prosecute any business sometimes for days together."

But his sensitive conscience allowed him no relaxation from his constant and difficult task of instructing his Indians — "What contributes much towards this difficulty is, that I am obliged to spend *much* time in communicating a *little* matter to them; there being oftentimes many things necessary to be premised, before I can speak directly to what I principally aim at."

He had reason for his complete and full explanations. Some of his Indians were all too ready to deceive themselves. "They are now generally awakened," he said, "and it is become so disgraceful, as well as terrifying to the conscience, to be destitute of religion, that they are in imminent danger of taking up with any appearances of grace, rather than to live under the fear and disgrace of an unregenerate state."

Though troubled with spirits that were "very low and flat" and a sense of shame and barrenness, he continued methodical indoctrination through catechising. He found this method very profitable, although he had feared it would tend "only to enlighten the head, but not affect the heart." It proved quite otherwise, for another "powerful period of grace" occurred at the close of his catechising session on Sunday night, January 19.

A week earlier he had preached from Isaiah 55:6, *Seek ye the Lord while he may be found,* and this Sunday he had continued with the next verse, *Let the wicked forsake his way . . . for he will abundantly pardon.* While he was "inviting sinners to come to Christ naked and empty, without any goodness of their own to recommend them," conviction and distress overtook an apparently young husband and his wife who "had long been striving after this view of things, supposing that this would be an excellent frame of mind." Brainerd stated that the man used to make a bargain with Christ, to give up his heart to Him that he might have eternal life, but now he saw "something that was unspeakably good and lovely," and it stole away his heart — "it went away of itself after that glory which he then discovered." It then seemed to him "unspeakably better to be saved altogether by the mere free grace of God in Christ," observed David, "than to have any hand in saving himself." His wife, however, continued under burden and concern at this time.

That week Brainerd enjoyed respite and spiritual refreshment as he went to Elizabethtown and met with his employers. He also preached at Connecticut Farms and had another meeting with Dickinson about the Indians' practical affairs. Their former excessive drinking at the white man's tippling houses and among themselves had brought them into such dire straits that their lands were in imminent danger of being confiscated by creditors. However, the Indians told Brainerd, they had been more frequently sued for debt and threatened with imprisonment since he had come than during seven years before.

His conference with Dickinson brought decision. From funds the commissioners had collected for the Indians, Brainerd was able to make a payment of 82 pounds, five shillings ("New Jersey currency at 8 shillings per ounce"). By June they had raised a hundred pounds, an amount equal to William Tennent's annual salary. The Presbyterians in New York contributed 23 pounds, ten shillings, and two pence. The balance came in small amounts from Jamaica on Long Island, Elizabethtown and Elizabeth Farms, Newark, Woodbridge, Morristown, Freehold, Shrewsbury and Shark River, Kingston, Neshaminy and places adjacent in Pennsylvania, Abington and New Providence "by the hand of the Rev. Mr. Treat," and also the Dutch Reformed congregations at Freehold, Middle-town, and in and about New Brunswick. The settlements in the Forks of Delaware and the congregation at Greenwich, New Jersey, are not mentioned.

The moneys collected by the churches was of utmost importance, as Brainerd explained. "If they imprison any *one* that embraced or hearkened to Christianity," he said, "the news of it would quickly spread among the pagans, hundreds of miles distant, who would immediately conclude I had involved them in this difficulty: and thence be filled with prejudice against Christianity, and strengthened in their jealousy, that the whole of my design among them, was to enslave them."

With a parcel of New Jersey, of *Schejachbi,* once more their own, David hoped that God would establish a church for Himself among them, "and hand down true religion to their posterity." It would seem from subsequent developments that the redeemed land included the tract he had visited late in October near Cranberry.

On the last day of January he realized an ambition he had cherished since his first days at Kaunaumeek. His Journal for Friday, January 31, reads: "This day the person I had made choice of and engaged for a *schoolmaster* among the Indians, arrived among us, and was heartily welcomed by my people universally. Whereupon I distributed several dozen of *primers* among the children and young people." On Saturday he recorded: "My schoolmaster entered upon his business among the Indians. He has generally about thirty children and young persons in the evening-school. The number of the latter sort of persons being less than it would be, if they could be more constant at home, and spare time from their necessary employments for an attendance upon these instructions."*

February was a month of much activity, and the schoolmaster's first day brought still another answer to Brainerd's prayers. Toward evening, as he disclosed in his diary, he had written two or three hours on I Corinthians 15:13-16, *But if there be no resurrection of the dead.* He was doubtless preparing for the Easter season, and was so refreshed by the intenseness of his "entertainment" that he could scarcely switch his mind to anything else. However, as recorded in the Journal, he conducted evening catechism, and toward the end of the lesson the old remarkable drunkard, conjurer and murderer suddenly experienced "acute anguish and utmost agony of soul." For seven months he had obstinately cherished the idea that he could do something for his own relief, until some time in January when, as Brainerd quoted him, "I drove him up into 'such a sharp corner,' that he had no way to turn." Now, through the night and into Sunday, the old stubborn powwow "trembled for hours together, and apprehended himself just dropping into hell, without any power to rescue or relieve himself," a fate he considered just right for him. "The devil," he declared, "has been in me since I was born."

Yet it was plain to Brainerd that despite severe self-condemnation, the old man continued to cherish a secret hope of mercy, "though imperceptible to himself." After his initial fears subsided this delusion kept him from genuine despair and, instead of being sad and dejected, "his very countenance appeared pleasant and agreeable."

Then, even as the old man continued to tremble on Sunday, February 2, Brainerd was himself unnerved. In his Journal he omitted all reference to this episode of "some ill-minded persons of the white people," who attacked him in a most scurrilous and vicious manner.

"After public worship, my bodily strength being much spent, my spirits sunk amazingly; and especially on hearing that I was so generally taken to be a *Roman catholic*, sent by the papists to draw the Indians into an insurrection against the English, that some were in fear of me, and others were for having me taken up by authority and punished. Alas, what will not the devil do to bring a slur and

---

* According to his biographers (Gillies, Tyerman, Belden, etc.), Whitefield visited the school in the spring of 1745. This date is obviously incorrect as David did not arrive "near Freehold" until June 9, 1745, and the schoolmaster arrived January 31, 1746.

disgrace on the work of God! Oh, how holy and circumspect had I need to be! Through divine goodness, I have been enabled to 'mind my own business,' in these parts, as well as elsewhere; and to let all men, and all denominations of men, alone, as to their *party notions*; and only preached the plain and necessary truths of *Christianity*, neither inviting to, nor excluding from, *my meeting* any, of any sort or persuasion whatsoever."

In his remarks to the First Part of his Journal, he had disclosed that all was not sweetness and light among the white people at Crossweeksung. As he phrased it: "Many attempts [were] made by some ill-minded persons of the white people to prejudice the Indians against, or fright them from, Christianity. They sometimes told them, the Indians were well enough already; that there was no need to all this noise about Christianity. . . . Sometimes they told them that I was a knave, a deceiver, and the like: that I daily taught them lies . . . and [would] sell them to England for slaves." In his Second Appendix he emphatically stated that these white people used "the most sneaking, unmanly, and false suggestions of things that had no manner of foundation but in their own brains." He could have added more, he said, of another nature, "had not modesty forbidden me to mention what was too obscene."

He never did explain, however, how complex and widespread the prejudice was against himself and his Indians. Those opposing him were not simply a few ill-minded individuals or people of a particular faith. Throughout the colony he and his Indians were under general suspicion for reasons which he could in no way control.

While he and Tattamy had been at the Susquehanna River in September, an ugly riot had occurred in Newark in protest over the arrest of a homesteader named Samuel Baldwin. This man had been jailed for refusing to give bail, pending his trial for cutting trees on land which he claimed as his own. His case was not uncommon.

Many New Jersey land titles were in a state of confusion after 1738 when that province was separated from the governorship of New York. This was especially so because many early homesteaders had bought land directly from the Indians without securing proper titles. Later, as wealthy persons secured legal title to large tracts of land and ignored the prior claims, feeling ran high as one after another settler lost his land. Thus it was on September 19, 1745, when approximately 150 men armed with clubs, axes and crowbars broke into the Newark jail to release Baldwin. Several of the rioters had boasted that they would re-appear with twice their number *and a hundred Indians.*

The threat was considered "ridiculous and impossible." Hardly fifty Indian males lived within thirty miles of Newark. Beyond that radius only two Indian men, Andrew and Peter, lived within fifty miles, "near Cranberry on the Navesink Side of the Raritan." However, it was alleged that in February the one called Andrew had informed "the Committee of the Rioters" that he expected a large number of Indians, perhaps as many as three hundred, would come to live near him, "on some lands he claims as his." Thus, although the threat of a hundred Indians invading Newark seemed remote, suspicion and rumor were rife, and so malicious that the evil effects were evident in Aaron Burr's congregation. And the only sizable body of Indians in New Jersey was the growing community of Brainerd's people at Crossweeksung.

The general state of alarm resulted in petitions to the Legislature, in which the above phrases appear. With obvious agitation Governor Lewis Morris wrote to his House of Representatives: "I send you also an Account of a Notorious Riot, Lately Committed at Newark, if it be not Something worse, If the Indians can be prevailed on to joyn in Attempts of the Kind, we may soon have a war with them in our own bowells, encouraged by the King's Subjects; The threat is of Dangerous Consequence."

Although King George's War was also still in progress, even though Louisbourg had been conquered, the charge that Brainerd had been sent "to draw the Indians into an insurrection," would seem to have been made without justification. Twice the number of the September rioters had again invaded Newark in January, less than a month ago, but not one Indian had accompanied them as they had threatened would be the case. It would thus rather seem that the white people should have been reassured that Brainerd's Indians were peaceable and well-behaved and that his presence among them guaranteed their good behavior, rather than the contrary.

The damaging fact was that David's opposers had capitalized on another inflammatory report which just at that time was the topic of buzzing conversation in every private and public house. A month earlier, on January 8, it had been confirmed by seapost and publically announced that a rebellion had broken out in Scotland against the King's government. The rebellion was the last significant effort of the Jacobites, the supporters of James Edward Stuart (the old Pretender), the son of James II who had been deposed in favor of Protestant William III during the Bloodless or Glorious Revolution of 1688. In September 1745 the Old Pretender's son, brave and charming Charles Edward (the Young Pretender), better known in ballad and song as "Bonnie Prince Charles," had gathered a Highland force to aid his exiled father to regain his throne. He had invaded England as far as Derby, and had thereby caused a near panic in London. The drive was unsuccessful, however, and after the Jacobite troops were defeated on April 16, 1746, young Charles escaped to France, later to roam about Europe as an aimless, unregarded drunkard.

Brainerd's spirits were "much sunk" and grieved over the devilish charges that he was working, as he stated it, "in the *Pretender's* interest." In the evening of that dismaying day he took refuge with his people in the words of Psalm 45: *God is a present help in time of trouble* — "although the wicked world should slander and persecute me, or even condemn and execute me as a traitor to my king and country." What hurt him most was the realization of the total lack of appreciation regarding the transformation of the former shiftless Indians on the part of the white people and their repudiation of his Christian mission. He was in an "extremely weak state" that week, and the affair also caused him to examine his own past conduct.

"This put me upon searching whether I had ever dropped any thing inadvertently, which might give *occasion* to any to suspect that I was stirring up the Indians against the English; and could think of nothing, unless it was my attempting sometimes to vindicate the rights of the Indians, and complaining of the horrid practice of making the Indians drunk, and then cheating them out of their lands and other properties; And once, I remembered, I had done this with too much warmth of spirit, which much distressed me; thinking that it might possibly prejudice them against this work of grace, to their everlasting destruction. God, I believe, did me good by this trial, which served to humble me, and show me the necessity of watchfulness, and of being 'wise as a serpent,' as well as 'harmless as a dove.'"

Prejudice knows no bounds. In Appendix Two Brainerd explained: "What they pretended gave them reason for this opinion, was, that they understood I had a commission from Scotland. Whereupon they could with great assurance say, 'All Scotland is turned to the *Pretender,* and this is but a popish plot to make a party for him here." In England, John Wesley disclosed in his journal for November 1745 that he too found it necessary to deny the same malicious rumor: "that Mr. Wesley was now with the Young Pretender, near Edinburgh."

A degree of anxiety about the affair remained with Brainerd, but Sunday, February 9, was apparently a normal day as he baptized a child and two adults. Several who had been "remarkably stupid and careless" were awakened, and in the evening "one who had been a vile drunkard" appeared to be in a great anguish until near midnight. It was probably the ancient conjurer, for later that week he finally experienced a genuine "lively soul-refreshing view of the excellency of Christ and the way of salvation by him." And the troubled young mother, the wife of the man whose heart "went away of itself," was also brought to the assurance of her salvation in Jesus Christ.

27. NOT FROM ANY GROSS IMAGINARY NOTIONS

ALTHOUGH FOUR MONTHS HAD PASSED since his last visit to the Forks of Delaware, Brainerd had not forgotten its obdurate natives, and on Monday, February 10, he again visited them. He made his way "under great weakness and some pain," and arrived at his Forks house on Friday.

He had chosen "half a dozen of the most serious and knowing" Crossweeksung converts to accompany him as evangelists. Beside the advantage of having these new Christians speak in their own language (David never mastered the Delaware speech although he could understand most of it), their very presence piqued the profane Indians, while others who would not otherwise have stopped to listen, now had face-saving reason to appear interested. He noted: "Some of them who had, in times past, been extremely adverse to Christianity, now behaved soberly, [although] others laughed and mocked. However, the word of God fell with such weight and power, that sundry seemed to be stunned, and expressed a willingness to 'hear me again of these matters.'"

On Sunday he prayed with and addressed the white people of Hunter's Settlement while his helpers worked among the Indians, and he remarked: "Enjoyed more resolution and courage for God, and more refreshment of spirit, than I have been favoured with for many weeks past." On Monday when he preached about Philip and the unclean spirits in Samaria, several of the Indians were awakened, and the Crossweeksung men "continued with them day and night . . . and sometimes prayed and sung psalms among them." This indirect approach seemed more effective than their direct attempts to instruct them.

On Tuesday he preached to his Scotch-Irish friends at Craig's Settlement, but on Thursday and Friday he addressed complete strangers. These were High and Low Dutch people whom, he stated, "had seldom heard the gospel preached, and were, some of them at least, very ignorant."

Some of these "Dutch" people had come eight or ten miles to hear him. They were probably recent German immigrants who were then settling in the Forks of Delaware. Mennonites and Reformed groups had built the pretty village called the German Town, north of Philadelphia, already before the turn of the century. They were the early German arrivals and were, for the most part, well-organized artisans. After 1700, however, thousands of Reformed and Lutheran peasant folk arrived, the High Dutch from the upper provinces of Germany and the Low Dutch from the Palatinate and the Lower Rhine Valley provinces. A great many of them were practically destitute. Many were indentured servants (as were many English and Scotch-Irish), and hundreds of their families had been fragmented through death, victims of the sickening conditions aboard the small ships on which often a third of the passengers died during the months-long passage across the Atlantic. Christopher Sauer, the Germantown newspaper and book publisher who printed the German Bible in 1743, estimated that in a single year two thousand of his countrymen had died on their way to America.

After Zinzendorf's ecumenical plan to unite all the German colonists had failed, the Lutherans' organizing genius, Henry Melchoir Muhlenberg (who married Conrad Weiser's daughter Anna Maria), had arrived in 1742 and had made some progress, but the Swiss leader of the Reformed people, Michael Schlatter, would not arrive under the auspices of the Reformed Church in the Netherlands until August, a half-year after Brainerd's present visit to the Forks. And although a Reformed congregation had been established in Germantown under John Philip Boehm already in 1719 and the Dutch Reformed Church of New York strove to serve as their spiritual mother, these German colonists had little spiritual leadership for many years. Schlatter reported as late as 1751 that only six pastors served the 30,000 Reformed in all of Pennsylvania. In the meantime, numerous sects, served by Sauer's printing presses, thrived and created much disharmony and confusion. Even Sauer's wife left him and her son to live at Beissel's Ephrata Cloisters for fourteen years.

Brainerd's heart went out to these people, particularly to the High Dutch to whom he first preached on Thursday. He wrote: "I could not but be affected with their circumstances; they being as 'sheep not having a shepherd,' and some of them appearing under some degree of soul-trouble, standing in peculiar need of the assistance of an *experienced* spiritual guide."

"They gave wonderful attention, and some of them were much affected under the word, and afterwards said, (as I was informed), that they never had been so much enlightened about the way of salvation in their whole lives before. They requested me to tarry with them, or come again and preach to them. And it grieved me that I could not comply with their request."*

Although his physical strength was "much wasted" that week, David stated that his spirits were "much supported" and he was especially gladdened with the interest and awakening of some of the Indians who now seemed "much cured" of their prejudices and former jealousies against Christianity. "God has been very generous to me this week," he wrote in his personal diary. The efforts of his six Crossweeksung evangelists had proven very effective, and of no little help was the ancient conjurer who was one of them!

"His zeal for the cause of God was pleasing to me," Brainerd wrote. "There being an old Indian at the place where I preached, who threatened to *bewitch* me and my religious people who accompanied me there, *this* man presently challenged him to do his worst, telling him that himself had been as great a *conjurer* as he, and that notwithstanding, as soon as he felt that word in his heart which these people loved, (meaning the word of God), his power of conjuring immediately left him. 'And so it would you,' said he, 'if you did but once feel it in your heart; and you have no power to hurt them, nor so much as to touch one of them.' So that I may conclude my account of him by observing, (in allusion to what was said of St. Paul), that he now zealously defends and practically 'preaches, the faith which he once destroyed,' or at least was instrumental of

---

* After two hundred years, in 1961, the descendants of Lutheran and Reformed Germans in the Evangelical and Reformed Church and Brainerd's Christian Congregationalists merged into the United Church of Christ.

obstructing. *May God have the glory of the amazing change he has wrought in him!"*

On February 23, his second Sunday at the Forks, David again urged the Forks Indians to move to Crossweeksung where they could hear the Gospel and be "free from the scoffs and temptations of the opposing pagans." Some who had been "kindly disposed" toward him were glad that he had returned to them but, he stated, "They had been so much attacked . . . by some of the opposing Pagans, that they were almost ashamed or afraid to manifest their friendship." Some of these now promised to go to Crossweeksung. He left them on Monday, but several of his evangelists remained to nurse one of their number who had become dangerously ill.

Brainerd did not return directly to Crossweeksung but spent "the whole week till Saturday on his journey" and "preached on the way every day except one." He may have re-visited Hopewell, Amwell and Maidenhead, and other churches also. But, does the vague editorial note that he preached every day except one conceal Brainerd's visit to his Moravian neighbors? In his *Narratives* the Moravian historian John Gottlieb Ernestus Heckewelder (1743-1823) stated that David at one time visited Bethlehem and the Moravian Indian town of Gnadehutten.

Heckewelder wrote: "About this time the Brethren also paid a visit to the Rev'd David Brainerd, missionary to the Indians in New Jersey, and rejoiced at the success with which that faithful servant of God had been blessed in preaching the gospel to the Indians; and some time after this, that worthy man, accompanied by some of his converts, visited both Bethlehem and Gnadenhutten, much to his satisfaction."

Brainerd's only convenient opportunity to make a return visit to the Moravians after his success at Crossweeksung and accompanied by several of his converts, would have been on this last journey from the Forks of Delaware. However, it is evident that Heckewelder confused David with his brother John. His statement that David visited Gnadenhutten on the Lehigh River three miles below Mauch Chunk and some forty-five miles west of Hunter's Settlement is certainly in error, for Gnadenhutten was not established until July of that year 1746. It is more likely, therefore, that Heckewelder was recalling John Brainerd's visit there in 1749 when four hundred Indians lived in the village.

If, however, David did visit the Moravians at their headquarters in Bethlehem before leaving the Forks of Delaware, how would he have reacted to the Brethren? There is no doubt that he would have loved them for their compassion for the Indian which matched his own in zeal and devotion. The *Unitas Fratrum,* the spiritual descendants of the Pre-Reformation martyr, John Huss of Bohemia, were even then spearheading the modern missionary advance throughout the world — in North America, in Africa, in Surinam, among the slaves of the West Indies where 160 Moravian missionaries died in fifty years, and in the North Atlantic. In 1749 the citizens of Philadelphia were amazed to see a Moravian missionary ship carrying a complete pre-fabricated house for erection in Greenland.

However, as a Congregationalist and New Side Presbyterian, David would also have some rather definite reservations about the Brethren of his day, a reservation guardedly expressed by John Brainerd on October 16, 1749, when on one of his visits to them he said, "I could not but fear they worshipped the human nature of Christ." Whereas the Calvinistic Congregationalists and Presbyterians had been swept into activistic revivalism, the Brethren were misled to an extravagant emphasis on the physical aspects of Christ and His suffering, and of mental visions or apparitions suggestive of His personal, physical appearance to particular individuals. Their deep piety and quiet faith and their lively sense of Christ's presence which had warmly influenced John and Charles Wesley in Georgia ten years earlier and had also initially attracted George Whitefield, had degenerated into sentimentalism, until their deviations were corrected largely through the leadership of Bishop Spangenberg. But especially from 1745 to 1750 which they called their "Time of Sifting," their extreme emphasis led to Whitefield's and Gilbert Tennent's disapproval of the Bethlehem Brethren. It also forced the revivalists to re-examine and amend their own enthusiasms.

Concerning "strong impressions on the imagination," Edwards wrote that David was "quick to discern when anything of that nature arose, though in its first buddings and appearing under the fairest and most plausible disguises." Brainerd had witnessed and had been deceived by "false appearances and counterfeits of religion," and he now deplored all extravagant claims, and, in the light of the Moravian subjectivism at this time, one of his reiterated warnings becomes less puzzling. That is to say, when John Brainerd later remarked about the Moravians that "the spring and foundations of their love to the *Saviour* was because He suffered and died for sinners, *and them in particular,*" John was but repeating one of David's constant concerns, literally to his dying day, as Edwards took pains to emphasize.

Brainerd's theology of evangelization was, in a manner of speaking, also more objective than that of the Moravians. His was the literal command, the Great Commission: *Go ye into all the world,* and, *compel them to come in that my house may be filled.* The Moravian zeal has always been expressed in the words of Isaiah's prophecy: *to win for the Lamb that was slain, the reward of his sufferings.* One emphasized the glory of the Father; the other the rewards due the Son for His sufferings — *He shall see his seed.* Yet both sought both. The last words of Brainerd's diary, "the last words which are written in it either by his own hand, or by any other from his mouth," said Edwards, were these: "O that his kingdom might come in the world; that they might all love and glorify him, for what he is in himself; and that the blessed Redeemer might see the travail of his soul, and be satisfied! Oh, come Lord Jesus, come quickly! Amen."

Wherever Brainerd may have been during the week after he left the Forks of Delaware, he was gratified to return to his own congregation at Crossweeksung. "I know of no assembly of Christians," he wrote, "where there seems to be so much of the presence of God, where brotherly love so much prevails, and where I should take so much delight in the public worship of God, in the general, as in my *own congregation.*" It would seem that in his delight he disclosed an intriguing commonplace, the type of frivolous remark he seemed so scrupulously to avoid — that his people lived in a compact group and were therefore "easily and quickly called together with only the sound of a conkshell." He added, parenthetically, "a shell like that of a periwinkle." One feels he would have liked to add that it was very similar to the tropical shells which graced the fashionable New England parlors of his day and the same he had seen Metocsin blow for John Sergeant at Stockbridge.

On March 9, his second Sunday after his return, he explained the story of listening Mary and her busy sister Martha. His people were so moved during his first prayer ("in the Indian language as usual"), that he dispensed with catechising in the afternoon and made "further improvement" of his message. As a result there was more agitation among them than had occurred for many weeks. Then, while they were singing at his house after the service, a young woman became ecstatic. She was the young mother who had found peace the night before he had left for the Forks of Delaware. Now she cried incessantly, "sometimes in English, and sometimes in Indian," that Christ might come and that she might be allowed to die. Her main desire was to die immediately, and her "grand argument" was that if she lived she should sin. And, although her husband was then critically ill, she avowed she could part with him and with their infant child:

"God will take care of it."   She continued in this manner for more than two hours before she was able to get to her house.

Brainerd considered her case a genuine manifestation of initial conviction of sin.   It is significant that he then especially emphasized the reason for her ecstasy.   It had arisen, he seems to imply strongly, from some other cause than such apparitions which the Moravians experienced.   Her ecstasy, he said, "appeared to spring from a true spiritual discovery of the glory, ravishing beauty, and excellency of Christ . . . not from any gross imaginary notions of his human nature, such as that of seeing him in such a posture, as hanging on the cross, as bleeding and dying, as gently smiling, and the like; which delusions some have been carried away with."

He also described the young mother's elation as "truly a joy in the Holy Ghost," in distinction from the "bodily agonies, convulsions, frightful screamings, swoonings, and the like" which he abhorred when such phenomena had swept Connecticut and against which he jealously guarded his Indians.   All in all, he seems to say, she had a *pure* apprehension of the Glorious Divine Being.   Her experience had duplicated his own in the Haddam grove which he had still to describe in his introduction to his diaries.   When he did so, he emphasized that he also had not imagined himself as transported "somewhere in the third heavens," nor had he had a vision of Christ or "of any one person in the Trinity, either the Father, the Son, or the Holy Spirit."

He baptized the woman on the following Sunday and, he stated, she lived thereafter as a devout and humble Christian, exemplary in life and in conversation.   On the evening of her baptismal day the Indians thronged into his house, "insatiable in their thirsting after Christian knowledge," and he was again near exhaustion from his constant ministering to them.

28. BETHEL — THE HOUSE OF GOD

BRAINERD WAS VERY ILL and despaired of his future usefulness during the week of March 17, but was "somewhat relieved" by medicines prescribed by his physician, perhaps pious Dr. LeCount, a member of Tennent's church.   He may have gone to Freehold to see this doctor, for when the ailing Indian evangelist returned from the

Forks of Delaware on Wednesday, David was absent and the school-master therefore led the congregation in thanksgiving. But the fact that he was away is of greater interest when viewed in the light of the deposition which the New Jersey Provincial Council received a short time later from one James Blain. Dated April 9, 1746, the reference which this document makes, to "about three weeks" prior to that date, coincides very closely with Brainerd's absence from Crossweeksung.

Was David also at Cranberry at the time? Was it Tattamy who wore the blue Laced Coat?

"April 9th, 1746. The Council received information that tho' for Six years past, no Indian men had lived near Cranberry, but Andrew & Peter, and that only two more had lived for many years before that, who both, for misdemeanors by them Committed, re-moved thence to Crosswicks, yet, within a few weeks before that infor-mation, there were come *forty fighting men of Indians* to Live there; that, about three weeks before that Information, one Indian came there who had a blue Laced Coat on; which, it was Said, he had got, as a present from the Governor of Canada, and he Lodged on the Informant's house one Night; and Some of the other Indians told the Informant that he was a King of some Indians on Delaware, and that he was come to View that place, and was come to settle there with his Indians, and they expected they would be about Three Hundred Indians there, in all, that the Neighbours there about were extremely Alarmed, at this Number of Indians Coming to Settle there, where its Esteemed impossible for such a Number to live, without Stealing or killing their Neighbours Creatures.

"That the Cause pretended, for Such a Number of Indians coming to Live there, is, that they are to be taught the Christian Religion, by one *Mr. Braniard*, and for that purpose they are to build a Town, a Church, and a School house, upon the Land there of one John Falconar, of London, Merchant. . . ."

"Whatever truth there may be in the pretense for those Indians gathered together, in that place, near the very Center of the Province," the lengthy document continued, it was plain that "the said Mr. Braniard" had made no application or given any notice of such intent. What seemed very significant to Blain was the infor-mation that the Andrew mentioned was "the head of them, and pre-tends to give those Indians the Land they are to Live upon," and that it was this same Andrew with whom a Committee of the Newark Rioters had negotiated prior to their raid on the jail in September

1745, at which time they had threatened to return with the assistance of a hundred Indians. And so "its Submitted how probable it Seems that this gathering of those Indians there may be in Consequence of what has been Concerted between the said Andrew and said Committee. . . ."

Up till now Brainerd had not mentioned definite plans for the removal of his Indians to Cranberry. But as of Sunday, March 23, he wrote that strange Indians "still continued to arrive." At least some of these newcomers, it may be supposed, had been urged to settle at the new Indian town which he was planning. The deposition of Blain, though ineffective, emphasizes how the arrival of these strange Indians to the region aroused the suspicions of the white people, especially during that spring of 1746 when provisions were finally completed to send five hundred New Jersey militia to the French-Canadian border.*

With fifteen strangers present that Sunday in the house where the Indians usually worshipped, Brainerd exhorted his people from Hosea 13:9 — *O Israel, thou hast destroyed thyself; but in me is thy help.* Although it is his only recorded sermon from the prophet of love, it may have been an exception to the "harangues of terror" which he eschewed. The very idea embodied in his text was probably most repugnant, especially to the profane visitors. Smoldering in their Delaware hearts was their undying and mounting hope of redemption from their odious status as "women" under Iroquois rule. Perhaps the prospect of Brainerd's new village and the even larger establishment which the Moravians were concurrently planning at Gnadenhutten on the Lehigh River was even then causing the Delaware fires of hope to mount.

Brainerd soon discovered that his message that day failed to "affect" his Christian Indians and left the strangers unimpressed,

---

* Again, Brainerd made no references in his Journal to the Newark riots or to Blain's complaint. But that he was aware of these matters is evident from his Appendix Two where he stated: "And some, I am informed actually went to the *civil* authority, with complaints against me, but only laboured under the unhappiness, that when they came, they had nothing to complain of, and could give no colour of reason why they attempted any such thing, or desired the civil authority to take cognizance of me, having not a word to allege against my *preaching* or *practice,* only they *surmised* that because the Indians appeared so very *loving* and *orderly,* they had a design of imposing upon people by that means, and so of getting a better advantage to cut their throats. And *what temper* they would have had the Indians appear with, in order to have given *no occasion,* nor left any room for such a suspicion, I cannot tell . . . ."

even though he had previously directed some of his "serious persons" to disperse themselves throughout the compound "so that wherever the strangers went, they met with some instructive discourse and warm addresses respecting their salvation." Near sunset he was still so "uncommonly concerned" that he resorted to "private discourse," until finally, in one of the houses, some of the strangers became "awakened" and "seemed at once to put off their savage roughness and pagan manners, and became sociable, orderly, and humane in their carriage." Their cries of lamentation or joy attracted the congregation who gathered immediately, and Brainerd preached to them: *The Son of man is come to seek and to save that which was lost.*

"Many tears and heart-affecting sobs" continued to be manifest at various meetings, Brainerd had observed shortly after his return from the Forks of Delaware. "God has made these things *common* with us," he said. However, he was not deceived by the mere appearance of religiosity, for he realistically appraised this phenomena and he assured his readers: "I am far from thinking that every appearance, and particular instance of affection, that has been among us, has been truly genuine, and *purely* from a divine influence. I am sensible of the contrary; and doubt not but that there has been some *corrupt mixture*, some chaff as well as wheat; especially since religious concern appeared so common and prevalent here."

With his Indians conveniently located in the Crossweeksung colony, he was able to take a census on Monday and counted 130 persons, old and young, plus perhaps fifteen or twenty who were absent. The day of that count, March 24, was the last day of the legal Old Style calendar, and the Indians excluded from the census were those who had left early in the morning to clear their lands for spring planting and settlement at Cranberry, "above 15 miles distant," and just over the line in Presbyterian East Jersey. Their Crossweeksung land, blandly stated the former Connecticut farmer, "was of little or no value for that purpose." Just before their departure and after he had stressed the importance of their being "laborious, diligent and vigorous," and not "slothful in business" as they had been in their pagan state, ("the season of planting being now near"), he had concluded their devotions by explaining and singing to them the words of Psalm 127, "common metre, Dr. Watts' version":

> If God to build the house deny
> The builders work in vain;
> And towns, without his wakeful eye,
> An useless watch maintain.

Before the morning beams arise,
Your painful work renew,
And 'till the stars ascend the skies
Your tiresome toil pursue;

Short be your sleep, and coarse your fare,
In vain, till God has blessed;
But if his smiles attend your care,
You shall have food and rest.

His hour of prayer after he had dismissed them had been the "dearest hour" he had enjoyed for many days, if not weeks. "After the Indians were gone to their work, to clear their lands," he wrote in his diary, "I got alone, and poured out my soul to God, that he would smile on these feeble beginnings, and that he would settle an Indian town, that might be a *mountain of holiness.*"

The next day his schoolmaster became very ill and he was forced to spend most of the week caring for him. Edwards wrote that in Brainerd's own weak state the task was an almost crushing load, "he being obliged constantly to wait on him, from day to day, and to lie on the floor at night," and his spirits and strength sunk under the burden.

During that week, however, he continued his private visits to certain individuals and stated that he found "particular and close dealing" to be often "very successful." After he catechised as usual on the Saturday evening before Easter he said the divine truths distilled upon his hearers "as the refreshing showers upon the new mown grass." On Easter Sunday, March 30, he probably chose the Easter theme from the first part of his scripture reading, Matthew 25:31-40, *When the Son of man shall come in his glory,* and as a concrete application and in direct reference to their sick schoolmaster he may have dwelt more weightily on the last verse: *Inasmuch as ye have done it unto one of the least of these my brethren, ye have done it unto me.*

Early on Easter Monday he again impressed upon the Cranberry workers the necessity of industrious labor, before he sent them to the site of their new village. Then as the schoolmaster continued ill and other necessary business occupied his time, Brainerd felt diverted from and fruitless in spiritual affairs — "my days pass away as chaff! . . . Oh that I were a spirit: that I might be active for God!" — and, "God deliver me from clogs, fetters, and a *body of death*, that impede my service for him." The next day he complained bitterly of the corruption of his heart.

Another week passed. At public worship on the first Sunday in April an adult male came under deep concern for his soul, and that afternoon Brainerd "opened" to his people the discipline of Christ in His Church, and how offenders were to be dealt with. The religious people were especially impressed when they heard that the offender, "continuing obstinate," must finally be considered and treated "as a heathen man." He noted: "Of this they seemed to have the most awful apprehensions; a state of heathenism, out of which they were so lately brought, appearing very dreadful to them." In his regular Monday evening meetings he also began to instruct them in the Lord's Supper and "the qualifications and preparations necessary to the right participation of that ordinance."

His Journal does not indicate that he left Crossweeksung on Tuesday and was gone for almost two weeks. He attended a meeting of the Presbytery in Elizabethtown, and on Sunday he preached to Dutch and English worshippers on Staten Island. The diversion raised his spirits considerably, for on Monday, back in Elizabethtown, he noted: "Oh, how free, how comfortable, cheerful, and yet solemn, do I feel when I am in a good measure freed from those damps and melancholy glooms, that I often labour under!" Although he was again under his "daily affliction and heavy load" on Tuesday, the "gloom and damps" lifted again before his return to Crossweeksung, and he was "animated" in his work.

On his twenty-eighth birthday, Sunday, April 20, he belatedly expounded the Easter story from Luke 24, *On the first day of the week, at early dawn, they came to the tomb.* He was himself free from "gloomy discouragement," according to his diary, and whimsically referring to Gideon and perhaps the drought of the past year, he wrote, "This was a sweet and blessed season, like many others that my poor people have been favoured with in months past. God has caused *this little fleece* to be repeatedly wet with the blessed *dew* of his divine grace, while all the earth around has been comparatively dry."

After another week it would be eight months since the first glorious baptismal day in August, and Sunday, April 27, would be the day for his Indians' first observance of the Lord's Supper. He had designated the preceding Friday, "having taken advice of some of the reverend *correspondents* in this solemn affair," as a day of fasting and prayer to renew their dedication "to God the Father, Son, and Holy Ghost." Recently there had been some "withdrawment" of God's manifest Spirit, he said, and also a "rising appearance of carelessness, and vanity, and vice" among his Indians. He also used the occasion for special prayer concerning the peaceable settlement of their Cranberry lands.

On Saturday he again instructed them, prayed with a dying child, baptized the man who had earlier in the month shown concern and also another adult, and closed the week with their regular Saturday evening catechism. On Sunday morning they had fellowship with Christ in the mystery of His Supper. Brainerd administered the ordinance to twenty-three of his Indians, "the number of the men and women being nearly equal." About five or six others who could have communed with them were away at the Forks of Delaware. Those who did attend, stated David, did so with great solemnity and with a most desirable tenderness and lively affection — "as if Christ had been really crucified before them . . . as if the Lord Jesus Christ himself had been present, and had personally spoken to them."

His concluding sermon on Monday was *If ye love me, keep my commandments,* and he exclaimed: "O, how free, how engaged and affectionate did *these* appear in the service of God! they seemed willing to have their 'ears bored to the door-posts of God's house,' and to be his servants forever." He then told them that they should renewedly enter into covenant before God, and "that they should watch over themselves and one another, lest they should dishonour the name of Christ by falling into sinful and unbecoming practices." He especially warned them again to watch against the sin of drunkedness, "the sin that most easily besets them." They "cheerfully complied with the proposal," he said, "and explicitly joined in that covenant." He also baptized six children that blessed day.

He left for another Presbytery meeting in Elizabethtown on Tuesday, and when he returned on Saturday, May 3, he joined his Indians not at Crossweeksung, but at Cranberry, "whither they are now removed, and where I hope God will settle them as a Christian congregation." He was a bit upset, however, because he now again had no house of his own and was therefore "obliged to board with an English family at some distance from them." The locale of their settlement which his brother John later called Bethel, *the House of God,* was a pleasant, level country of light sandy soil, between one and two miles northeast of Cranberry, at the head of Wigwam Brook. The stream was fed by two or three good springs, and a few miles toward Freehold was a medicinal spring which the Indians frequented. Close by Cranberry was a small lake.*

---

* On October 20, 1905, the *New York Times* reported: "The ladies of Cranbury, N. J., today, named the pond in their village Brainerd Lake, after David Brainerd, a missionary to the Indians in the dim distant past."

Since the time the Indians had begun to work their Cranberry land they had been the object of malicious rumors and villification. Their peaceable settlement had therefore been one of Brainerd's chief concerns during their day of prayer and fasting prior to the Lord's Supper — "that they might be a commodious congregation for the worship of God; and that God would blast and defeat all the attempts that were, or might be, made against that pious design." He summarized the situation in a footnote: "There being at this time a terrible clamour raised against the Indians in various places in the country, and insinuations as though I was training them up to cut people's throats. Numbers wished to have them banished out of these parts, and some giving out great words, in order to fright and deter them from settling upon the best and most convenient tract of their own lands; threatening to molest and trouble them in the law; pretending a claim to these lands themselves, although never purchased of the Indians."

It is plainly evident, however, that Brainerd never ascribed all villainy to the white man and only virtue to the Indian, and as far as the Indians' prospects were concerned, he surely was not blinded. He did not imagine that simply to civilize them would insure their eternal or even their temporal salvation, although, on both counts, he would certainly and capably challenge the view that "he scarcely saw that to Anglicize the Indians was all the more to jeopardize their existence."*

His realistic appraisal of his Indians' plight is well stated in the following paragraphs from his Appendix Two. His "dear ignorant people" whom he loved were not a noble race. Nor had they known the idealized life of the forest and stream evoked by later writers. Anything done toward civilizing them was better than allowing them to die away in their demoralized paganism.

"The Indians" he wrote "are a very poor and indigent people, and so destitute of the comforts of life, at some seasons of the year especially, that it is impossible for a person who has any pity to them, and concern for Christian interest, to live among them without considerable expense, especially in time of sickness. . . . And while they retain their pagan tempers, they discover little gratitude, amidst all the kindnesses they receive. If they make any presents, they expect double satisfaction. And Christianity itself does not at once cure them of these ungrateful tempers.

* Roland H. Bainton: *Yale and the Ministry*. N. Y. 1957, Charles Scribner's Sons, page 28.

"They are in general unspeakably indolent and slothful. They have been bred up in idleness, and know little about cultivating land, or indeed of engaging vigorously in any other business. . . . They have little or no ambition or resolution. Not one in a thousand of them has the spirit of a man. And it is next to impossible to make them sensible of the duty and importance of their being active, diligent, and industrious in the management of their worldly business; and to excite in them any spirit of promptitude of that nature. . . . It is to be hoped, that time will make a yet greater alteration upon them for the better."

The first wonderful event at Bethel occurred on Friday, May 9. It was the baptism of the old conjurer from the Forks of Delaware. Almost two years had passed since Brainerd had challenged the powwows of the Forks to do their worst — to bewitch and poison him if they could, "that God might be glorified." During those many months he had endured great discouragement and despondency. But now, ten months after the great visit of the Spirit at Crossweeksung, even this ancient powwow had confessed his faith in Jesus Christ. He was baptized under the spring sky, "in the open wilderness: the Indians having as yet no house for public worship in this place, nor scarcely any shelter for themselves." "In all respects," stated David, "so far as I am capable to judge, he bears the marks and character of one 'created anew in Christ Jesus to good works.'"

That week-end, according to his personal diary, David assisted Charles McKnight in the serving of the Lord's Supper at nearby "Allens-town." On Saturday afternoon he was displeased with his exposition of Titus 2:4, *Who gave himself for us* — that he had treated so excellent a subject in so defective a manner. He decided: "If my discourse had met with the utmost applause from all the world, (as I accidentally heard it applauded by some persons of judgment), it would not have given me any satisfaction."

On Sunday, only after fervent prayer, was he able to feel equal to the task of leading the people at this place — "God helped me to wrestle for his presence in prayer. . . ." As soon as he got under way about Moses and Elijah who appeared in glory to speak to Christ about His decease at Jerualem, he discovered that he was given "special freedom," and it remained with him. "Things pertinent to the subject were abundantly presented to my view, and such a fulness of matter, that I scarce knew how to dismiss the various heads and particulars I had occasion to touch upon. And, blessed be the Lord, I was favoured with some fervency and power, as well as freedom;

so that the word of God seemed to awaken the attention of a stupid audience, to a considerable degree."

Perhaps some of those who opposed him and his Indians were not outside the church of Christ in that stupid audience between Cross-weeksung and Cranberry. Perhaps he had merely missed the immediacy and the audible response of his own people at Bethel.

Book Five

The Saint

His religion was not like a blazing meteor, or like a flaming comet, (or a wandering star, as the apostle Jude calls it), flying through the firmament with a bright train, and then quickly departing into perfect darkness, but more like the steady lights of heaven, constant principles of light, though sometimes hid with clouds.

—Jonathan Edwards

29. AS A FLAME OF FIRE

No PORTION OF BRAINERD'S DIARY reveals his complete commitment in grace more than the spring of 1746 when the settling of his Indians at Bethel confronted him with the future of his own way. His early anxious pressing of God had matured into a mystical union, a trustful, constant walk with Him, although sometimes obscured, "sometimes hid with clouds." His self-surrender also was not the grim asceticism he had once harbored in froward anticipation of martyrdom. It had dissolved into an assurance of his salvation and the acceptance of God's will for the salvation of others. His innermost knowing was that he would fulfill his Maker's transcendent will. But the manner in which he should go filled his daily thoughts and earnest prayers.

Even as St. Paul did not stay with the congregations he organized but was constrained to travel from place to place as he pressed forward in his great calling in Jesus Christ, Brainerd faced the particulars of his responsibility to his Christian Indians over against his longing desires for those along the Susquehanna River and beyond. Late on Friday afternoon, May 16, he conferred about this matter with "a dear minister," most probably William Tennent or Charles McKnight, and, in the evening, after long hours of ejaculatory prayer, he arrived at a preliminary conclusion: "Lord, use me as thou wilt; do as thou wilt with me; but O, promote thine own cause!"

"When I attempted to look to God, respecting my worldly circumstances, and his providential dealings with me, in regard to my settling down in my own congregation, which seems to be necessary and yet very difficult, and contrary to my fixed intentions for years past, as well as my disposition — which has been, and still is, at times especially, to go forth, and spend my life in preaching the gospel from place to place, and gathering souls *afar off* to Jesus the great Redeemer — I could only say, 'The will of the Lord be done; it is no matter for me.'"

The next morning he reflected how discouragement hindered his fervency, but that when he felt he did something for God, "this refreshes and animates me, so that I could break through all hardships, undergo any labours, and nothing seems too much to do or to suffer. But oh, what a death it is, to strive, and strive;

to be always in a *hurry*, and yet do *nothing*, or at least nothing for God!"

On Sunday as he began to preach from Revelation 3:20, *Behold, I stand at the door and knock*, he felt "peevish and provoked" with the rude conduct of the white people who crowded in between him and his Indians. "But blessed be God!" he exclaimed, "I got these shackles off before the middle of my discourse, and was favoured with a sweet frame of spirit in the latter part." In the evening, grieving again that he had done so little for God, he longed that he could be "a flame of fire," as the writer of the Book of Hebrews had declared that God had so made His angel-servants.

As the "appearance" of his audience that Pentecost Sunday was "comparatively discouraging," he wrote: "I was ready to fear that God was about to withdraw the blessed influence of his Spirit from us." On Monday, as lively affections seemed still to be generally lacking, he labored to impress upon his people the necessity of religious fervency and devotion, "without which religion will be but an empty name and a lifeless carcass," and he specifically warned them about the "idolatry, self-gratification and disagreeableness" of self-induced demonstrations. He seemed to be constantly concerned with this counterfeit religion. But were they puzzled, even alarmed, that the text he had chosen for that day was from Paul's farewell address to the elders of Ephesus? How intently he had privately pondered those words: *from the first day I came*, and, *Now, behold I go*.

But all must have seemed quite normal to them as each day he left his boarding house to visit them at their new land and homes and to supervise their daily affairs. They were incapable of managing their tasks and petty differences, he said, without his constant care and advice, "as if they were a company of children." However, they seemed definitely ambitious to learn the English language, and to master it some of the adults frequently spoke it among themselves and attended the English classes conducted by the schoolmaster. Their interest gave Brainerd much satisfaction.

He was also more than pleased with the interest his teacher displayed toward the Indians. As Paul said of his helper Timothy, he knew of "no man like-minded who will naturally care for their state." In his General Remarks he wrote with evident satisfaction: "The children learn with *surprising* readiness; so that their *master* tells me, he never had an English school that learned, in general, comparably so fast." Although some were very young, no more than two children failed to learn all the letters in the alphabet only three days after they began attending classes in the school-church building which had by now been constructed. The children were also instructed twice a week in the Shorter Catechism and were encouraged to engage in personal prayer. "Most of them constantly attend it night and morning," Brainerd noted, "and are very careful to inform their master if they apprehend that any of their little school-mates neglect that religious exercise."*

Nor is the reader of Brainerd's diaries and Journals rewarded with the names of his Indians, except Tattamy. However, some of the little schoolmates' parents must certainly have been among the signers of the Crosswicks Conference of 1758 at which old Tattamy represented his former "mountain" or Minisinks people. The Indian signers from Cranbury were Thomas Store, Stephen Calvin, John Pompshire, Benjamin Claus, Joseph Wooley, Josiah Store, Isaac Still, James Calvin, Peter Calvin, Dirick Quaquay, Ebenezer Wooley, and, lastly, Sarah Stores ("widow of Quaquahela"). Of these family names some recorded traces remain. A young Joseph Wooley attended Eleazar Wheelock's Indian School (Dartmouth College) in 1757 and was licensed to teach in 1765, but while preparing to extend his services to the Iroquois in New York he died of tuberculosis on November 27 of that year, "greatly mourned by the Indians." His brother Jacob received the same educational opportunities but became an apostate to the Christian religion. The shining light was Stephen Calvin, the husband of Weequehela's daughter. He was an elder in the Indian church throughout his years and saw his sons grow up under the Christian teachings of John Brainerd. One of his sons, Hezekiah Calvin, taught a Mohawk school and held great promise in 1766, but five years later John despaired of him: "he seems to choose to be a useless creature." Another educated son was reared on the Calvin farm near the New Jersey Brotherton Reservation. A third son, Bartholemew S. Calvin, attended the college at Princeton until the Revolutionary War closed the school. He became an exemplary leader and teacher but was not experientially

---

* Brainerd did not reveal the name of the schoolmaster who pleased him so well. We like to think that he was the person mentioned in *The New York Gazette Revived* or *The Weekly Post Boy* of July 30, 1750: "All Persons indebted to the Estate of Mr. Ebenezer Hayward, Indian School-Master at Bethel, in New-Jersey, deceased, are desired forthwith to pay the same: And those that have any Demands against the said Estate, are desired to bring in their Accounts, that they may be adjusted. JOHN BRAINARD, Executor."

converted until he was near seventy years old and living at Stockbridge where he had led his people.*

These encouraging and hopeful prospects of both adults and children had also led Brainerd to consider his future as well as a further pleasing matter closely related to his permanent settling at Bethel. For two years he had longed for a companion, and although the schoolmaster had joined him, he was now considering marriage. This, too, had been a principal factor in his Friday night wrestling.

His thoughts during that month of May in New Jersey are easy to imagine. Only a few miles away William Tennent lived in domestic bliss with the widow Noble and their three young sons. It was this spring, too, that Charles Beatty and Charles McKnight decided to forsake bachelorhood. Beatty's marriage to Anne Reading was to take place in a month, on June 24. This union of the popular preacher of Neshaminy with the daughter of John Reading, president of the Council and acting governor of New Jersey that year, would certainly be thoughtfully considered by the Bethel bachelor. Charles McKnight would marry Elizabeth Stevens on August 19.

Brainerd had continued his reflections in his diary for Friday, May 16 — "The same frame of mind I felt with respect to another important affair I have lately had some serious thoughts of: I could say, with utmost calmness and composure, 'Lord, if it be most for thy glory, let me proceed in it; but if thou seest that it will in any wise hinder my usefulness in thy cause, oh prevent my proceeding: for all I want, respecting this world, is such circumstances as may best capacitate me to do service for God in the world.'"

Two days later, as if in answer to these intimate thoughts, he had confessed to his diary on Pentecost Sunday: "God made me to see that I was a *child*; yea, that I was a *fool*."

Now, Thursday, May 22, as he sat in his room in the evening, he experienced what he described as "a frame somewhat remarkable."

---

* He had removed to New Stockbridge on Oneida Lake, New York State. As a lone surviving chieftain of the Delawares, Bartholemew petitioned the New Jersey Legislature for settlement of the last Indian land claims in the state. The sum of $2000 was paid in final extinguishment in 1832. Bartholemew, then 76 years old, thanked the Legislature in valedictory: "Not a drop of our blood have you spilled in battle, — not an acre of our land have you taken but by our consent. These facts speak for themselves, and need no comment: they place the character of New Jersey in bold relief and bright example to those States within whose territorial limits our brethren still remain. Nothing save benisons can fall upon her from the lips of Leni Lennapi." As Thomas Brainerd remarked: "It does full justice to New Jersey; perhaps a little bit more."

It has been suggested that what he wrote that night was addressed to Jerusha Edwards, but Edwards submitted it as an integral part of his diary. Not that young Jerusha was not foremost in his heart and mind, or that he did not transcribe these exact thoughts in an intimate and heart-breaking letter to his betrothed. Delicate and serene, less tempermental than her older sister Sarah and less vivacious perhaps than Esther, two years her junior, Jerusha Edwards was in her father's estimation the flower of his large family. When Jonathan Edwards later wrote, "She was a person of much the same spirit with Brainerd," he also disclosed that Brainerd had often expressed his opinion of Jerusha as a Christian and as a saint who "by the temper of her mind, was fitted to deny herself for God and to do good, beyond any young woman whatsoever whom he knew."

In soul-transparent words David revealed that he had given considerable thought to accomplish and even hasten his settling at Bethel. The idea had grown on him. The anticipation of "quiet settlement, the certain place of abode, the tender friendship, which I thought I might be likely to enjoy in consequence of such circumstances" appeared desirable and extremely pleasing to him. Yet he was not fully convinced, "never quite pleased with the thoughts of being settled and confined to one place," even though God had enabled him to gather Bethel from among the pagans. "For I never, since I began to preach," he declared, "could feel any freedom to 'enter into other men's labours,' and settle down in the ministry where the 'gospel was preached before.' I never could make that appear to be my province."

But, he persisted, was it *God's* plan to provide him with a permanent home? There was but one answer for him. "But now these thoughts seemed to be wholly dashed to pieces; not by necessity, but of choice." It appeared to him that God's dealings toward him had fitted him for a life of solitariness and hardship. "It appeared to me just right, that I should be destitute of house and home, and many comforts of life, which I rejoiced to see others of God's people enjoy." For the advancement of Christ's kingdom he was willing to be "a pilgrim or hermit in the wilderness." He prayed: "Send me even to death itself, if it be but in thy service." All his dreams of home and domestic comfort "vanished as stars before the rising sun," and he was done with them though he desired them. His choice was final and it was beyond himself. All his miserable hours and days of loneliness and dejection and the prospects of more to come did not matter: "I was constrained, and yet chose, to say, 'Farewell, friends and earthly comforts, the dearest of them all, the very dearest, if the Lord calls for it; adieu, adieu; I will spend my life, to my latest moments, *in caves and dens of the earth*, if the kingdom of Christ may thereby be advanced.'" And again he expressed his longing to be as a flame of fire — "continually glowing in the divine service, preaching and building up Christ's kingdom, to my latest, my dying moment."

These things he wrote in his diary, "only for his own private use," as Edwards said, "and not to obtain honour and applause in the world, nor with any design that the world should ever see it, either while he lived, or after his death."

He continued to prevail in prayer that night until he feared he should disturb the family in the house where he lodged — "With what reluctancy did I feel myself obliged to consume time in sleep!" — and he prayed not only for Bethel and for his friends, but especially that the Kingdom of God would be extended among the Indians far remote.

It was in perhaps even a greater spirit of exultant dedication — "to burn out in one continued flame for God" — that his brother John found him the following day, May 23. John was one of only twelve students who graduated from Yale that year. He was now twenty-six years old and still single. There is no personal record of his life up to this time, but his later life as David's successor reveals a man of quiet opinion and steady action. He was certainly less impetuous than David and also less prone to periods of deep melancholy, but he was not altogether free from them. Although David later declared, "I love him the best of any creature living," only a single sentence records their visit. David wrote: "In the evening was visited by my brother John Brainerd; the first visit I have ever received from any near relative since I have been a missionary."

The remainder of the Second Part of his Journal reveals that on Sunday, June 1, he baptized five adults and five children, his largest group since November. He noted that "those comforted of late seem to be brought in, in a more silent way." At the end of that week, on Saturday, his Indians went with him to Freehold to observe the Lord's Supper on June 8. There they communed with the white people in the holy ordinance, Brainerd observing in his diary: "A number of my dear people sat down by themselves at the last table." Apparently somewhat abashed, they were less "refreshed and feasted" than in their own observance, but to the people of God at Freehold who had earlier invited some of them and "who had longed to see this day," it was a most satisfying and blessed time. Walter Ker, the old patriarch of the Jersey pinewoods, headed the list of officers whose statement was appended to Brainerd's Journal.

"We whose names are underwritten, being elders and deacons of the Presbyterian church in Freehold, do hereby testify, that in our humble opinion, God, even our Saviour, has brought a considerable number of the Indians in these parts to a saving union with himself. . . . This we are persuaded of, from a personal acquaintance with them, whom we not only hear speak of the great doctrines of the gospel with humility, affection, and understanding, but we see them walk, as far as man can judge, soberly, righteously, and godly. We have joined with them at the Lord's Supper, and do from our hearts esteem them as our brethren in Jesus. . . ."*

Early on Monday morning his Indians met by themselves in a quiet place in the woods and "prayed, sang, and conversed of divine things," and to conclude the sacramental season David then repeated the sermon he had once preached on Long Island, *And Enoch walked with God.* Although his strength was "lengthened out even to a wonder," he was "spent and his spirits exhausted" on Tuesday, and by Wednesday he complained of "vapoury disorders, and dejection of spirit, and of enjoying but little comfort or spirituality." But on Thursday he was again praying especially for the Indians "far back in the wilderness" — mounting evidence that his eight months absence from the Susquehanna River weighed upon his mind. On Friday he baptized two more children and three adults, including the very aged and childish woman whose rationality had so amazed him the day after Christmas. Although she could still not understand anything he asked of her, "she could give a very distinct and particular relation" of her experience and conviction of salvation when he allowed her to tell her story in her own way.

On June 14-16, for the third time in five weeks, Brainerd participated in the Lord's Supper. This time it was several miles to the northwest, at Kingston, to assist Eleazar Wales, the first pastor who had served the Forks of Delaware. During the Saturday afternoon service, he wrote in his diary, he almost fainted while preaching in Wales' pulpit, "yet God strengthened me when I was just gone." On Sunday, before he blessed the bread and wine, he made his old

* The first Freehold log church was built in 1692, some seven miles south of Raritan Bay. In 1730 the building in which Brainerd preached and assisted in the Lord's Supper, was erected seven miles farther south on White (Oak) Hill. The third beautiful "Old Tennent" which still stands was built in 1751. Among its prized furnishings is the time-worn Communion Table from which Brainerd served the sacrament to his Indians.

familiar complaint: "Was in a dejected, spiritless frame, that I could not hold up my head, nor look anybody in the face." But as he preached "to a vast multitude" he found that he addressed them with such freedom, fluency and clearness, "as commanded the attention of the great."

Since Kingston and its Black Lion Inn were on the Trenton-New Brunswick stage route (nearby Princeton was then hardly more than a cross-roads), "the great" may have been some visiting dignitaries, either political or ecclesiastical. More than likely they were the latter, for on Wednesday Brainerd went farther west to a meeting of ministers at Hopewell. And, on Thursday, June 19, two of his employers, most probably Dickinson and Burr, visited him at Bethel, on the first anniversary of his arrival at Crossweeksung.

"This day makes up a complete year from the first time of my preaching to these Indians in New Jersey. What amazing things has God wrought in this space of time for this poor people! . . . They 'who were sometimes darkness, are now become light in the Lord.' May they 'walk as children of the light, and of the day!' And now to him that is of power to stablish them according to the gospel, and the preaching of Christ — To God only wise, be glory, through Jesus Christ, for ever and ever! Amen."

30. YET A LITTLE WHILE

BRAINERD'S MANY ILLNESSES and apparent rapid recoveries which at times strain the credulity of his readers, vexed his own mind and conscience to no small degree. However, his diaries (which Edwards resumed in fuller detail after the close of the Journals) leave no doubt that in his public records David continually failed to mention his poor physical health. As Edwards remarked: "he purposely concealed in what he published."

"On June 20th, as well as on the next day," Edwards now reported, "he was very ill; though, with great effort, he was enabled to preach to his people on Saturday. His illness continued on the Sabbath, but he preached, notwithstanding, to his people both parts of the day. . . . But he was extremely wearied with the service of the day, and so ill at night, that he could have no bodily rest. . . . On Monday he continued very ill."

Edwards then discontinued Brainerd's daily account for that week, stating only that Brainerd "continued very feeble, and for the most part dejected in mind." The reader is thus left to wonder whether or not David witnessed the wedding of Charles Beatty and Anne Reading on Tuesday.

One feels, however, that at this time Brainerd began to prepare his congregation for the days ahead. His sermon on the last Sunday in June was from John 14:19, *Yet a little while, and the world seeth me no more,* and his Indians probably sensed how well it applied to him. Several, said Brainerd, were "powerfully revived" and one man was awakened who "appeared before as stupid as a stock."

As for himself, Brainerd considered that God had again and amazingly renewed and stretched out his strength that day. "I was so spent at noon," he wrote, "that I could scarce walk, and all my joints trembled; so that I could not sit, nor so much as hold my hand still; and yet God strengthened me to preach with power in the afternoon; although I had given out word to my people that I did not expect to be able to do it. . . . Returned home with more health than I went out with; although my linen was wringing wet upon me, from a little after ten in the morning till past five in the afternoon."

So it continued through July with intermittent periods of both physical and spiritual relief. On July 1, as one of his Indians lay at the point of death, Brainerd preached from Hebrews 9:27, *It is appointed unto men once to die.* He was able to attend a meeting of the Presbytery in Newark, and was gone for a week. He celebrated the Lord's Supper in Elizabethtown on Sunday afternoon and preached his familiar message, *I have no pleasure in the death of the wicked.* On Monday evening, probably at Dickinson's home, he had the most agreeable conversation which he could remember in all his life, "upon God's being *all in all,* and all enjoyments being just *that* to us which God makes them, and no more." He rode home on Tuesday and to William Tennent's for a social evening on Wednesday. He noted that night: "My heart was dead to all below; yet not through dejection, as at some times, but from views of a better inheritance."

Saturday was prayer and fast day at Bethel preparatory to the congregation's second observance of the Lord's Supper on July 13. This time thirty-one Indians participated and Brainerd commented: "There was scarcely a dry eye among them when I took off the linen, and showed them the symbols of Christ's *broken body.*"

After reporting Brainerd's routine entry for the thanksgiving sermon on Monday, Edwards stated only that David spent the week journeying to and from Philadelphia, all the while "under a great illness of body and dejection of mind." When he returned he preached to his people on Sunday, "with great clearness and plainness," but it was Monday before he disclosed to them the most plausible reason for his trip to the Quaker City. In view of his poor health, it must have appeared unbelievable to them.

"I proposed my design of taking a journey speedily to Susquehannah," he said, and although he did not intend to leave until after three weeks, that same day he chose six evangelists to accompany him. As he disclosed later, he intended to be gone "a considerable time."

The next day he became extremely depressed. Whether it was merely his physical condition and his descent from the joys of his anniversary, or a disquiet over his bold decision to again visit the Susquehanna, is not said. It was his thorn in the flesh, that like the Elijah of the juniper tree, he was now again overwhelmed by his dark clouds of gloom. In plaintive desperation he longed for and did attain some desire for living to God and wearing out life for Him, but he wanted more than anything else simply to finish his earthly course — "I wanted to wear out life, and have it at an end."

During the remainder of the week as he attended still another Presbytery meeting at Elizabethtown, his gloom prevailed and he was, said Edwards, "distressed with a senselessness of all good, so that the whole world appeared empty and gloomy to him." Regardless of temporal successes or spiritual rewards, it had remained with him as Edwards had warned his readers: "he was, by his constitution and natural temper, so prone to melancholy and dejection of spirit, though he often spoke of the very harmful nature of that *disease* which afflicted him."

After Saturday, however, except for physical weakness on Monday, he enjoyed unusual peace and bouyancy, especially during the last week of July. On Friday the first day of August, he seemed to shout it out: "Oh how serene was my mind at this season! How free from that distracting concern I have often felt!" But were his Susquehanna plans uppermost in his mind that day when he saw that God was infinitely wise, "and could not do anything amiss, as I was in danger of doing?"

As "powerful impressions" were made upon "both saints and sinners" on Saturday, and he continued free from "sinking damps" over the week-end, he was again filled with thanksgiving: "*O what a mercy is this!*" And even on Tuesday, August 5, when he conducted the funeral of an Indian Christian, the nervous headache and dejection that seized him soon passed. His text was Isaiah 57:2, *He shall enter in peace.*

On Thursday he rode to his hut at Crossweeksung to fetch some things he needed for his Susquehanna journey. It was his last visit to the scene of his reward where, he said, "God so marvellously visited with the showers of his grace." He was refreshed to see it once again: "O how amazing did the *power of God* often appear there!"

He spent Saturday in straightening out his Indians' affairs, "as much as possible," and on Sunday he baptized three adults and three children. He was weak and weary but full of tenderness for the people he was about to leave. With Charles McKnight he observed Monday as a special day of worship, farewell, devotions and admonitions.

He spoke to his people from Psalm 2: *I shall give the heathen for thine inheritance*, and Psalm 110: *He shall judge among the heathen.* During his first prayer the Indians were already impressed and, concerning his main discourse from Acts 4:31, *And when they had prayed the place was shaken*, he remarked: "God helped me, and my interpreter also; there was a shaking and melting among us; and divers, I doubt not, were in some measure 'filled with the Holy Ghost." Then, after McKnight had prayed, David "opened" the last stanzas of the metrical arrangement of Psalm 72, and there were tears and sobs as he led his Indians in the song:

> See springs of life in thirsty deserts flow,
> And savage tribes the immortal Saviour know,
> Prostrate in dust his humbled foes shall lie,
> Or send their hymns of transport to the sky;
> And each blest land rehearse his praises o'er,
> 'Till moons shall walk their evening round no more.

31. THAT I MAY ACCOMPLISH MY COURSE

EARLY ON TUESDAY, August 12, Brainerd and the six Indian evangelists he had chosen to go with him left for his fourth trip to the Susquehanna River. That his Indians traveled on foot may have slowed his progress. However, it would seem that he made several delaying visits, for he covered less than eighty miles in four days as he traveled from Cranberry to Philadelphia and along the Schuylkill River on the Great Road to Norriton Mills and Charlestown.

Edwards explained: "He took his way through Philadelphia; intending to go to Susquehannah river, far down, where it is settled by the white people, below the country inhabited by the Indians; and so to travel up the river to the Indian habitations. For although this was much farther about, yet hereby he avoided the huge mountains, and hideous wilderness, that must be crossed in the nearer ways. . . . He rode this week as far as Charlestown, a place of that name about thirty miles westward of Philadelphia; where he arrived on *Friday*; and in his way hither was, for the most part, in a composed, comfortable state of mind." It is possible that he also stopped at Richard Treat's home at Abington, north of Philadelphia, and that they rode together to Charlestown, for it was there that Treat and Brainerd together conducted services on Saturday and Sunday.

The old township of Charlestown in Great Valley, one of the earliest centers of American Presbyterianism, was located on the south side of the Schuylkill River, between present Phoenixville and Valley Forge. It is now known as Schuylkill. Prior to 1741 Great Valley had been served by the Lower Providence and the Old Norriton Church which, built in 1698 and still intact, is probably the oldest Presbyterian church in America today. Treat had supplied both these churches for ten years. But when John "Hell-fire" Rowland came to take charge and the Old Siders at Norriton locked the doors of their meetinghouse against him, his New Side supporters withdrew and built the Charlestown church about five miles west of Norriton. This was probably the "New-Providence" church which with Treat's Abington congregation had collected ten pounds and five shillings for Brainerd's Indians in New Jersey. That Treat was now again officiating at Charlestown would seem to support the assumption that Rowland, hardly thirty years old, had already died.

Brainerd tarried with Treat over Saturday and Sunday, heard him preach, preached himself both afternoons, and partook of the Lord's Supper with five of his six evangelists. He was "much spent" by Sunday evening after preaching for the third recorded time, *I have no pleasure in the death of the wicked*, but he was "something renewed" when he spent the evening, almost till midnight, in prayer and devotions. On Monday he set out on the remaining 135 odd miles to Shamokin.

"Weak and disordered," he traveled by way of either Lancaster or the Ephrata Cloisters where, as the effusive dedication to their hymn book stated, lived several hundred "solitary turtle-doves cooing in the wilderness as a spiritual harp." He reached the Susquehanna River on Tuesday after he had passed through the territory served by the Presbyterian church at Derry (now Hershey) and Paxton (Peshtonk, Peixtan, Paxtang, Paxtong, all meaning swampy). In this area east of present Harrisburg lived the Irish minister John Elder who in the Indian war eight years later would command all the block houses from the Forks of Delaware to the Susquehanna River, as well as the "Pextony boys" who against Elder's explicit commands massacred every Indian at Conestoga and Lancaster.

Could Brainerd's strange remark that day, that he had met "with none that I thought godly people" stem from the fact that John Elder looked with scant indulgence upon the evangelistic New Siders, and resented the encroachment of other preachers into his scattered frontier parish? Elder had been the pastor of the Paxtang congregation for only two years when in 1740 the Old Side-New Side controversy had split his church. He had then become the pastor of the Old Side party at Derry, while the New Side elements of both churches called John Roan, an Irish graduate of the Log College, who settled there in 1745. The churches, including Mount Joy, served a very large area east of the Susquehanna River and north and south of Swatara Creek. On his return trip it would seem that Brainerd met some whom he did consider godly people for he was twice importuned to preach in this region. On both ocassions, however, he had to refuse their earnest solicitations.

During Tuesday night and on Wednesday he continued in poor health. "Having lain in a cold sweat all night," he wrote, "I coughed much bloody matter this morning, and was under great disorder of body, and not a little melancholy; but what gave me some encouragement, was, I had a secret hope that I might speedily get a dismission from earth, and all its toils and sorrows." He rode on Wednesday "to one Chamber's" on the east bank of the Susquehanna. This would be Chamber's Mills at Fishing Creek, a trading post forty miles south of Shamokin. There he lodged and was "much afflicted" in the evening with an "ungodly crew," he said, who were drinking, swearing, and apparently carousing in the typical rough ways of the frontier. "O what a *hell* it would be, to be numbered with the *ungodly!*" he wrote; but he did enjoy "some agreeable conversation" with a traveler who seemed to have "some relish of true religion."

On Thursday he rode up the river about fifteen miles and lodged with a family "that appeared quite destitute of God." He tried to talk with the man about religion but found him "very artful" in evading such conversation, and exclaimed: "Oh, what a death it is to some to hear of *the things of God!*" However, he was less dejected that day.

There is no record that he stopped at the Juniata island, simply that he continued up the river on Friday, "my people now being with me, who before were parted from me." As he got beyond the last English settlements he camped at night in the open woods "and slept with more comfort than while among an ungodly company of white people." Finally, near night on Saturday, he arrived at Shamokin.

On Sunday (August 24) he visited and discoursed about Christianity with some of the Delawares and with the king and others who seemed disposed to hear, but he spent most of Monday in writing, having sent out his evangelists to talk with the Indians, to "contract a friendship and familiarity with them," that he might have a better opportunity of dealing with them later. "Some good seemed to be done by their visit this day," he observed, "divers appeared willing to hearken to Christianity." In fact, by Tuesday noon, as he discoursed to a considerable number, he thought that the situation actually appeared as encouraging as it had at Crossweeksung. "I pressed things with all my might," he wrote, "and called out my people, who were then present, to give in *their testimony* for God; which they did." But Wednesday was a very poor day for him.

"There having been a thick smoke in the house where I lodged all night before, whereby I was almost choked, I was this morning distressed with pains in my head and neck, and could have no rest. In the morning, the smoke was still the same; and a cold easterly storm gathering, I could neither live within doors nor without any long time together. I was pierced with the rawness of the air abroad, and in the house distressed with the smoke. I was this day very vapoury, and lived in great distress, and had not health enough to do anything to any purpose."

On Thursday he was visited by some who wanted to hear him and, he stated, he "laboured to persuade them to *turn to God,*" but he sensed a degree of failure — "Scarce ever saw more clearly, than this day, that it is *God's work* to convert souls, and especially poor *heathens.* I knew, I could not *touch* them; I saw I could only speak to *dry bones,* but could give them no *sense* of what I said. My eyes were up to God for help: I could say, the *work* was *his;* and if done, the *glory* would be *his.*"

He visited the Delawares on Friday but found few at home, and he felt poorly. On Saturday he spent the afternoon in visiting a trader who "came down the river *sick*; who appeared as ignorant as any Indian." He spent some time on Sunday, the last day of August, in reading and expounding Scripture and in singing and prayer with his evangelists, his "dear family." He also preached to some few of the Susquehanna Indians, but he felt somewhat less than happy about any progress, stating, "Oh, how heavy is my work, when *faith* cannot take hold of an *almighty arm,* for the performance of it! Many times have I been ready to sink in this case. *Blessed be God that I may repair to a full fountain!"*

His plans were laid, however, and he followed them with stubborn determination. He had never gone farther west than Shamokin in his earlier Susquehanna trips, but this, despite his desperately poor health, was now his goal — to strike out on a hazardous five-day, one-hundred-mile journey through the wild mountain country along the west Branch of the Susquehanna, beyond Ostonwackin (Montoursville), the village of Madame Montour and her son Andrew, to the Shawanese Indians at Big or Great Island, the site of present Lock Haven. Government documents disclose that the tribe at this place was considered especially treacherous because some of them under their half-breed leader, Peter Chartiers, had very recently defected to the Canadian French.

"Monday, September 1. Set out on a journey towards a place called *the great island,* about fifty miles distant from Shaumoking, on the north-western branch of Susquehannah. Travelled some part of the way, and at night lodged in the woods. Was exceeding feeble this day, and sweat much the night following.

"Tuesday, September 2. Rode forward; but no faster than my people went on foot. . . . I was so feeble and faint, that I feared it would kill me to lie out in the open air; and some of our company being parted from us, so that we had now no axe with us, I had no way but to climb into a young pine-tree, and with my knife to lop the branches, and so made a shelter from the dew. But the evening being cloudy, and very likely for rain, I was still under fears of being extremely exposed: sweat much in the night, so that my linen was almost wringing wet all night.

"Wednesday, September 3. Rode to the Delaware-town; found divers drinking and drunken. Discoursed with some of the Indians about Christianity; observed my *interpreter* much engaged and assisted in his work; some few persons seemed to hear with great earnestness and engagement of soul. About noon rode to a small town of Shauwaunoes, about eight miles distant; spent an hour or two there, and returned to the Delaware-town, and lodged there. Was scarce ever

more confounded with a sense of my own unfruitfulness and unfitness for my work, than now. Oh, what a dead, heartless, barren,
unprofitable wretch did I now see myself to be! My spirits were so
low, and my bodily strength so wasted, that I could do nothing at all.
At length, being much overdone, lay down on a *buffalo-skin*; but sweat
much the whole night.

"Thursday, September 4. Discoursed with the Indians, in the
morning, about Christianity; my *interpreter*, afterwards, carrying
on the discourse to a considerable length. Some few appeared well-
disposed, and somewhat affected. Left this place, and returned towards Shaumoking; and at night lodged in the place where I lodged
the Monday night before; was in very uncomfortable circumstances
in the evening, my people being belated, and not coming to me till
past ten at night; so that I had no fire to dress any victuals, or to keep
me warm, or keep off wild beasts; and I was scarce ever more weak
and worn out in all my life.

"Friday, September 5. Was exceeding weak, so that I could
scarcely ride; it seemed sometimes as if I must fall off from my horse,
and lie in the open woods: however, got to Shaumoking, towards
night: felt something of a spirit of thankfulness, that God had so far
returned me; was refreshed to see one of my Christians, whom I left
here in my late excursion."

On Saturday he was even more completely confused, guilty, and
ashamed than on Wednesday. The river of his fondest expectation,
he seemed to say, was for him the river of final frustration. This
trip broke him. Yet despite his great weakness and ill health he
had chosen, perhaps persisted against superior advice, to take this
journey. Why did he do it?

Five years later his brother John was also thoroughly discouraged
on these same banks of the Susquehanna. His measured words can
answer for both brothers, even as they have and continue to answer
for the vast host of Christ's ambassadors through the years. John
wrote: "If it should be wondered why I incline to take such journeys,
so remote from the people of my more peculiar charge, and be looked
upon as desiring to run before I am sent, I answer: These people
among whom I chiefly reside are but a handful in comparison with
those who live remote from the white inhabitants . . . where the
people are *perishing for lack of vision.* . . . A missionary might well
be employed wholly among these people. . . . Nor could he content
himself to be confined to one little spot, when whole countries are
dying for want of knowledge."

But John's firm confidence did not readily fill David's soul that

Saturday night, September 6, 1746, as he clung to life at Shamokin, "coughing and spitting blood," and having little appetite for any food he had brought with him, and "very little life or heart to speak for God." His agonized mind flagellated him.

"Was scarcely ever more ashamed and confounded in myself than now. I was sensible, that there were numbers of God's people, who knew I was then out upon a design (or at least the pretence) of doing something for God, and in his cause among the poor Indians; and they were ready to suppose, that I was *fervent in spirit*: but oh, the heartless frame of mind that I felt filled me with confusion! Oh (methought) if God's people knew me, as God knows, they would not think so highly of my zeal and resolution for God, as perhaps now they do! I could not but desire they should see how heartless and irresolute I was, that they might be undeceived, and 'not think of me above what they ought to think.' And yet I thought, if they saw the utmost of my flatness and unfaithfulness, the smallness of my courage and resoluteness for God, they would be ready to shut me out of their doors, as unworthy of the company or friendship of Christians."

The bitter-sweet of saints! Seventeen years later John Woolman visited the Indians at Wyoming and he was also in great distress as he lay in a hut along the Susquehanna. He wrote: "I grew jealous of myself, lest the desire of reputation, as a man firmly settled to persevere through dangers, or the fear of disgrace arising on my returning without performing the visit, might have some place in me. Thus I lay full of thoughts during the great part of the night . . . until the Lord, my gracious Father, who saw the conflicts of my soul, was pleased to give me quietness."

After a listless and afflicted Sunday during which he did, however, preach "a little" to the Indians, but mostly mourned that he could do so little for God, Brainerd abandoned his plans and made his last farewells to Sassoonan, Shikellamy, and the tri-village of Shamokin. After he had ridden a few miles down river on Monday afternoon his assurance in some degree returned and he reflected: "Whether the issue of it would be the setting up of Christ's kingdom *there,* or only the drawing of some few persons down to my congregation in New Jersey; or whether they were now only being prepared for some further attempts, that might be made among them, I did not determine; but I was persuaded the journey would not be lost. *Blessed be God, that I had any encouragement and hope.*"

"Monday, September 8. Spent the forenoon among the Indians; in the afternoon, left Shaumoking, and returned down the river, a few miles. Had proposed to have tarried a considerable time longer among the Indians upon Susquehannah; but was hindered from pursuing my purpose by the sickness that prevailed there, the weakly circumstances of my own people that were with me, and especially my own extraordinary weakness, having been exercised with great nocturnal sweats, and a coughing up of blood, in almost the whole of the journey.

"Tuesday, September 9. Rode down the river, near thirty miles. Was extremely weak, much fatigued, and wet with a thunder-storm. Discoursed with some warmth and closeness to some poor ignorant souls, on the *life* and *power* of *religion;* what were, and what were not the *evidences* of it. They seemed much astonished when they saw my Indians ask a blessing and give thanks at dinner; concluding *that* a very high evidence of grace in them; but were astonished when I insisted that neither that, nor yet secret prayer, was any sure evidence of grace. Oh the ignorance of the world! How are some empty outward *forms*, that may all be entirely *selfish*, mistaken for true religion, infallible evidences of it! The Lord pity a deluded world!

"Wednesday, September 10. Rode near twenty miles homeward. Was much solicited to preach, but was utterly unable, through bodily weakness. Was extremely overdone with the heat and showers this day, and coughed up a considerable quantity of blood.

"Thursday, September 11. Rode homeward; but was very weak, and sometimes scarce able to ride. Had a very importunate invitation to preach at a meeting-house I came by, the people being then gathering; but could not, by reason of weakness. Was resigned and composed under my weakness; but was much exercised with concern for my companions in travel, whom I had left with much regret, some lame, and some sick.

"Friday, September 12. Rode about fifty miles; and came just at night to a Christian friend's house, about twenty-five miles westward from Philadelphia. Was courteously received, and kindly entertained, and found myself much refreshed in the midst of my weakness and fatigues."

Certainty about this place "twenty-five miles westward of Philadelphia" as Charlestown is obscured because Edwards had earlier stated that Charlestown was about thirty miles west of the city. It seems likely, however, that David returned to the same house where he had lodged before, for on Saturday as he continued to be "agreeably entertained with Christian friendship, and all things necessary," he again heard Richard Treat preach in the afternoon and conversed with him in the evening. Treat and the people also asked Brainerd to preach on Sunday. He complied by expounding his ordination text "both parts of the day (but short)": *Go into the highways and hedges.* . . . He was very tired in the evening but, he remarked with generous extravagance, "I was comforted with the most tender treatment I ever met with in my life."

It appears that Brainerd definitely differentiated between Treat and the Christian friend at this place who cared for him so solicitously, but the identity of this person remains a mystery. We yearn to believe that it was John Rowland, that he was still alive though perhaps incapacitated, and that it was he who comforted the exhausted Yankee. Rowland was a powerful evangelist, exactly the type whom Brainerd would recognize as a brother in Christ. Whitefield said of Rowland: "There is much of the simplicity of Christ discernible in his behaviour." And Rowland was also the kind of controversial figure which Edwards seemed to have discreetly deleted from his Brainerd story.*

Brainerd and Treat spent all of Monday in helping to settle a difference among certain persons in the congregation. One can only wonder whether perhaps Rowland was involved in the dispute. There seemed to be a blessing on their endeavors, stated David. In the evening he baptized a child, and, afterwards, spent the time in religious conversation till late into the night, and he wrote; "This was indeed a pleasant, agreeable evening." Then, although he was "very weak, unable to perform any business, and scarcely able to sit up" on Tuesday, September 16, he and Treat rode the twenty-five or thirty miles into Philadelphia on Wednesday — "still very weak, and my cough and spitting of blood continued."

Once in the city, where would he and Treat lodge? He enjoyed some agreeable conversation with friends there, but he added, he personally wanted more spirituality. Would they not go to the home of Gilbert Tennent? He was still preaching at "Whitefield's Tabernacle," the *New-Building* which would soon become the "Academy," later the University of Pennsylvania. Had they perhaps read the following news item in *The Pennsylvania Gazette* of the previous Thursday?

* The time, place, and manner of Rowland's death is unknown today. Although one historian (Murphy) states that Rowland died "not later than 1745," another of equal authority (Sprague) declares that he was still alive in 1746, if the words that he died "before the autumn of 1747" can be so interpreted. In support of the possibility that Rowland was still alive and that he may have entertained Brainerd we can note that John Campbell did not become pastor of the Great Valley churches until 1747.

"*Philadelphia, Sept* 11. Last night the Rev. Mr. Whitefield returned hither, after an Excursion of 9 Days into the East-Jerseys; during which he preached 4 times at Cape May, once at Cedar Bridge, once at Woodbury, and 3 times at Greenwich, to very large and affected Auditories. He purposes, God willing, to preach Tomorrow Evening when he intends to take his leave."

What a treasure, had the possible meeting of these great ones been preserved! Here was the mature Whitefield, age thirty-two, a Church of England priest who embraced Presbyterians, Congregationalists, Dutch Reformed, Lutherans, Baptists and Quakers as his co-laborers. Across from him sat the still younger Presbyterian missioner, the former Congregationalist who had eschewed all party spirit in his quest for souls among the Indians of the river valleys. As the Great Awakener of Britain and America faced the gaunt, feverish Yankee did he have the heart to declaim his life-long conviction, as Eleazar Wheelock revealed it in 1764, "that the Pagans of America, are Canaanites, to be cut off before God's people, and never to be gathered into his Family"? And their older host: what influences had quietly made their mark on Gilbert Tennent? Less than three years later he published his *Irenicum* and became a prime mover in the reconciliation that reunited the New Side and Old Side Presbyterians in 1758.

After tarrying for the day and night in Philadelphia, Brainerd spent Thursday night at Treat's home in Abington where Whitefield, perhaps now again, was a house guest on more than one occasion. On Friday he remounted his horse and rode east, passing near William Penn's Manor and into New Jersey, to "Mr. Stockston's, at Princeton." Here he spent the evening with some degree of satisfaction. He was then but eight miles from home. On the following day, the fortieth day of his fourth wilderness journey, he arrived again among his own people, "just at night." He found them praying together and went in and gave them an account of God's dealing with him and his companions in the journey. "I then prayed with them," he wrote, "and thought the divine presence was amongst us."

The day of his return to Cranberry was Saturday, September 20. On the previous day his ardent friend, Samuel Buell, was installed in the church at East Hampton, Long Island. Buell had recovered from a year's serious illness after his graduation from Yale and his initial successes at Northampton and other New England places, and he had married in May. Starting out on a preaching tour to the Southern Colonies, he had stopped at Newark where he met Aaron Burr, only a month after Burr had assured the East Hampton people that he would furnish them with a minister. Buell was the man. The distressed congregation accepted him unanimously, and no less than Jonathan Edwards preached the installation sermon, choosing for his text, Isaiah 62:4, 5, *Thou shalt no more be termed Forsaken*. Thus it was, too, that Edwards knew from first-hand appraisal that it was from East Hampton, "the fairest, pleasantest town on the whole island, and one of its largest and most wealthy parishes," that the now cough-racked, consumptive Brainerd had elected to go, rather than stay.

Thirteen years later, on August 30, 1759, Buell preached the sermon at the ordination of Samson Occom. It was at East Hampton, the first church which Brainerd had served, that this swarthy son of New England became the first Indian minister in the Presbyterian Church, and Buell said: "He is an ornament to the Christian Religion and the glory of the Indian nation."

He could have said the same about Brainerd, and perhaps he did.

Of the Yale trio distinguished for their zeal, only Buell reached old age. David Youngs of Setauket died at thirty-three, five years after Brainerd, but Buell served East Hampton for fifty-two years. He was a colorful figure all his life, particularly during the Revolutionary War when the British occupied Long Island. He preached ten thousand sermons in his lifetime and when he died in 1798 at eighty-two, he had outlived two wives and eight of their nine children. The mother of his tenth child was some fifty years his junior and survived him for forty-six years.

32. I COULD DO NO MORE

BRAINERD'S INCREASING ALLUSIONS to his coughing of blood meant only one thing. The tuberculosis of his lungs which had felled him during his first year at Yale College was relentless and would eventually destroy him. He may have felt guilty, finally, that he had recklessly injured his health or aggravated his illness, as Edwards intimated. Actually, his zeal and outdoor life probably prolonged his days.

After his return from the Susquehanna, however, he was but one of thousands, of both white people and Indians, who fell victim to a general and nasty plague of dysentery (flux) and malarial-type

illness (ague) which wrought havoc in Central New Jersey and Pennsylvania during the autumn of 1746. He confirmed this fact when he
had mentioned at Shamokin that he left the Indian capital, not only
because his own health was impaired, but also in view of the general
sickness that prevailed there. Some of his evangelist companions
had also become ill.

For a fortnight after his return, he was too weak to preach
to his Indians. However, on Sunday afternoon he rode to them and
sat in his chair and told them, "None of us liveth to himself."
His nausea and pain in his chest and back allowed him little sleep
at night, and throughout the first week his violent cough continued
and he had high fevers. He had no appetite for food and frequently
could not retain it. That he more and more neglected his diary
from this point on, as Edwards approvingly emphasized, underscores
his truly miserable condition.

Brainerd was able to ride to his people, about two miles each
day, but he was not able to sit up any whole day. "Whether I
should recover or no, seemed very doubtful," he said, "but this was
many times a comfort to me, that *life* and *death* did not depend upon
my choice. I was pleased to think, that he who is infinitely wise, had
the determination of this matter. . . . I could with great composure
look *death* in the face, and frequently with sensible joy."

On the second Sunday, September 28, he tried to preach but had
to stop after a turn of faintness, and was hardly able to ride back
to his boarding house in Cranberry. There, as he lay in a burning
fever and almost delerious for several hours, he seemed to have
realized that he had come to the end of the road. As he recorded
his thoughts he first rather naively remarked: "I have often been
feverish, and unable to rest quietly after preaching; but this was
the most severe, distressing turn that ever preaching brought upon
me." But the conclusion he reached that day comes as a preliminary
benediction, a "well-done," upon the consciousness of a faithful servant who knows he has performed his task. "I felt perfectly at
rest in my own mind," he said, "because I had made my utmost
attempts to speak for God, and knew I could do no more."

And he was entirely free from dejection and melancholy, those
"unhappy glooms," and from "a peevish froward spirit."

He still rode, "a little every day," and visited the workmen building
his house. Then, on Friday afternoon, he felt "wonderfully revived."
It was the day he moved into his fourth little house among the
Indians. It was also the day of preparation for his congregation's
third observance of the Lord's Supper which he had planned for the

first Sunday in October, and concerning which he had given notice to his people and to those of the Forks of Delaware in particular. His Friday sermon, "Examine yourselves," was a continuation of his un-completed sermon of the Sunday just past. But when he finished he immediately had to go to bed, "for such speedy relief and refresh-ment as I could not well have lived without." In the evening he conversed to his people on divine things from his bed. He did the same on Saturday evening after he had again preached to them.

Sunday, October 5, 1746, was Brainerd's last blessed day of the Lord's Supper with nearly forty of his converts, "besides divers dear Chris-tians of the white people." The detailed outline of his sermon that day reveals that he preached *Behold the Lamb of God.* After the service he baptized his last two adults. His final harvest was now gathered in — a total of eighty-five Indians, of whom forty-three were adults and forty-two were children.

When he was ready to go home he could hardly traverse the some three hundred feet to his house, but was supported and led and tenderly laid upon his bed where he lay in pain till the evening, when he was able to sit up. As he discoursed with friends he could hear his Indians, "till near midnight, praying and singing praises to God, in one or other of their houses."

That week, by covering the thirty miles in two days, he rode to Elizabethtown to attend a meeting of the New York Synod, but it had removed to New York. Two weeks passed before he could return to Bethel because he was "seized with an ague," followed by a high fever. Physician Dickinson and perhaps his youngest daughter Martha cared for him, and he was ashamed, "to see so much concern about so unworthy a creature." Before the week ended they may also have convinced him that he actually was a sick man, for he wrote that he now realized and was fully convinced of his being really weak and unable to perform his work, "whereas at other times my mind was perplexed with fears, that I was a misimprover of time, by conceiting that I was sick, when I was not in reality so."

During his second week in Elizabethtown he reiterated that he was willing either to die or to live, but gradually he began again to fret over the passage of "misimproved" time, and he found it difficult to be reconciled to "thoughts of living *useless.*" He may have had some of his aged Indians and their plight in mind when he exclaimed, "Oh that I might never live to be a burden to God's creation; but that I might be allowed to repair *home,* when my *sojourning* work is done!"

By covering a short distance for several days he finally rode back to his house by Wednesday, October 23 and set things in order. He was weak and he was lonely. On Thursday he spent the day supervising the Indians who were mending a fence around their spring wheat. Forty of their eighty acres of farm land were for "English grain" and forty for Indian corn. Their clearing was a half mile long and a quarter mile wide. The success of such tasks and other business still seemed entirely to depend on him, he said, but it refreshed him to be able to do something useful, for he could no longer serve his people as he had in the past.

All day Sunday he was pained to see his people "wandering as sheep not having a shepherd," waiting and hoping that he would preach to them before night. When he felt a little better at the close of the day, he called them to his house and sat down and read and explained the Beatitudes from Matthew 5:1-16, especially the last verse: *Let your light so shine before men, that they may see your good works, and glorify your Father which is in heaven.* It was his final, "faintly delivered" sermon to them, and they humbly realized their shortcomings. One who had been drunk some time before was especially grieved over his sin and misconduct.

He spent all of Monday in again overseeing the fence-mending project, except that in the afternoon, he was visited by "two dear friends." Although William Tennent and Charles McKnight come readily to mind, these friends may have been others who came to invite him to the home of John Stockton in Princeton where he had stayed overnight on his way back from the Susquehanna. Whatever the case, the next day, Tuesday, October 28, he rode to Princeton, but before he could cover the eight miles his weakness and a violent fever forced him to alight and lie down in "a friend's house," probably Eleazar Wales' in Kingston.

Stockton's home in "Prince-town" was beautiful Morven, now the official residence of the Governor of New Jersey, which stands on Stockton Street, a few minutes walk from Princeton University. It received its name after Brainerd's day, but the house was then already some forty years old. His host, a son of the purchaser of the original five-hundred-acre estate, was a gentleman of wealth and influence and the presiding judge in the Court of Common Pleas of Somerset County. He was the father of Richard Stockton, the persecuted and imprisoned signer of the Declaration of Independence, whose wife Annis Boudinot gave their little "kingdom" its mythical Gaelic-Norse name. Richard was sixteen years old when Brainerd visited Morven.

"Near night" several guests arrived, apparently with the express purpose of visiting Brainerd. They were Richard Treat, Charles Beatty and his bride Anne, and a fourth, an enigmatical "another friend."

Brainerd remarked, "My spirits were refreshed to see them; but I was surprized, and even ashamed that they had taken so much pains as to ride thirty or forty miles to see me." He was able to sit up most of the evening and spent a comfortable time with them.

Had these loyal friends consulted each other about Brainerd's grave physical plight and had they come determined to persuade him to discontinue, if only for a time, the impossible life he seemed determine to pursue, despite his own realization that he could do no more? Treat and the friend, perhaps Rowland, who had nursed him twenty-five miles west of Philadelphia had doubtless shaken their heads while he tarried with them. Perhaps, too, the Charles Beattys had gasped when they saw their wasted, coughing horseman dismount in the yard of their Neshaminy parsonage on his way home from Susquehanna.

The identity of the other friend, one may again suspect, may have been concealed to avoid mention of a controversial name. It could again have been John Rowland. He was well known to John Stockton, for Stockton's testimony in court had freed Rowland of the charges against him in the Tom Bell horse-stealing affair at Freehold. George Whitefield's presence is ruled out as he was in Maryland after the middle of that month. But is it impossible that James Davenport attended the party that night? After writing his "Retraction" in New England in 1743, Davenport had practically disappeared from public view as he moved to and was married in New Jersey. He had also petitioned the New Brunswick Presbytery to accept him as a minister and, after much delay, he had been finally recognized on September 22, just a month ago. It is even possible that it was Davenport to whom David had alluded at Kingston when he said he had "commanded the attention of the great."

In his lifetime Davenport paid dearly for his misguided fanaticism, and in history he is remembered for little else. Yet he had been and again became a solid preacher with a genuine evangelistic spirit. In later years when he and John Brainerd became fast friends, John considered James "a sweet and zealous soul," and when Davenport died in 1757 he wrote of "our dear wrestling Jacob — I mean that man of God, the Rev. James Davenport. Oh, we exceedingly want such gap men!"*

* John was perhaps referring to Charles Wesley's rapturous hymn, "Wrestling Jacob," which had gained immediate popularity when it first appeared in *Hymns and Sacred Poems* in 1742 — "Come, O Thou Traveler Unknown . . . . With Thee all night I mean to stay and wrestle till the break of day."

Davenport served the New Jersey churches at Maidenhead and Hopewell during the last three years of his life, and died when he was forty years old. For two centuries his now forgotten grave in the peaceful New Jersey countryside about a mile west of Pennington bore these glowing lines as a last reminder of the zealous, fevered heart that beat within him.

> Oh, Davenport, a seraph once in clay,
> A brighter seraph, now in heavenly day.
> How glowed thy heart with sacred love and zeal!
> How like to that thy kindred angels feel!
> Clothed in humility thy virtue's throne,
> In every eye illustrious but thine own.
> How like thy Master on whose friendly breast
> Thou oft hast leaned and shall forever rest.

On Wednesday David rode about ten miles with his fellow saints, probably to a Delaware River crossing, and they departed from him, "all but one, who stayed on purpose" to keep him company, and to cheer him, as he continued weak and feverish throughout the day. On Thursday he rode three or four miles to Kingston for a final visit with Eleazar Wales. When he left Princeton again about Saturday noon, he returned home, "to my own house," and he wrote, "Was much disordered in the evening, and oppressed with my cough; which has now been constant for a long time, with a hard pain in my breast, and fever."

On Sunday he was totally unable to preach or even to sit up, and he was grieved, "and almost sunk," to see his Indians destitute of the means of grace. They could not read and were therefore under great disadvantages for spending the Sabbath comfortably, he said, and he thought he could be contented to be sick if only his poor flock had a faithful pastor to feed them. "A view of their want of this was more afflictive to me, then all my bodily illness."

The next day, Monday, November 3, 1746, was his last day as pastor of the flock he had gathered from the fields and pinewoods of New Jersey.

"Being now in so weak and low a state, that I was utterly incapable of performing my work, and having little hope of recovery, unless by much riding, I thought it my duty to take a long journey into New England, and to divert myself among my friends, whom I had not now seen for a long time. And accordingly took leave of my congregation this day.

"Before I left my people, I visited them all in their respective houses, and discoursed to each one, as I thought most proper and suitable for their circumstances, and found great freedom and assistance in so doing. I scarcely left one house but some were in tears; and many were not only affected with my being about to leave them, but with the solemn *addresses* I made them upon divine things; for I was helped to be *fervent in spirit* while I discoursed to them.

"When I had thus gone through my congregation, (which took me most of the day,) and had taken leave of them, and of the school, I left home, and rode about two miles, to the house where I lived in the summer past, and there lodged. Was refreshed, this evening, in that I had left my congregation so well-disposed and affected, and that I had been so much assisted in making my farewell-addresses to them."

David Brainerd's Book of his work among the Stockbridge, Delaware and Susquehanna Tribes of Indians was finished. It was precisely on November 4, four years after November 5, 1742, the probable date of Ebenezer Pemberton's letter which desired him to speedily come to New York to consult about the Indian affairs in those parts, that David withdrew from Cranberry and the vicinity of his work. It was less than sixteen months after he had heard of some Indians at a place called Crossweeksung and "determined to make them a visit, and see what might be done towards Christianizing them."

Yet, there was another day, after the long winter which he had been forced to spend in Elizabethtown, rather than with his friends and kin in New England. Having ridden from Dickinson's home under a great dejection on Thursday, he rose early on the morning of Friday, March 20, 1747, and walked among his people in Bethel near Cranberry. He inquired about their state and concerns, "and found an additional weight and burden . . . upon hearing some things disagreeable." "I endeavoured to go to God with my distresses," he wrote, "and made some kind of lamentable complaint; and in a broken manner spread my difficulties before God; but, notwithstanding, my mind continued very gloomy. About ten o'clock I called my people together, and after having explained and sung a psalm, I prayed with them. There was a considerable deal of affection among them; I doubt not, in some instances, that which was more than merely natural."

The sun had not reached its zenith when he said good-bye to his Indians that early spring morning. He left his people of Bethel and they saw him no more. He departed as he had come, rather melancholy and apprehensive and distressed, for he was a melancholy saint, and wise for his years in spiritual and practical experience, and he knew his dear, ignorant, slothful people would suffer much tribulation before their millennium would come.

33. I SHALL BE SATISFIED

To THOSE who breathe his wine-strong spirit, David Brainerd has hardly been an enigma, despite the need to join with him in distinguishing his soul-striving from his constitutional melancholy which Thomas Brainerd has shown to have been a family trait. His contemporaries and those who followed him in his century knew him readily.

"Let every preacher read carefully over the life of David Brainerd," directed John Wesley who printed and distributed an abbreviated "Life" of Brainerd to all his Methodist societies: "Let us be followers of him, as he was of Christ, in absolute self-devotion, in total deafness to the world and in fervent love to God and man."

Francis Asbury who became the Missionary of Methodism to America in 1771, urged that Brainerd's life be made known to every minister under his jurisdiction. Thomas Coke, Wesley's appointee as superintendent of the Methodist Church in America in 1784, pointed to Brainerd as his inspiration. So also did William Carey, the Baptist shoemaker who in 1793 became one of the first missionaries to India and was responsible for the translation of the Scriptures into forty languages and dialects.

As the nineteenth century opened a brilliant student at Cambridge discovered Brainerd in the autumn of 1802. Henry Martyn wrote: "I long to be like him; let me forget the world and be swallowed up in a desire to glorify God." His diary reveals that on the day he reached Calcutta in 1806 he echoed Brainerd's passionate desire: "Now let me burn out for God." Before his short intense service ended in 1812 during his feverish dash for Europe, Martyn had translated the New Testament into Hindustani and supervised the translation of other Scriptures into Persian and Arabic. The years are replete with evidences of the inspiration of Brainerd in the annals of the modern missionary advance, so that W. W. Sweet rightly observes in his *Story of Religion in America*: "Indeed, David Brainerd dead was a more potent influence for Indian missions and the missionary cause in general than was David Brainerd alive."

Jim Elliot who was killed with his flying missionary companions in 1956 by the Auca Indians of South America bore eloquent tribute to Sweet's statement when he wrote in his journal: "Confession of pride — suggested by David Brainerd's Diary yesterday — must become an hourly thing with me." To his Elisabeth he wrote, "Tell your father I was deeply impressed with Brainerd's Diary." And, after he reached Ecuador at the Shell Mera camp and witnessed "that body-jolting sob of children . . . all confessing faith in Jesus and sorrow for sin," he wrote to his parents: "A very simple thing, and very 'sweetly moving,' as Brainerd would say. . . ."*

After he had taken leave of his Indians on November 4, 1746, Brainerd had lodged at John Pierson's parsonage in Woodbridge for the night, and proceeded to Dickinson's manse in Elizabethtown on Guy Fawkes Day. There he became so ill that he could not return to New England. On the 24th of November he wrote to his brother Israel that he had several symptoms of consumption. In December he mentioned an asthmatic disorder and his inability to digest food. As he lay confined throughout that cold winter in New Jersey, his companion-nurse may again, quite probably, have been Dickinson's youngest daughter Martha, then twenty-one years old. She was declared by a contemporary to have been very serious and religious, a most agreeable companion, "and intellectually superior to most of her sex."

Although his friends "for some time together" thought Brainerd could scarce live another day, they were mistaken. Before spring he again rallied, and on February 24 he traveled the short distance to Newark where he presumably visited his friend Aaron Burr. On Saturday of that week one of his Indians, perhaps Tattamy, visited him, and on Wednesday, March 4, he "met with reproof from a friend," which he thought he did not deserve. A week later, on a day of public fasting and prayer in Elizabethtown, he attended church for the first time since December 21. He made his last visit to his Indians on March 18-20.

On Tuesday, April 7, he again rode to Newark and officiated at the marriage of Dickinson to Mary Crane. Dickinson who that month became the first president of the College of New Jersey conducted in his home, was fifty-nine; his second bride was twenty-seven. Two days later Brainerd again went to Newark to attend a Presbytery

---

* Elisabeth Elliot: *Shadow of the Almighty, the Life and Testament of Jim Elliott.* N. Y. 1958, Harper & Brothers, pp. 105, 109, 183.

meeting, the ordination of a Mr. Tucker (a Harvard man who died the following December), and the examination for licensure of a former classmate, Caleb Smith, the fiancee of Martha Dickinson. Smith was employed as the first tutor at the College of New Jersey.*

Back in Elizabethtown, on Monday, David assisted in examining his brother John, and he visited with Eliab Byram, the companion of his first Susquehanna journey. On the following day he said good-bye to his brother John as he left to care for the Bethel Indians. Seven years later John sorrowfully witnessed the dissolution of Bethel. After years of lawsuits and pressure from some of the white people, he finally deeded the land at Wigwam Brook to a Peter Deremer in July, 1754. During his sixty-three years, John also served as an army chaplain in the Indian wars and for fifteen years he was pastor-missionary at Brotherton, New Jersey's first and only Indian reservation. The last Indians moved from the reservation to New York, between 1802 and 1804, and to Green Bay, Wisconsin, in 1822.

According to Edwards' great-grandson and biographer, Sereno Edwards Dwight, it was also in April that Jonathan Edwards (or Jerusha?) invited Brainerd to Northampton. On Tuesday the 21st, the day after his twenty-ninth birthday (spent mostly in bed), David therefore bid farewell to Mary and Martha and Jonathan Dickinson. As they watched their frail guest depart for New England from whence he had come, they certainly did not expect that Jonathan would die first, two days before David. Dickinson and Edward Vaughn, his Anglican townsman and friend who was also sick, exchanged notes during their illness, and they died within days of each other. Timothy Johnes of Morristown was with Dickinson in his last hours.

Brainerd traveled slowly and came to Haddam and its environs where he could have visited more than a score of nephews and nieces in the homes of Hezekiah and his four sisters. Jerusha's ninth child had died in January. As this favorite sister watched him ride away, she may have made the same error as had the Dickinsons. Two months later in Boston it was he who received from his brother Israel the totally unexpected news of *her* death.

He headed his horse toward Northampton and came to the Edwards'

---

* Aaron Burr succeeded Dickinson as president of the college. He married Esther Edwards in 1752 and died on September 24, 1757. Jonathan Edwards succeeded Burr, but died on March 22, 1758, before he could actually undertake his duties. A fortnight later, on April 7, Esther died, age 26; and her mother, Mrs. Edwards, died on October 22. All are buried at Princeton.

hospitable home on May 28, "apparently vastly better" and cheerful. The Edwards' tenth child was then but three weeks old. Here he was almost overcome by Edwards' Pentecost sermon of June 7 on the saving grace of God's Spirit. Here, too, Northampton's Doctor Mather plainly told him of his "confirmed, incurable consumption" and said he could not long live but should ride to lengthen his days. Edwards then disclosed that David prayed at least one petition in each family prayer, "that we might not outlive our usefulness."

After much deliberation in the family he left for Boston on Tuesday, June 9. He and Jerusha, together at last, started on their three-day journey on horseback through the June countryside. She was seventeen; and she nursed him for nineteen weeks, "devoting herself to it with great delight," said her father, "because she looked on him as an eminent servant of Jesus Christ."

In Boston he enjoyed his visits with ministers and perhaps also the acclaim accorded his Journals. But after three days his lungs ulcerated and he became desperately ill, so that Jerusha wrote from the home of Joseph Bromfield: "Dr. Pynchon says, he has no hopes of his life; nor does he think it likely that he will ever come out of the chamber; though he says he may be able to come to Northampton." But once more Brainerd rallied, and discoursed with many on the evil effects of party-spirit and the delusions of Satan that place the stamp of approval on imagination founded upon "heat without light." He conferred about Indian affairs with the Commissioners of the London Society who sought his advice; he received token gifts for his people at Bethel from the trustees of a legacy; and he wrote lengthy letters which he signed "Your dying brother."

He admonished his brother John not to overtax his strength as he had done, and later he told him never to go to the Susquehanna country without a missionary companion. But more so, he warned John against false religion, especially among his Indians. "Let me tell you," he exhorted, "it is the devil transformed into an angel of light; it is a fiend of hell, that always springs up with every revival of religion, and stabs and murders the cause of God, while it passes current with multitudes of well-meaning people for the height of religion."

To young, indecisive Israel he wrote: "Do not be discouraged, because you see your elder brothers in the ministry die early, one after another. . . . I would not have spent my life otherwise for the whole world." To a young ministerial candidate, most probably Nehemiah Greenman, he wrote: "I have a secret thought . . . that God may perhaps design you for some singular service."

While he was confined he also edited printer's proofs of a recently-discovered diary of "old" Thomas Shepard (1605-1649), that remarkable New England parson whose short life included three wives. It was Shepard's *Select Cases Resolved* which Edwards cited when he noted approvingly that David neglected his diary after his last trip to the Susquehanna — that a saintly person had once been deluded by Satan to aggravate his illness by his fretful attention to a diary "of his hourly life," until a Christian friend had convinced him of his "erroneous conscience." We do the Sage of Northampton an injustice if we fail to recognize his mild satire in this instance. It has been noted that in his *Treatise Concerning Religious Affections* Edwards also quoted Shepard no less than seventy-five times.

On Sunday, July 20, David was carried in a chaise chair to the Old South Church. He heard Joseph Sewall and Thomas Prince preach and he partook of the Lord's Supper, "as one who anticipated his next Supper in eternity." On Monday he had a public debate with one who taught "that the essence of saving faith lies in believing that Christ died *for me in particular,*" the shibboleth Brainerd had learned so well to recognize and to fear. After the debate he declined honorary escort out of town. One "honourable person," however, rode with him for several miles, perhaps to Roxbury where John Eliot, the first apostle to the Indians, had labored for forty years; and in the cool of the day he and Jerusha, and Israel who had come posthaste from Yale, continued on the first lap of their five-day journey back to Northampton. There, according to his brother John, "he was, on his return from Boston to New Jersey, detained by the increase of his disorder."

Actually, he was happy to have escaped the pomposity of a Boston funeral, and from the time of his arrival he expressed no desire to return to New Jersey, nor did he express any hope for recovery. As he lingered for eleven weeks at the Edwards' King Street home he was at first able to ride two or three miles a day, but this lasted only a fortnight. In Edwards' absence on Tuesday, August 11, he prayed with the family for the last time, and he took his last ride on Thursday. He could not attend church that Sunday, and by the following Friday he could no longer climb stairs, and a room on the first floor was set aside for him. He went to church for the last time on Wednesday, September 2, "the last time that he ever went out of our gate alive," said Edwards.

While he could, he kept busy. He wrote a treatise against self-love as his preface to Shepard's diary, and he penned a long letter of counsel for Eliab Byram's church. Although he could not finish them himself, he also wrote long letters to Boston: to the men who had provided and pledged additional funds for a second schoolmaster at Bethel and for a mission to the Six Nations, and to the Commissioners of the London Society to recommend to them Job Strong of Northampton and Elihu Spencer, his double cousin, as missionaries to the Indians. Both letters were successful, but neither of the young men chosen was able to stay on the job for long.

On September 7, John came unexpectedly from New Jersey and brought David his diaries. These he read with pleasure and blessed God "for what passed long ago," and after he was persuaded not to destroy them he began with Israel's help to write the account of his early life and conversion. But he never left his room after September 17 when Israel had returned from Yale, and he longed to be gone — "O why is his chariot so long in coming? why tarry the wheels of his chariot?" He wished it to come on a Sunday, the day on which he was born, and born anew in Christ. He was impatient, too, for the promised re-appearance of John who was detained at Bethel where the chariot was carrying away many Christian Indians who died in the terrible smallpox epidemic that swept the Delaware and Susquehanna tribes that year.

His last days were appalling, and Edwards described them with clinical detail. His feet had been swollen for a month and had grown worse; his pain and discomfort was constant, and his condition nasty — "a constant discharge of purulent matter" — "very inward pain and distress" — "broken whispers" — "agonies of body." Ten days before he died he asked to hear part of Psalm 102, and in the house so often gay with the girls' irrepressible spirits and their mother's lilting songs, he heard them sing: *Hear my prayer, O Lord, and let my cry come unto thee — for my days are consumed like smoke, and my bones are burned as a hearth — But thou, O Lord, shall endure for ever.*

Through all his dismal hours his faith and testimony remained strong. It never wavered and he could talk of little else. But he asked others to pray that God would support and give him patience that he might not dishonor Him, for at times he could hardly bear the thought of another moment. During his last day he was "much disordered as to the exercise of his reason," and "the pain of his body continued and increased." He had so often longed for death with pleasure even when he was well, but he had not then fully considered the physical pain he would be required to suffer. In that respect, he said that night, "it was another thing to die, than people imagined."

Mercifully, John had fulfilled his promise to see him once again.

He had come back from New Jersey two days ago and it was with this brother who had taken up his mantle and whom he loved most of all that David talked late into the night, about the Indians and about their congregation at Bethel. Then, as *the* day began to dawn, on Friday, October 9, 1747, his eyes became fixed, and he lay immovable, and the chariot came.

On Monday a great concourse of people gathered to mourn his passing and they filled the meetinghouse where they had aforetime seen him, and they heard Jonathan Edwards' paraphrase from St. Paul's second letter to the Corinthians — In him whose death we are called to consider and improve, we have not only an instance of mortality, but, as we have all imaginable reason to conclude, an instance of one, who, *being* absent from the body, *is* present with the Lord. . . .

It was just before the ground hardened with the freeze of winter that they buried him in the peaceful Northampton graveyard, near the banks of his Connecticut, sixty miles upstream from Old Haddam. Little did his last saddle companions anticipate their early rendezvous as they witnessed his interment. Israel joined his brother on January 6 and was buried in New Haven. On February 14, before the spring showers could soften the Northampton soil, she joined them, she whom Edwards esteemed the flower of his family. Her body was laid next to that of the Haddamite who on his last Sunday had confided to her: "Jerusha, if I thought I should not see you, and be happy with you in another world, I could not bear to part with you. . . . We shall spend a happy eternity together."

On the slab of the table-top marker of Brainerd's grave they described him well: "A faithful and laborious missionary." But on Jerusha's headstone the stonecutter chiselled the words which she and her father, like the people of Neshaminy, had so often heard from the lips of their beloved Yankee —

> *I shall be satisfied,*
> *when I awake,*
> *with Thy likeness.*

Selected Sources

(In addition to Black's Edition of *The Works of Jonathan Edwards* mentioned in the Preface to this volume).

Alderfer, E. Gordon, assisted by Wilkinson, Norman B., and Harris, Johanna Alderfer, *Northampton Heritage* — The Story of an American County. Maps by Peter Maxwell. Easton, Pa., The Northampton County Historical Genealogical Society, 1953.

Bacon, Leonard, *Thirteen Historical Discourses,* on the Completion of Two Hundred Years, from the Beginning of the First Church in New Haven, with an Appendix. New Haven, 1839.

Bainton, Roland H., *Yale and the Ministry.* New York: Harper and Brothers, 1957.

Beck, Henry C., *Fare to Midlands — Forgotten Towns of Central New Jersey.* New York: E. P. Dutton & Co., Inc. 1939.

Beck, Henry C., *Forgotten Towns of Southern New Jersey.* New York: E. P. Dutton & Co., Inc. 1936.

Belden, Albert D., *George Whitefield — The Awakener:* A Modern Study of the Evangelical Revival. Nashville, Tenn.: Cokesbury Press, 1930; New York: The Macmillan Co., 1953.

Brainard, Lucy Abigail, *The Genealogy of the Brainerd-Brainard Family in America, 1649-1908,* Vol. 1 and Vol. 2 (especially Part VII). Hartford: The Hartford Press (The Case, Lockwood & Brainard Company), 1908.

Brainerd, Thomas, *The Life of John Brainerd, the Brother of David Brainerd, and His Successor as Missionary to the Indians of New Jersey.* Philadelphia: Presbyterian Publications Committee, 1865.

Day, Richard Ellsworth, *Flagellant on Horseback — The Life Story of David Brainerd.* Philadelphia: The Judson Press, 1950.

DeSchweinitz, Edmund, *The Life and Times of David Zeisberger, The Western Pioneer and Apostle to the Indians.* Philadelphia: J. P. Lippincott & Co., 1870.

Dexter, Franklin Bowditch, *Biographical Sketches of the Graduates of Yale College,* First Series, Oct. 1701-May 1745. New York: Henry Holt & Co., 1885.

Documents Relating to the Colonial History of New Jersey, First Series. Especially Vol. vi, 1738-1747, re: Deposition of James Blain, Newark Riots, Governor's letter of 9-28-45, Population Records of 1745; Vol. ix; Vol. xi, re: Wequalia; Vol. xii, re: Ebenezer Hayward obituary.

Dunaway, Wayland F., *The Scotch-Irish of Colonial Pennsylvania.* Chapel Hill, N. C.; University of North Carolina Press, 1944.

Dwight, Sereno E., *The Life of President Edwards.* New York: G. & C. & H. Carvill, 1830.

Edwards, Jonathan, *Memoirs of the Rev. David Brainerd; Missionary to the Indians on the Borders of New-York, New-Jersey, and Pennsylvania: Chiefly taken from his own diary.* By Rev. Jonathan Edwards, of Northampton. Including His Journal, Now for the First Time Incorporated with the Rest of His Diary, in a Regular Chronolgical Series. By Sereno Edwards Dwight. New Haven: S. Converse, 1822. (Dwight made many changes in phraseology, wording, grammar and punctuation.)

Edwards, Jonathan, *Memoirs of Rev. David Brainerd, Missionary to the Indians of North America;* Based on the Life of Brainerd prepared by Jonathan Edwards, D.D., and Afterwards Revised and Enlarged by Sereno E. Dwight, D.D. By J. M. Sherwood. New York.: Funk and Wagnalls Co., 1884. (Based on Dwight's "corrected" version.)

Edwards, Jonathan, *The Life and Diary of David Brainerd;* Newly Edited, and with a Biographical Sketch of President Edwards. Philip E. Howard, Jr. Chicago: Moody Press, 1949. (Based on Black's 1817 edition).

Eliot, John, *A Biographical Dictionary, Containing a Brief Account of the First Settlers and Other Eminent Characters Among the Magistrates, Ministers, Literary and Worthy Men in New England.* Boston, 1809.

Fisher, Sydney George, *The Making of Pennsylvania.* Philadelphia: J. B. Lippincott Co., 1906.

Gausted, Edwin Scott, *The Great Awakening.* New York: Harper and Brothers, 1957.

Gillies, John, *Memoirs of the Rev. George Whitefield.* Revised Edition: New Haven: Whitmore & Buckingham and H. Mansfield, 1834; Hartford: Edwin Hunt & Son, 1853.

Haddam Vital Records: Connecticut State Library, Hartford, Conn.

Halsey, Francis W., editor, *A Tour of Four Great Rivers, the Hudson, Mohawk, Susquehanna and Delaware in 1769,* Being the Journal of Richard Smith of Burlington, New Jersey, edited with a Short History of the Pioneer Settlements. New York: Chas. Scribner's Sons, 1906.

Hanzsche, Wm. Thomson, *Forgotten Founding Fathers of the American Church and State.* Boston: The Christopher Publishing House, 1954. (Includes chapter on David Brainerd)

Harper, George McLean, *John Morley and Other Essays* (includes: "David Brainerd: Puritan Saint"). Princeton: Princeton University Press; Oxford University Press (London), 1920.

Heckewelder, John, *History, Manners, and Customs of the Indian Nations Who once inhabited Pennsylvania and the Neighbouring States.* New & Revised Edition, with an Introduction and Notes by the Rev. Wm. C. Reichel. Philadelphia: Publications Fund of The Historical Society of Pennsylvania, 1876.

Henry, Stuart C., *George Whitefield: Wayfaring Witness.* New York: Nashville: Abington Press, 1957.

Humphreys, M. G., *Missionary Explorers Among the American Indians.* New York: Chas. Scriber's Sons. 1913. (Includes chapter on David Brainerd)

Johnson, Willis Fletcher, on David Brainerd, in: *Historical Background of the Pageant of Union City, New Jersey,* 1928.

Klett, Guy Soulliard, *Presbyterians in Colonial Pennsylvania.* Philadelphia: University of Pennsylvania Press, 1937.

McGiffert, Arthur Cushman, Jr., *Jonathan Edwards.* New York: Harper and Brothers, 1932.

Murphy, Thomas, *The Presbytery of the Log College, or, The Cradle of the Presbyterian Church in America.* Philadelphia: Presbyterian Board of Publication, 1889.

Page, Jesse, *David Brainerd, The Apostle to the North American Indians.* London: S. W. Partridge & Co., 1903.

Parker, Joseph, Address delivered in the Presbyterian Church, Mount Holly, N. J., April 22, 1886 (unpublished: N. J. State Library).

Peabody, Wm. B. O., *Life of David Brainerd, Missionary to the Indians.* Vol. viii, The Library of American Biography, Conducted by Jared Sparks. New York: Harper and Brothers, 1837.

Pennsylvania Magazine of History and Biography, The, published by The Historical Society of Pennsylvania. Volume I — Journal of Wm. Black; Volume II — Spangenberg's Notes on Travels to Onondaga, Signers of Conference of 1758.

Pemberton, Ebenezer, *The Knowledge of Christ Recommended,* A Sermon Preach'd in the Public Hall at Yale-College in New Haven, April 19th, 1741. New London: T. Green, 1741.

Proceedings of the New Jersey Historical Society, 2nd Series, 1886-7, vol. ix, Nos. 3 and 4: "Historic Old Tennent"; New Series, Oct. 1917, vol. ii, No. 4: "The Lenni Lenape or Delaware Indians"; Observers and Travellers": Oct. 1920, vol. v, No. 4: "Early Newark As a Puritan Theocracy in Colonial New Jersey"; "The Dutch Trading Post at Trenton"; Jan. 1926, vol. xi, No. 1: "The Early Dutch Maps of Upper Delaware Valley."

Rankin, Jeremiah Eames, *Esther Burr's Journal.* Washington, D.C.: Howard University Print, 1903. (Reprinted: Fisher, Josephine, editor, "The Journal of Esther Burr," New England Quarterly, 1930, III, pp. 297-315.) This work is fictitious to October 1, 1754 entry.

Sipe, C. Hale, *The Indian Chiefs of Pennsylvania.* Butler, Penna.: The Ziegler Printing Co., Inc. 1927.

Slosser, Gaius Jackson, editor, *They Seek A Country: The American Presbyterians* (McKinney, Wm. W., Beginnings in the North). New York: Macmillan Co., 1955.

Smith, Samuel, *The History of the Colony of Nova-Caesaria, or New Jersey.* Burlington, N. J., 1765. (Trenton: State of New Jersey, 1877.)

Sprague, Wm. B., *Annals of the American Pulpit;* Volume 1, Trinitarian Congregationalists; Volume III, Presbyterians. New York: Robert Carter & Brothers, 1857 and 1858.

Sweet, Wm. Warren, *Religion in Colonial America.* New York: Chas. Scribner's Sons, 1951.

Sweet, Wm. Warren, *The Story of Religion in America.* New York: Chas. Scribner's Sons, 1930.

Thompson, A. C. *Protestant Missions: Their Rise and Early Progress.* New York: Student Volunteer Movement for Foreign Missions, 1903.

Tracy, Joseph, *The Great Awakening: A History of Religion in the Time of Edwards and Whitefield.* Boston: Congregational Board of Publications, 1841.

Trinterud, L. J., *The Forming of an American Tradition — A Re-Examination of Colonial Presbyterianism.* Philadelphia: Westminster Press, 1949.

Tyerman, L., *The Life of the Rev. George Whitefield,* Volume Two. Hodder & Stoughton, (London), 1876.

Van Den Berg, Johannes, *Constrained by Jesus' Love: An Inquiry Into the Motives of the Missionary Awakening in Great Britain in the Period between 1698 and 1815.* Kampen, The Netherlands: J. H. Kok, 1956. (This study devotes considerable attention to David Brainerd.)

Wallace, Anthony F. C., *King of the Delawares — Teedyuscung, 1700-1763.* Philadelphia: University of Pennsylvania Press, 1949.

Walton, Joseph S., *Conrad Weiser and the Indian Policy of Colonial Pennsylvania.* Philadelphia: Geo. W. Jacobs & Co., 1900.

Whitney, Janet, *John Woolman: American Quaker.* New York: Little Brown, 1942.

Winslow, Ola Elizabeth, *Jonathan Edwards, 1703-1758.* New York: The Macmillan Co., 1941.

Woolman, John, *A Journal of the Life, Gospel Labours, and Christian Experiences of that Faithful Minister of Jesus Christ, John Woolman.* Philadelphia: Friend's Bookstore, 1845.

Index